# Far Out

## Sailing into a Disappearing World

BY

# CORINNA WEYRETER

FAR OUT: SAILING INTO A DISAPPEARING WORLD

ISBN# 978-1-907984-09-9

First published in Great Britain in 2012 by Boathooks Books
www.sunpenny.com (Sunpenny Limited)

MORE BOOKS FROM SUNPENNY:

Watery Ways, by Valerie Poore (non-fiction)
The Skipper's Child, by Valerie Poore (young adult)
My Sea is Wide, by Rowland Evans (non-fiction)
A Little Book of Pleasures (non-fiction, memoirs)
Dance of Eagles, by JS Holloway (thriller/adventure)
Going Astray, by Christine Moore (thriller)
The Mountains Between, by Julie McGowan (literary saga)
Just One More Summer, by Julie McGowan (women's fiction)
Someday Maybe, by Jenny Piper (literary)
Blue Freedom, by Sandra Peut (inspirational romance)
Embracing Change, by Debbie Roome (inspirational romance)
A Flight Delayed, by KC Lemmer (inspirational romance)
Redemption on Red River, by Cheryl R Cain (historical romance)
If Horses Were Wishes, by Elizabeth Sellers (children/young adult)

*For Gjalt,*
*and the family and friends*
*who shared our adventure*

*Over 40 percent of the world's oceans are heavily affected by human activities, and few if any areas remain untouched.*

– National Center for Ecological Analysis and Synthesis,
  February 2008


*Not only are we already experiencing severe declines in many species to the point of commercial extinction in some cases, and an unparalleled rate of regional extinctions of habitat types (e.g. mangroves and seagrass meadows), but we now face losing marine species and entire marine ecosystems, such as coral reefs, within a single generation. Unless action is taken now, the consequences of our activities are at a high risk of causing, through the combined effects of climate change, overexploitation, pollution and habitat loss, the next globally significant extinction event in the ocean.*

– International Programme on the State of the Ocean,
  June 2011

STELLA MARIS
Make: Westerly Oceanlord
Year Built: 1999
Length overall: 40.5 feet
Main breadth: 13.5 feet
Draft: 5.5 feet

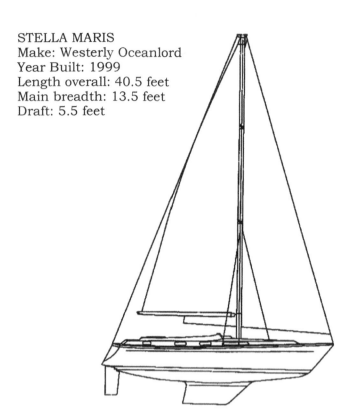

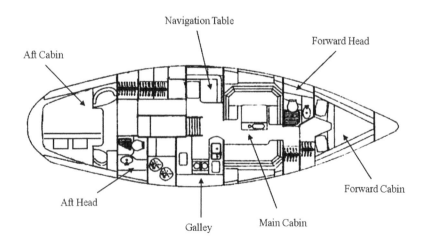

Navigation Table

Forward Head

Aft Cabin

Aft Head

Galley

Main Cabin

Forward Cabin

# ROUTE FROM TEXAS TO THE GALAPAGOS ISLANDS THROUGH THE WESTERN CARIBBEAN AND THE PANAMA CANAL

USA

Kemah

Gulf of Mexico

Mexico

Isla Mujeres

Cuba

Chinchorro Bank

San Pedro

Belize

The Bay Islands

Vivarillo Cays

Honduras

Nicaragua

Isla de Providencia

Colón

Pacific Ocean

Panama

Colombia

Isabela

San Cristóbal

Ecuador

Galápagos Islands

500 miles

# ROUTE ACROSS THE SOUTH PACIFIC FROM THE MARQUESAS ISLANDS TO AUSTRALIA

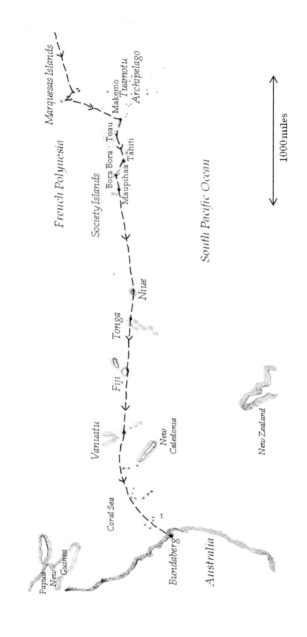

Papua New Guinea

Coral Sea

Bundaberg

Australia

New Caledonia

Vanuatu

Fiji

Tonga

Niue

New Zealand

South Pacific Ocean

Society Islands

French Polynesia

Bora Bora  Toau

Maupihaa  Tahiti

Makemo

Tuamotu Archipelago

Marquesas Islands

1000 miles

# Prologue

I 'd held out for as long as I could, but desperation finally forced me below deck. I had to leave behind the fresh air and predictable motion of the cockpit, both of which prevented me from feeling sick. Nausea was waiting for me at the bottom of the ladder, and the moment I stepped off the fourth and final rung, it struck. The main cabin, normally a cosy haven of warm oak and comfortable seats, now seemed airless and in need of an exorcism as it lurched erratically in unpredictable directions. I urgently needed to get to the toilet in the forward head, a mere four strides away, but one wrong move and I'd be taking a close look at the teak floor.

The weather conditions during the first two days of our week-long crossing of the Gulf of Mexico were identical to those of every training trip we'd made on that particular stretch of water: relentless head winds screaming over deck, steep waves biting at the bow like rows of razor-sharp shark teeth, and a heavy blanket of ominous grey clouds threatening worse to come. The simplest tasks were irksomely demanding: dressing, undressing, walking, cooking, washing-up, and going to the toilet in particular, all strained my temper and tested my conviction that sailing wouldn't always be like this.

I braced myself and set off across the cabin, moving from one strategically placed handhold to the next like a monkey swinging between trees. The movement exerted strange gravitational effects on my body, adding weight to my stomach and removing it from my head. I felt as though I'd swallowed several litres of molten lead and my brain had been replaced with air. I had to sit down before I fainted and collapsed into the regurgitated contents of my own stomach.

I opened the door to the head, pulled myself into the room that was roughly the size of a narrow wardrobe, and quickly closed the door again before it started slamming back and forth on its hinges. I plonked down onto the toilet with a certain relief at having made it that far, although I was acutely aware that the worst was yet to come. My skin felt hot and clammy as I embarked on the next stage of an operation that on dry land would have been 'piss easy': getting undressed.

As it was the middle of December, when even in Texas temperatures plummet (that year it snowed in Houston just before Christmas), I had several layers to peel away. Whenever my hands were busy unzipping or removing a particular article of cold weather gear, the boat would invariably crash into a wave and I'd be hurled against a hard surface. By the time I eventually landed on the seat with the requisite amount of clothing removed, I was frustrated to the point of despair. I immediately pushed my hand against the door to stabilise myself, closed my eyes, and rested my head on my outstretched arm to quell the growing urge to vomit. Going to the toilet was such an ordeal that I always put it off until I simply couldn't wait any longer, but that didn't mean relief was just around the corner.

The only window in the forward head was a small hatch in the ceiling, so every violent plunge into the choppy waves came as a shock. All my muscles instantly tensed up as I fought to stop myself from slipping off the seat. Sailing upwind taught me an interesting fact about water: in order to pass it, each muscle involved in the process has to be completely relaxed. It sometimes took more than half an hour of focussed meditation to coax my body into cooperation, by which time the pressure on my bladder had become so painful I was close to tears. It was at times like these that I really didn't like sailing.

Gjalt was oblivious to these basic struggles, thanks to a piece of marine equipment he'd bought called 'Little Johnny'. This was essentially a plastic bottle with a long neck that ballooned out into a handy catchment area. It had a flat base in case you wanted to let the contents stand around and mature and a convenient carry handle in case you didn't. This simple receptacle allowed Gjalt to relieve himself in the cockpit, where he was able to anticipate every boat movement and so avoid both nausea and frozen bladder plumbing.

Although I was jealous of Gjalt's ability to urinate in the open air, I couldn't complain that the makers of Little Johnny had ignored the plight of the female sailor when manufacturing their device. At no extra cost, they supplied an intriguing blue attachment that slotted easily into Little Johnny's red neck. Shaped like a dust mask (but made of non-porous material, obviously), it was essentially an unusually shaped funnel. Unfortunately, the apparatus didn't come with any operating instructions – a simple sketch would have been handy, not to mention amusing – and although it was clear where to position the dust mask, I wasn't sure if it was supposed to be used like a urinal or a toilet. I couldn't picture myself standing in the cockpit with my trousers around my ankles and the dust mask in my hand even at the best of times, let alone in adverse conditions. My muscles would have contracted with every abrupt pitch and roll, and I was almost certain to fall over at some point during the process; and as for sitting down, a similar lack of dignity and potential for leakage over-shadowed any benefits the attachment offered. In both cases, there was the added hygienic aspect of having to clean the adapter after each use to consider.

Gjalt was sympathetic to my predicament, so before we set off he constructed his own version of an outdoor toilet for my personal use. The best inventions are often simple, and his was certainly that, comprising mainly – it has to be admitted – of a bucket. But this wasn't just any old bucket: it was 'Homer's All-Purpose Bucket', a fact Homer had proudly emblazoned on its bright orange exterior, and it had a soft rim that Gjalt had fashioned from a long piece of pliable foam. I doubt even Homer had envisaged just how all-purpose some people thought his bucket could be, and I'm not sure how proud he would have been had he known, but Gjalt took him at his word. Still, although I did appreciate Gjalt's efforts, I didn't find his home-made portable toilet any more dignified than Little Johnny's dust mask, and as awful as it was to go below deck to the head, it was the best option I had.

None of this unpleasantness would exist on the 'warm route', Gjalt often assured me. We were heading for the Pacific, where friendly trade winds would push us along like a fluffy cloud floating through a blue sky: no thermal underwear, no upwind sailing into hostile seas, no cramp-ing bladder muscles; nothing but sunshine, crystal-clear water, and palm tree-lined beaches on tropical islands.

Once we'd crossed the 700-mile Gulf between the United States and Mexico, the most difficult part of our trip to Australia would be behind us, I was told. It was my belief in this promise that got me through the bad times.

CORINNA AND GJALT BESIDE STELLA MARIS IN TEXAS

# 1.

## Independence Day

*The dead zone in the Gulf of Mexico, now the world's second largest, covers 21,000 square kilometres, an area the size of New Jersey. Dead zones are areas where the dissolved oxygen levels are so low that no marine life can be sustained (other than micro-organisms). Moreover, these biologically dead areas are expanding due mainly to high nutrient pollution levels brought in by rivers and streams and washed off coastal land. Since the 1960s, the number of dead zones around the world has doubled every decade.*

– Peopleandplanet.net, 2011

The trouble with work is that it dominates your life and all the things you'd rather be doing have to be squeezed in around it. With your schooldays finally over, you leap into a career at twenty, pause briefly to take stock at forty, and then carry on regardless until you hit sixty, when you retire. Sitting in your comfortable armchair, grey-haired and worn out, you look back on your life and try to work out where it went. Too late you realise that at some moment you failed to notice at the time, the years began to accelerate and run into each other. They disappeared in a blur while you haplessly sleepwalked through them, oblivious to how precious they were. And now you find that the slippers fit your feet so snugly they're impossible to take off, and the only dream you might still have energy to fulfil is the planting of an herbaceous border in the back garden. This was the grim future we feared would be ours if we didn't break free at the taking-stock stage. For Gjalt and I this stage arrived as we neared the end of a four-year posting working for Shell in Houston, Texas. By then we'd spent a combined total of thirty-three years with the company and that felt like quite long enough for both of us.

If I could have had the job I'd really wanted when I left university, I would have become an astronaut. Had I been born in America, I would probably have given it a go, but as I wasn't the only chance I ever got was to be the first Briton in space on a Russian mission. Along with around 13,000 others, I answered an advertisement that read: 'Astronaut wanted, no experience necessary'. It appeared in 1989, just as I obtained my degree in astrophysics from the University of Birmingham (perfect timing, I thought), but another woman, Helen Sharman, got the job instead. (She worked for Mars, the chocolate company – an inter-planetary connection that possibly gave her an edge.)

Having lost out on the astronaut job, I had to come up with something else. I didn't know what I wanted to do, but I was sure I didn't want to sit at the same desk in the same office for the next forty years. A desk like that seemed too much like a coffin to me; one day the lid would open, I'd be pulled inside, and that would be that. Instead, I sought another job that promised excitement, one I wouldn't have to compete with 13,000 other people to get. I found it when I picked up a Shell recruitment brochure at university and saw pictures of offshore drilling rigs and people working in sunny climes, their office windows offering exotic vistas. A quick investigation revealed that oil industry salaries weren't bad either. Here was a company prepared to pay me to fly in helicopters and work abroad. I knew nothing about oil or how people went about getting it, but I was prepared to find out. *If I don't like it, I can always quit,* I thought.

But it turned out that I did like it. Shell whisked me offshore to the unseen world of North Sea oil exploration and showed me what it took to drill for oil. I spent two exciting years working two weeks on, two weeks off. What better way to ease into the rigours of working life than having a fortnight's holiday every month, especially when I loved being on the rig so much that I rarely wanted to get off? I was gradually transformed from an astrophysicist into a petrophysicist, someone who analysed data from inside the earth instead of from outer space, someone who could determine the porosity and permeability of rock and how much oil, if any, was in it. Postings to Holland, Oman, Norway, and America followed, and fifteen years passed before I felt the time had come for me to move on to the next adventure. By then I'd reached a point in my career when I was expected to start slowly climbing up the long managerial ladder, away from the well site, but I just wasn't interested in doing that.

If Gjalt could have had the job he really wanted, it would have been as a solo sailor. His father had taught him to sail when Gjalt was just a young boy, first in a small boat and then in a Mirror dinghy he built for Gjalt and his two brothers. As a family, they progressed to a thirty-foot yacht, building experience on the lakes of their native Friesland, in the northern Netherlands, before moving on to the Ijsselmeer and then the Waddenzee, a 430-mile long intertidal zone in the southeastern North Sea that seemed as vast as an ocean to the young boys. Gjalt was fascinated by the tales of such sailing adventurers as Bernard Moitessier, Robin Knox-Johnston, and Bill Tilman. Like them, he wanted to sail across oceans to magnificent and remote places without anyone but himself to rely on. When he was seventeen, sailing alone through Friesland one evening, he was struck by the thought that nothing could ever really get him down because he could always go sailing.

Even today, the prospects for becoming a professional sailor aren't good, but back then they were unheard of. Besides, Gjalt had been raised to make the most of his education – not to pursue his favourite pastime as a career – so he had search elsewhere for adventure that came with a salary.

This quest began in the Mining Engineering Department of the Technical University in Delft. He had planned to study mathematics, but veered from this path when he discovered it would probably land him behind one of those coffin-like desks I dreaded. Mining engineers, however, tended to join Shell, the Anglo-Dutch oil giant, and spread throughout the world, moving to a new country every three or four years.

Having specialised in geophysics, Gjalt began his career looking for oil through the acquisition and interpretation of seismic data, the reflections of sound waves sent through the earth that, when processed, provide maps of the subsurface. Basically, his job was to decide where to drill, while mine was to say whether he'd been right to drill there. His career started as adventurously as he'd hoped, with brief assignments to Argentina, Eastern Turkey, and

Abu Dhabi, followed by postings to Burma (now Myanmar), Oman, Scotland, and then America. Over time, he shifted away from the technical side of the industry into economics and then into developing new business for Shell. It was a shift he enjoyed until the company procedures for approving projects became so cumbersome and protracted that they hampered his ability to close deals. Sailing away from it all became increasingly appealing.

Although Gjalt and I met in Oman, we only moved in together four years later, in America. From Oman I was sent to Stavanger in Norway, and since there were no jobs there for Gjalt, he ended up in Aberdeen, Scotland. After years of flying across the North Sea every fortnight to spend the weekends together, we wanted to be posted to the same country. Arranging this, however, proved to be a challenge.

This was because Shell had recently replaced its colonial model of simply sending staff wherever it thought best with a modern one involving a certain amount of personal choice. This sounded like progress in theory, but for couples needing two jobs in the same place at the same time, the process was a nightmare. Just finding an operating company with a simultaneous requirement for both an economist and a petrophysicist was difficult enough, but for each of us to then independently get those jobs proved nigh on impossible. The old godfatherly role of a central staff planner had been thrown out with the proverbial baby and its bath water, and no one was interested in helping us. Finally, after many phone calls, a lot of persuasion, and six long months, we both got jobs in Houston. It wasn't an experience we were prepared to go through again and for the first time we considered leaving our jobs to go sailing.

What stopped us back then was an innate tendency to be sensible. We were both brought up by sensible parents who guided us through our educations and into sensible jobs. Although we did look at a few yachts in Scotland during those six months, we knew that buying one quickly and setting off ill-prepared and ill-equipped would not be wise. At that point, my sailing experience with Gjalt amounted to a two-week bareboat charter in the British Virgin Islands and one week in Croatia – not nearly enough to embark on a Pacific crossing. We needed more financial security, more time to choose the right boat, and more time to get the vessel and its sailors ready for long-distance cruising. Some people are eccentric, they do set off on a whim, but we aren't whimsical types. Being sensible might be more dull, but it's generally less hazardous.

It's the easiest thing in the world to slip into the American dream. We rented a large house with a double garage for our two cars and a swimming pool in the back garden. It was in a suburban neighbourhood so immaculately manicured and in such glorious Technicolor it almost didn't seem real, as if we were living on a Hollywood film set. We soon discovered that this pristine perfection was ensured by the iron fist of the neighbourhood's Garden Committee. This shadowy group patrolled the streets undercover, looking for the first signs of dereliction of duty. At the merest hint of a weed gaining ground in a flowerbed, you'd get a warning letter in your mailbox advising you to take corrective action or face the consequences. When our jobs took us abroad for stints that were too long for us to maintain our property to their required standards and we received a second warning letter (gardens need a *lot* of attention in Houston), we knew we had to get help. We turned to Alberto, a congenial Mexican who subsequently came every week to make sure our front garden never fell foul of the Committee again.

We saw as much of the States as we could during our vacations and were gradually seduced by its unique grandeur. Everything was big, bigger than anywhere else: the landscape, the sky, the buildings that scraped it, the cars, the highways, the fast food portions, even the people. Modesty and moderation were alien concepts. You could get anything you wanted and too much that you didn't, and most of it was cheap, that sly accomplice of temptation. It was easy to settle into the human melting pot that is Houston, a place where practically everyone comes from somewhere else.

Still, Gjalt's desire to go sailing was not suppressed by any of this. Two pivotal things happened the year we bought our boat. The first was a trip to San Diego, California, where it seemed to Gjalt that every single resident had their own yacht. While I enjoyed the ideal climate, the ocean, and the laid-back atmosphere, Gjalt sank into a deep depression. As far as he was concerned, his boatless status meant his life was as good as in the toilet. The second thing happened one morning in our glorious Technicolor neighbourhood. As Gjalt was taking out the garbage (a chore known to upset men's testosterone levels), he glanced down the street and saw a staggeringly rotund man on the outer limits of middle age doing exactly the same thing. For Gjalt it was an epiphany: he had looked into the future, and the future was bleak. He was sure that if he didn't act soon, he'd be taking out the garbage in suburbia for the next twenty years, steadily gaining weight in the process. At that very moment, all his disparate frustrations merged into a full-blown crisis, and as he lowered the lid onto the dustbin, he decided to buy a yacht.

We found her for sale at Clear Lake, an hour's drive south from Houston, on the Fourth of July 2001; Independence Day. She was a forty-one-foot Westerly Oceanlord, a yacht distinguished in sailing magazines as 'a pedigree blue-water cruiser'. Since it was a British design foreign to the U.S. market, she'd waited months for a buyer and as a result, the asking price had fallen dramatically.

We both fell in love with her at first sight. Gjalt was drawn in by her beautiful hull shape, her strong lines, sturdy mast, teak deck, and centre cockpit. She was solidly built to withstand heavy weather, he could see how well she would cope with big seas. Just standing behind her steering wheel, simply gazing at her winches, took him to those places he'd always dreamt of going: across oceans, to uninhabited islands, completely self-sufficient.

Down below, her interior was similarly prepared for adventure. The chart table was immediately to the left of the stairs, it was broad and solid, we could sit behind it securely, even in the roughest conditions. On the other side was the galley, a compact space we could cook in safely while the boat coursed through the waves. The main cabin had handholds in all the right places, so we could move about without falling over. And hidden from view was a fifty-four horsepower engine and tanks that could hold 500 litres of fresh water and 320 litres of diesel. This was a yacht designed to venture far beyond the marina.

With a meagre three weeks of sailing to my credit, I was captivated by her other, more superficial qualities. The first of these was the colour of her hull; shallow, but true. "Look, they've got a blue one," I said to Gjalt when we arrived at the brokerage.

She was also brand new, which was incredibly appealing. I wouldn't have to scrape charred remnants from the cooker, or sit on a toilet with a long history of unknown, salty backsides. I loved the idea that we would be her first owners, that she would truly be ours.

I felt at home the moment I stepped onboard. When I sat in the cockpit, I could picture us anchored in tropical waters. Her interior was inviting, a warm blend of oak cupboards and dark blue upholstery. There was a double bed in the aft cabin and not just one head complete with shower, but two; I wasn't going to have to rough it. When Gjalt said she was a safe boat to take to sea, it seemed like a bonus, but of course it was her beauty and homeliness that were bonuses to her seaworthiness, something I would come to appreciate soon enough.

She was the best boat we had looked at by far, and a bargain at the reduced price. Even so, she was expensive.

"We can afford it if we each pay half," I said, which took Gjalt by surprise. As sailing across the Pacific was his dream, the most he'd hoped for was that I would go with him; he hadn't expected me to chip in financially.

But it was an easy dream to share, and I was happy to buy into it. Besides, our posting had three years left so if I decided I hated sailing, we could just sell the boat. Having spent our working lives abroad, however, moving to a new country every three or four years, travel had become part of our lives. We were modern-day nomads, and we grew uncomfortable if our surroundings stayed the same for too long. It seemed cruising would fit us perfectly and might even help me achieve a dream of my own.

I'd always wanted to be a writer – the real kind whose books got published, since I was already one whose books didn't. After two novels were turned down (for good reason, I realised in hindsight), I began to write short stories instead. As these were far less time-consuming, rejection was somewhat easier to take. But I did win a major competition called the Bridport Prize, had a second story published, won a smaller competition, and was runner-up in another. It wasn't much, but it was enough to make me wonder if I could write a worthwhile book, if only I had the time. It wasn't easy to be creative after a long day in the office, and weekends were filled with other things. Sailing across the Pacific appealed to my sense of adventure, but I also hoped it would give me the time and inspiration to write. I didn't want to get to the end of my life and regret not having tried.

After as much careful deliberation as prospective parents give to naming their baby, we called our boat *Stella Maris*. Gjalt's surname is van der Zee, which means 'from the sea' in Dutch, and I had studied the stars, so we chose 'The Star of the Sea', expressed more poetically in Latin.

We spent time getting to know her on the shallow, protected waters of Galveston Bay before we ventured further out onto the adjacent Gulf of Mexico. As an avid racer, Gjalt was overjoyed to discover that, despite her being a solidly built thirteen-and-a-half-ton cruising boat, she was also fast. He loved the in-mast furling system but had to get used to the shape of the mainsail, the outer edge of which was slightly concave so it could fit inside the mast. With the genoa on a roller furler, both sails could be handled from the cockpit – a safe design for rough weather.

Meanwhile, I became accustomed to the motion of the boat, to the fact that it was possible for her to heel over in strong winds and not capsize, something I doubted at first. On sunny afternoons, there was a peacefulness that came with gliding effortlessly across the bay, the rush of water past the hull the only sound. In time we ventured along nineteen miles of the Houston Ship Channel to pass between the Galveston Jetty breakwaters and into the Gulf of Mexico. The Gulf would prove to be a hard taskmaster, exposing us to conditions we didn't expect to encounter in the Pacific. If we and *Stella Maris* could cope there, we'd be well prepared for what lay ahead.

We were tested the first time we spent the night away from the safety of our berth at Kemah. The weather was good when we dropped the anchor in a sheltered spot beside the Galveston Marina, close to the Jetties and the Gulf. We watched the sun go down and enjoyed being at anchor, away from houses and cars, away from people. A cold front was forecast for the following afternoon, but we intended to be in Freeport by then, the next safe haven along the coast, some forty miles southwest.

But the front followed a different schedule, arriving twelve hours early at three in the morning, with enough force to rip our anchor out of the mud. Gjalt woke up instantly and rushed on deck while I remained fast asleep. The wind had shifted 180 degrees and put us on a lee shore. Gjalt shouted for me to get on deck and raise the anchor. I hurried up the stairs and ran forward, my pyjamas whipping around me in the strong wind, getting drenched by heavy rain as I operated the electric winch on the bow. As the chain wound around it, I glanced up and saw a huge freighter crossing in front of us on its way into port; behind us, the monstrous concrete wall of the marina was waiting for us to drift onto it.

With the anchor safely up, we motored into the marina and found an empty berth directly behind the concrete wall. We slipped in, tied up, and made ourselves a couple of very stiff rum-and-Cokes. As we watched sea spray fly over the wall – which looked a lot better from this side – the realisation of how close we'd come to disaster sank in. If Gjalt hadn't woken up immediately, if the engine hadn't started, or if either of us had panicked, we could have lost *Stella Maris* that night. We'd been wrong to trust the accuracy of the weather forecast, but it wasn't to be the last time we were caught out by the unpredictable arrivals of cold fronts.

On our next trip, we sailed overnight for the first time to reach Matagorda Island, 110 miles southwest of Galveston. The night sky was so clear and decorated with such a glittering array of stars that we stayed up together for too long enjoying it. Gjalt needed to be alert when we made landfall the following morning, so I finally sent him to bed for a few hours. The weather was calm, and I felt confident to stay on watch alone.

We sailed relatively close to shore, over oilfields and amongst the hundreds of small, unmanned platforms that were busy extracting crude from beneath the sea. This made the Gulf a very good place to practice another important aspect of blue-water cruising: night watches. If we wanted to cross oceans, we'd have to sail at night, and that meant keeping a lookout for ships. The deadliest of these would be monstrously bigger than *Stella Maris* and significantly faster. A tanker sighted on the horizon and moving at a speed of twenty knots could run over us within twenty minutes if we were on a collision course. It would be complacent to rely on the ships' crews seeing *Stella Maris*.

We knew we were responsible for our own lives and so at least one of us was in the cockpit at all times keeping watch.

Early the next day, we left the Gulf waters through a channel beside uninhabited Matagorda Island. We tucked behind its eastern end, dropped anchor, and went straight to bed. Despite a few hours of snatched sleep, we were both shattered. That afternoon we moved a few miles in to a more protected and picturesque part of the island called Lighthouse Cove, where we were the only yacht anchored in the shallow waters. Since it was a wildlife refuge and state-designated natural area, there were no houses, no cars, no roads, and no lights. We spent a peaceful night there, but we had an unexpectedly rude awakening the next morning when another early cold front tore our anchor out of the mud once again.

We began drifting just after dawn, so at least it was light. Nevertheless, I found the situation daunting, but with the soft, muddy bottom the only hazard, Gjalt calmly motored into the howling wind and rain towards the island's small harbour. Unsure if the water there was deep enough to accommodate *Stella Maris*, Gjalt sent me down below to check the cruising guide. With the harbour approaching fast, I wanted to give him a quick answer and rushed to the stairs, but slick with rain they'd become as slippery as ice. My feet shot out in front of me, leaving me dangling by my right arm as my fingers gripped the handhold at the top of the companionway. Unfortunately my right shoulder wasn't up to the job of holding me there, having been in the habit of dislocating since I was fifteen. With the ball well and truly out of its socket, I instantly let go and plummeted onto the cabin floor a few feet below. I'd already been unnerved by the morning's events, but this latest incident seemed an injustice too far. I began to sob and feel incredibly sorry for myself, because I knew I had to get my shoulder back in its rightful place quickly so I could help Gjalt berth *Stella Maris*. I forced myself to get on my knees and felt quite heroic as I shouted up the stairs, "I'm okay! Don't worry about me. I don't need any help," although quite frankly help was the last thing I wanted.

I'd mastered the technique of popping the ball back into its socket the third time I dislocated it, inspired by a doctor's threat to have me sliced open and repaired the second time I'd gone to hospital seeking professional help.

It was something I had to do alone; I was terrified of good Samaritans arriving on the scene wanting to help. I braced myself the way you do before ripping a plaster from your skin, then quickly stretched out my arm and twisted it from side to side until I felt the reassuring jerk of the ball joint slipping back into place. I knew the soreness would come the next day, but at that moment the instant fix at least allowed me to be useful again. I was able to throw the mooring lines to the three people we unexpectedly found standing on the shore, while Gjalt manoeuvred *Stella Maris* into the small harbour.

Gjalt told me later that he didn't even realise I'd dislocated my shoulder, nor heard me shout because the wind was so loud.

"I couldn't have helped you anyway," he said. "I had to take care of *Stella*."

*Charming*, I thought, but of course he was right.

G jalt wanted us to make a long-distance trip before we committed ourselves to sail to Australia, so a year after buying the boat, we intended to sail 700 miles across the Gulf of Mexico to the Florida Keys. But the October weather didn't cooperate with our plan, and the prevailing winds forced us to sail southwest again, this time to Brownsville on the Mexican border.

As we filled up at the fuel dock, I wasn't desperately keen to head out to sea beneath a sky that was so menacingly grey, and I'd probably have resisted had I known that thunderstorms were in the forecast. Fearing this Gjalt kept the knowledge to himself; he wanted to see how well we and *Stella Maris* would cope in rough conditions. In those early days I really was just the idiot along for the ride, happy to leave everything to Gjalt: the weather, the route planning, the navigation. Practically the only contribution I made – besides companionship – was keeping watch. And this latest trip, which involved more than one night at sea, was supposed to give us the opportunity to test our watch schedule, to see how many hours we could each comfortably stay awake so the other could get a decent chunk of sleep.

But the weather was so bad – even worse than Gjalt thought it would be – that *we* were the ones tested, not the watch schedule. From the start, we had very strong following winds, and *Stella Maris* raced along under reefed sails, riding the waves with ease, unlike me. I felt seasick and unnerved by the heavy blanket of bulging grey clouds that stretched across the sky. On one occasion we sailed too close to a manned oil platform, and a sudden gust sent us speeding towards it. It was huge – a steel monster that looked especially grotesque in the miserable gloom – and, to make matters worse, a hostile standby boat chased us away. Down below I was unbalanced by every wave *Stella Maris* charged through. It was October, it was cold, I wore several layers to keep warm and each took a concerted effort to add or remove whenever I went to the toilet, or got in or out of bed. When Gjalt woke me up for my second night watch I snapped. "This might be your idea of fun, but it's not mine," I shouted. "You didn't tell me it would be like this. You said it would be fun, but it's not, it's horrible. I hate sailing. I want to sell the boat!" And Gjalt knew that I meant it.

The following day, conditions deteriorated. We decided to give up on Brownsville and head for Port Aransas instead; a destination that still required us to spend a second night at sea. On my watch, close to midnight, I sat in the cockpit, calmly watching the lightning display up ahead become increasingly dazzling. In my naivety, I thought nothing much of it, although I was careful not to touch anything made of metal in case I got electrocuted. It was only when one particularly bright flash of lightning made me think I'd seen a huge tanker very close to us that I woke up Gjalt. Before that, I'd been convinced that the lights I was keeping a watchful eye on belonged to distant fishing boats, but suddenly I was afraid they were actually on either side of a scarily wide and dangerously close tanker. Gjalt came topsides and agreed that the lights were as far away as I initially judged them to be, but he decided he didn't like the look of the lightning. He went back down below to check the size of the storm on the radar.

After too long waiting for his assurance that all was well, I pushed open the companionway hatch. "Is everything okay?" I asked.

"No, it isn't."

This was not what I wanted to hear.

An unbroken patch of black covered half the radar display, and it was just a few miles ahead of us. Gjalt tuned the VHF radio to the weather channel, and we heard a calm male voice announcing the approach of a severe thunderstorm. The man advised all listeners to move away from any windows and take shelter under the nearest table until he gave the all-clear. Although the idea of hiding under the table did hold a certain appeal, it wasn't a very useful suggestion in our particular situation. The eye of the storm was bearing down on us, and it was too big and moving too fast for us to sail out of its way.

I retreated below deck while Gjalt went into the cockpit to bring in the sails before the strong winds reached us. I was shocked to see him illuminated almost constantly by eerie bluish-white light. I desperately hoped he wouldn't be struck dead by lightning, leaving me alone in that dark night at the mercy of the elements. I was a complete beginner; I didn't have a clue what to do in such dire conditions, and with a grilled captain lying in the cockpit I would be reduced to a gibbering wreck. Thankfully, for Gjalt as well as me, obviously, he survived unscathed and joined me down below to see what the storm had in store for us.

I felt quite numb as I sat perched on the edge of a seat in the main cabin, knowing there was no escaping this nightmare. I considered praying, but it had been a good few years since I'd asked any favours of God, and I'd since convinced myself that He did not exist. Even though I could hear Death howling towards me, I knew it would be unethical to suddenly hedge my bets and pray to be saved just because I found myself in a tight squeeze.

So instead, my thoughts turned to the sentient being closest to God, as far as I was concerned – my mum. She had warned me against sailing and told me, "It will only make you feel sick, sick, sick!" She was right, as always, although the sickness in the pit of my stomach was fear and had nothing to do with the motion of the sea. While outside the wind grew steadily stronger, I wondered why I hadn't kept my feet firmly on dry land as my mum had told me to. It sounded terrifying as it tore through the rigging, whipping stays and halyards in a frenzied assault that reached a screaming climax when the storm passed right over us.

Gjalt sat at the chart table looking at the instruments but turned away from the wind speed indicator when it registered sixty-three knots. He didn't want to see it go any higher than that; the noise was bad enough without knowing any cold, hard facts.

Despite being bombarded by the wind and the torrential

downpour that came with it, *Stella Maris* was unfazed and remained steady in the water. Gjalt couldn't resist sticking his head out of the hatch to witness the storm's power. It was too brief to kick up any real waves, and the rain was so hard it literally flattened the surface of the sea, ironing out any potential ones. Although Gjalt was fearful of a direct lightning strike to the mast, which had the capacity not only to burn out the instruments but to sink the boat, he also thought, *This is as bad as it's ever going to get, and we're coping fine.*

After an hour, the wind had dropped to gale force, a mere stiff breeze compared to the preceding fury. It almost seemed calm.

"You know, sailors can go their whole lives without ever experiencing weather like that," Gjalt said, smiling proudly.

"Is that supposed to make me feel better?" I asked, incredulous.

"Well, at least you have to admit that *Stella* was a star," he persisted.

While that was certainly true, I was in no mood to admit to anything at the time. The trip had been traumatic enough before the storm, which had now blown away what had been left of my good will. "Well, you got us into this mess, so you can get us out of it," I said and proceeded to get into bed, where I stayed for the rest of the night.

My refusal to relieve Gjalt from the helm during the night left him completely exhausted the next morning when he steered us into harbour. I did eventually feel ashamed about this, although the guilt dissipated some months later when he admitted to having known about the forecast thunderstorms and kept quiet about it.

Safely berthed in Port Aransas, we discovered a knot in the genoa sheet so tight and complex it seemed that only a paranormal entity could have tied it; it took Gjalt an hour to unravel with his pliers.

The bad weather continued unabated for almost three weeks. I'd been promised a trip to Florida, and I got a Texan resort town out of season. It was wet, it was boring and the only way back to Galveston was via the Intracoastal Waterway. It wasn't pleasant, but with winds stubbornly persisting from the northeast, at least we managed to make it home.

Six months later, we decided to try again to reach the Florida Keys. If we could not only complete the 1,400-mile round trip but enjoy it too, we'd be ready for the 11,000-mile journey to Australia. It was May, almost summer, but the passage began as horribly as the last one. This time, though, we didn't turn away from the strong winds but sailed close to them, pounding into oncoming waves that were short, steep, and unforgiving. Seawater flew over deck with such persistence that the only way to keep moderately dry whilst on watch was to sit on the cockpit floor. Once again, I was seasick, and I only felt better when I could lie down. Gjalt stayed on watch as long as possible to spare me from the elements; he knew he had to thwart my threats of selling the boat.

But when conditions eased on the third day, we sailed into a different world. The angry sea became tranquil, a vast indigo carpet that rolled out to the horizon all around us. Away from land there was emptiness and solitude. During six days at sea, we only saw the odd ship in the distance and a smattering of unmanned oil platforms. We pretty much had the world to ourselves and, far from being bored, or lonely, we loved it.

Having spent many weeks on remote offshore drilling rigs, I wasn't surprised that I felt comfortable at sea; the yacht was just a tad smaller than the rig, that was all. We fine-tuned our night watches to three hours on, three hours off (two was too short, four was too long), and after a few days we'd grown used to the routine and no longer felt tired on that schedule. Then one bright, sunny morning, we arrived at Garden Key in the uninhabited Dry Tortugas, the westernmost islands of the Florida Keys. The tropical islet was dominated by Fort Jefferson, a massive hexagonal fortress that had been built in the nineteenth century to defend America's Gulf Coast.

As we dropped the anchor in the clear turquoise water, attracting a school of barracudas as it glistened in the sunlight on its way down, we realised Garden Key was just one of many fascinating places in the world that can only be reached by boat. We knew then that we wanted to sail to those places.

Gjalt was pleased that after six days at sea, neither of us felt the urge to escape the confined space of *Stella Maris* and rush to stand on dry land – nor were we starved for the company of other people. He was proud we'd made it and knew that Australia wasn't beyond our reach. So we spent our fourth and final year in Houston completing preparations for what would be the biggest adventure of our lives.

It was strangely fortuitous that while our sailing ambitions grew, our satisfaction at work declined. When we had first arrived in Houston, our jobs were challenging and interesting. Gjalt worked on developing new business opportunities for Shell within the United States and worldwide, a job that took him to China and Abu Dhabi. I was the operational petrophysicist for exploration wells drilled in deep water off the coasts of Brazil and Egypt, a job that regularly took me offshore.

But as time went by, a raft of middle managers drifted into the organisation, clogging up the system. There was a wearisome increase in office politics, and a seemingly never-ending series of project reviews were introduced. We no longer felt as if our efforts were appreciated, and there seemed to be a growing company-wide addiction to rambling, unproductive meetings that did nothing but sap our energy. Elvis Presley expressed our thoughts perfectly when he sang, "A little less conversation, a little more action please."

In the last year of our posting, we often found our spirits in need of lifting. Both of us were keen swimmers, so sometimes the endorphins produced during a long swim would be enough. Often, a trip to our local Mexican restaurant for a frozen margarita served in a glass the size of a goldfish bowl would do the trick. But the guaranteed cure for our despondency was the film *The Big Lebowski*: no matter how close to the brink we found ourselves, it never failed to pull us back.

In the Coen brothers' 1998 comedy, Jeff Bridges plays The Dude, a middle-aged hippy "the square community doesn't give a shit about", whose only concern in life is ten-pin bowling. The Dude is a man who goes to the supermarket in his dressing gown and writes a cheque for a sixty-nine-cent carton of milk he's already sampled in the aisle. Watching him lead a life as far removed from the petty stresses of the rat race as it's possible to get was not only comforting, it was inspiring.

One morning, The Dude's landlord pays him a visit to carefully broach the subject of overdue rent. "Dude, tomorrow's already the tenth," he says.

Sipping his breakfast of a White Russian cocktail, our hero replies, "Far out."

That was how laid-back we wanted to be; surely that was the attitude to have if we were to lead long and healthy lives. Deep down, we knew how insignificant those irritating work issues were, yet we took them all so seriously, we allowed them to upset us. Somewhere along the line we'd lost perspective, and the time had come to get it back. Life really is short, a mere blip on the timescale of the universe. Why waste it worrying about work? Nobody ever lay on their death bed wishing they'd spent more time in the office.

We didn't know if we would enjoy the cruising life or if we could live on a small boat for an extended period of time without bloodshed. In the event that we hated it, hated each other, or - less likely - missed work, we thought it best to leave our options open and so we requested a one-year sabbatical from the company. After all, we reasoned, Shell had invested a lot of money in us over the years, and the oil business was going to need more people as it headed into its sunset years. Most of the oil still in the ground is inclined to stay there – it's either hard to find, hard to get at, hard to get out, or all three – and extracting it will require skilled people. But despite support from our immediate bosses, somewhere up the long chain of command someone concluded that opening the golden cage doors for us would lead to a stampede by everyone else. Sabbaticals for studies? Yes. Sabbaticals for babies? Well, that was required by law. Sabbaticals for sailing? You must be joking! If we wanted a break to engage in such clearly frivolous pursuits, we had no choice but to resign.

This outcome disappointed and annoyed Gjalt, and he wasn't mollified by a concession that allowed us to apply for jobs through the internal system within two years. He felt responsible for my resignation and wanted me to be able to return if things didn't work out. I wasn't surprised by the decision (Shell was rather conservative and hated setting precedents), and I wasn't sorry, because I really didn't believe that we would want to return after only one year of freedom. I was convinced it would feel like a sell-out to take such a big step – to actually sail halfway around the world – and then simply return to a life that we knew no longer satisfied us, as if nothing had changed.

Resigning wasn't a brave choice; it was really the only

choice. Our expatriate life with Shell had been exciting and rewarding, but it had reached its natural end. In many ways, Houston was the high point of it all, and carrying on would only have taken us downhill; down to that armchair we dreaded, the one overlooking the herbaceous border in the back garden.

The list of things that needed to be done was extensive. Gjalt took on all the vital technical tasks required to turn *Stella Maris* into a blue-water sailing vessel. During the three years we'd owned her, he'd already installed all the equipment we needed to sail close to home, such as the VHF radio, the autopilot (so we didn't have to sit behind the wheel all the time), and a life raft.

The life raft had to be serviced before we left, and we went along to see it unpacked. It was supposed to accommodate four people, but was alarmingly cosy when we sat in it. It seemed a wholly inadequate contraption to entrust one's life to, and the accepted wisdom of only ever stepping up to your life raft became obvious. A basic survival pack was included that contained a knife with a flimsy blade, a small torch, and a plastic paddle that looked as if it had been stolen from a child's beach set. None of this mattered, though, because we prepared our own ditch bag and filled it with food, a hand-operated water maker that made seawater drinkable, a medical kit, sunscreen, hats, and even toothbrushes; if we were adrift for a long time, we didn't want to kiss our rescuers with bad breath. We kept the bag under the companionway steps, where it was easy to grab should that terrible need to abandon ship ever arise.

We only splashed out on the expensive blue-water cruising necessities when we knew for sure that we were actually going. A single sideband (SSB) radio would enable us to talk with other cruisers over long distances and e-mail our families and friends, a vital connection to the world beyond our small floating one. An emergency position indicating radio beacon (EPIRB) would transmit our location to the Coast Guard in the event we needed rescuing. A water purifier that used ultraviolet light to zap hostile bacteria would make the foreign water we put in the tanks safe to drink. A dinghy and outboard engine would take us ashore when at anchor, additional sails and a spinnaker pole would ensure we sailed well downwind in the trades. Solar panels placed on top of the bimini that provided shade in the cockpit would prevent us from having to run the engine to produce electricity, and a towing generator would provide extra power underway.

Gjalt installed everything himself, not only to save money, but also so he could learn about the ins and outs of all the equipment onboard. To this end, he paid a mechanic to come to *Stella Maris* and give him a crash course in her diesel engine; understanding and properly maintaining it was vital. To Gjalt, self-sufficiency was just as appealing an aspect of cruising as the freedom and adventure it promised. Help would mostly be scarce or non-existent and was certainly not something that could be relied upon.

We put together a comprehensive medical kit that could treat anything from a headache, to a bacterial infection, to a partially severed finger. We had aspirin, antibiotics, morphine, plasters, bandages, syringes, and the ability to suture. We even had surgical implements, just in case *Stella Maris* turned out to be the closest hospital to the patient and one of us had to morph into the nearest surgeon. Gjalt suggested I have all my old amalgam fillings replaced, but my dentist and I were of a different opinion. He even considered the merits of an appendectomy (his had been whipped out years earlier), but dropped the idea after he read that antibiotics could stave off any trouble long enough to reach a hospital. (I would never have agreed to it, obviously.)

We did both have comprehensive medicals, though; if our bodies were harbouring anything unpleasant, we wanted to know about it before we quit. We were inoculated against yellow fever, tetanus, diphtheria, polio, typhoid, and hepatitis B, and stocked up on malaria pills. We took out worldwide health insurance in case something happened to us underway. It was quite expensive, but the cost was insignificant compared to the bankrupting potential of serious medical treatment.

Everything on the list took longer to complete than expected – much, much longer. Even simple tasks could span days, and each one spawned a new set, so the list only ever seemed to get longer. Gjalt repeatedly felt overwhelmed by the number of things that needed to be done, while time steadily slipped away.

My main task was to obtain provisions for the months ahead. Once we left America restocking would become more difficult and more costly, especially in the Pacific. I read articles by cruisers about how to estimate the quantities of food required and heeded advice not to scrimp on things that were cheap in the States but monumentally expensive in the cruising waters beyond, such as toilet rolls and paper towels. From our own experience in the Gulf, I knew to avoid tinned meals, such as beef stew, chilli con carne, spaghetti meatballs, and that classic gourmet favourite, pork and beans. In a burst of misplaced enthusiasm, we'd bought these tins in bulk for our early trips, but as the flavour comes from excessive amounts of fat and sugar, they quickly become inedible. So we donated the remainder of our stock to the Houston Food Bank, doing our bit to expand the average American waistline.

What better place to find oversized supplies than in the USA? Another sailor directed us to Sam's Club, a wholesaler that primarily caters to small businesses but which fortuitously turned out to be the perfect ship chandler. The enormous warehouse was stacked to the rafters with tray upon tray of tinned foods, huge sacks of rice and pasta, bags of sugar, tea and coffee, boxes of Coca Cola cans, toilet rolls, paper towels, toothpaste, and even antiseptic hand sanitiser that didn't require water. It was a cruiser's heaven. We piled it all onto industrial-strength carts and as good as fork-lifted it into the boat, returning to get more as long as there was still space. I excelled at provisioning, filling up every available compartment, until Gjalt, horrified at the sight of *Stella Maris'* sinking waterline, stopped me.

To minimise the amount of litter we would produce as we ate our way through the supplies, I repackaged all the dry foods into reusable Ziploc bags. Although I'd read tips about preserving eggs by coating them in Vaseline and sealing tins with varnish, my laziness convinced me that such actions were unnecessary. I did make a spreadsheet listing everything we'd bought and where it was stored so we could keep track of stocks and find things easily. I soon stopped updating it, though, because we restocked whenever a good opportunity arose; besides, on a forty-one-foot boat, there are only so many places things can be.

Another store that doubled as a ship chandler was Bed Bath & Beyond – the Beyond inadvertently being the cruiser's section. I bought freestanding shelves and all manner of handy storage containers to convert *Stella*

*Maris'* interior into something as capacious as *Doctor Who's* Tardis. I spent an inordinate amount of time investigating the best electronic gadgetry we needed for the trip: laptop computer, digital camera complete with waterproof housing, camcorder, and an MP3 Walkman, something to keep me sane during night watches. I even bought a battery-operated cappuccino whisk because I didn't see why we should live without some luxuries, but the gadget never did see the light of day. We were about to sail away from one of the most enthusiastic consumer societies in the world and took full advantage of the incredible variety of low-priced products on offer while we still had the chance.

But the quantity of new possessions we acquired was far outweighed by the old ones we shed. For a while, we considered putting things in storage, but a critical close inspection of the quality and state of our belongings convinced us to part with them. This was one of our wisest decisions; it would have cost us around 1,500 dollars and necessitated a return to Houston to deal with it later into the bargain.

Instead, we ruthlessly scaled down our lives, keeping only what justified taking up space in our small sailing boat. We sold what we could, gave away what we couldn't, and stored the few remaining possessions we weren't able to part with in the attic of Gjalt's parents. We said goodbye to our two cars, our furniture, TVs, VCRs and DVD players, books, paintings, crockery, cutlery, pots, pans, kitchen appliances, plants, and a small mountain of clothes. A homeless man was the bewildered recipient of a Hugo Boss business suit, but I'm sure he didn't wear it whilst trying to raise money from the motorists who stopped at the traffic lights he called home.

In the end, some of my tasks slipped into Gjalt's domain because I just couldn't reduce the amount of time and energy I spent in the office during those last months. I did try to savour the fact that my colleagues' concerns were no longer of any consequence to me. I did try to be like The Dude when they asked me to do something:

"We need petrophysical evaluations of one hundred and fifty wells by Tuesday to evaluate this prospect."

"Far out."

"We must have a detailed data acquisition programme in time for next week's meeting."

"Far out."

But being as cool as The Dude just wasn't that easy – not in real life. I did say, "Far out," every now and then, but quickly explained the joke before agreeing to do whatever was asked of me. I worked hard right up until my last day, attempting to satisfy all the final demands that piled up as the end of my office life drew near. Producing a report that documented every detail of my four years of work on a project in Brazil almost became an obsession. Gjalt was struggling to complete his own tasks for the trip and then had to deal with those I neglected because I was dedicating myself to the death throes of my career. Instead of saying, "Far out" and meaning it, I couldn't bear the thought that the impression I'd leave with my colleagues was that I'd been a waster. It was obvious that the only hope I had of emulating The Dude was to leave my job behind and actually move far out: far out to sea and away from 'the real world' that I'd been conditioned to take so seriously.

Before I did, though, Gjalt and my boss convinced me to write my staff report for that final year, just so my CV would be up to date should I be back in the company any time soon. I knew it was pointless, and considering the amount of things I had to do before we left, it was also a terrible waste of time, but in the spirit of not being obnoxious and leaving bridges intact, I wrote it.

When I handed the finished article to my boss, he gazed at it with quizzical curiosity, as if seeing paper for the first time. "What should I do with it now?" he asked seriously, looking to me for guidance.

I had a suggestion, but I didn't make it. I think I know where it ended up.

I had no regrets about leaving, but I wasn't entirely convinced that would always be the case.

GARDEN KEY ANCHORAGE, DRY TORTUGAS, FLORIDA

DOLPHINS UNDER THE BOAT EN ROUTE TO THE DRY TORTUGAS, FLORIDA

# 2.

# Held Up in Mexico

*In the 1970s, 12 families lived on the 20 kilometre-long island of Cancun, Mexico. Today, Cancun has more than 20,000 hotel rooms, 2.6 million visitors a year, and a permanent population of 300,000, only 30 per cent of whom have homes with treated sewage.*

– Peopleandplanet.net, 2004

*Small reef patches, such as El Garrafon at Isla Mujeres and Punta Nizuc at Cancun, have been completely destroyed by tourism.*

– United Nations Environment Programme World Conservation Monitoring Centre Atlas, September 2001

The Gulf of Mexico lies in a zone of variable winds: not the steady and reliable trades that awaited us in the Pacific, but fickle, mischievous winds intent on making life hard for a small yacht wanting to sail south to Mexico. To get the better of them, we decided to take advantage of the kind of cold front that had twice dislodged our anchor and sent us drifting towards shore. These fronts regularly swept northerly winds down through the USA, and we planned to hang on to the tail of one to get us across the Gulf. This strategy meant sailing in strong winds, but we'd had plenty of practice doing that during our training trips, and even though it wasn't going to be much fun, the passage would at least be fast.

The bright sunshine couldn't warm us against the icy wind that was blowing the mid-December morning of our departure, but it did make me less reluctant to head out to sea. Wrapped up in cold-weather gear, we cast off the lines and left the marina for the last time. I'd expected to feel emotional, but it seemed no different from all the other times we'd left. For Gjalt, though, it was a memorable moment: his dream was becoming a reality.

After we cleared the familiar Galveston Jetties, we steered a course southeast towards our destination of Isla Mujeres, a small island some five miles east of Cancun and the nearest Mexican check-in port. Sailing in this direction took us out of the extensive matrix of unmanned oil platforms sooner than on our previous trips, giving us the rewarding feeling that we were making fast progress.

The first two days were intensely cold, wet, and rough, and with thirteen hours of darkness, the nights were long. Alone on watch, staring into the pitch darkness, Gjalt felt overwhelmed by the magnitude of the adventure we had embarked on. He couldn't believe it was really happening, that we had severed our ties and reduced our lives to fit on our small boat. It made him feel excited but also very small – too small to be taking on something so big.

The winds were strong and more easterly than we had hoped, leading to dispiritingly familiar upwind sailing. *Stella Maris* beat doggedly into the waves, rising to the challenging conditions for which she'd been built. Gjalt found his sea legs straightaway and did the cooking, washing-up, and navigation, tasks which were impossible for me at that early stage in our voyage. Despite taking anti-seasickness pills, I felt instantly nauseous whenever I left the fresh air of the cockpit to go down below. Going to the toilet remained my most unpleasant and infuriating challenge and always pushed me into such a black mood that I became desperate to get off the boat. But being on a sea voyage is like being on a fairground ride: once it starts, you can't get off until the end.

We did at least make the good progress we'd hoped for, sailing between seven and eight knots in the strong winds. The sunshine had disappeared soon after we entered the Gulf, but at the halfway point, three grey days later, it finally found its way through a chink in the thick blanket of clouds. We were closing in on Mexico, and I took it as a sign that the warm weather and idyllic sailing I'd been promised really did lie ahead of us. We peeled away the layers of our cold-weather gear and felt our spirits lifting right along with the temperature.

By now I was able to move around below deck without

feeling sick and could help with the cooking and washing-up duties. I also sent my first e-mail using the SSB radio and Winlink, a system developed by radio hams for radio hams – a special band of enthusiasts who erect towering antennas in their back gardens so they can communicate over vast distances with others who find the telephone as unexciting and mundane as they do. Winlink was a wonderful spin-off of this interest and allowed cruising sailors who'd earned their way into the select fold to send and receive e-mails for free. Gjalt needed no greater incentive than this to subject himself to the necessary exams, one of which proved so testing it caused lasting psychological damage.

This exam required a certain proficiency in the deciphering of Morse code, a level of ability the examiners thought modest and Gjalt thought monumental. He hated learning languages and this one, with its strange dot-dash sequences transmitted at insanely high speeds, was no exception. With a fair amount of complaining and ultimately a great deal of pride, he learnt every letter of the alphabet, numbers, and a host of punctuation marks. It was when all this was strung together to form words and sentences that the challenge proved too much for him.

The Morse code sequences were fired into Gjalt's ears like tap dancers from a machinegun. He simply didn't have enough time to decipher one letter before the next arrived, and he soon found himself adrift in a sea of incomprehensible clicks. He knew the only way he could pass the exam was to jot down the dots and dashes and translate them in his own good time. So, one Saturday morning, he filed into a classroom with a handful of other eager candidates, took a seat behind a school desk, and quietly confident, with his pencil at the ready, prepared to take the exam.

Unfortunately, though, the examiner was on to him and announced that the dots and dashes were not to be written down. People had obviously tried this flagrantly underhand trick before, and shortcuts to Hamdom were simply not allowed.

Gjalt protested vigorously, as if that would change the official rules being wafted under his nose. Finally he saw that he had no choice but to scoop up his pens, erasers, and good-luck charms from his desk and skulk home knowing that his brain would have to master the impossible if he were to get his licence.

An intense period of study followed, and there was much robotic dah-dahing of letters around the house before he finally dared to take the exam and translate the message 'on the fly'. Against all the odds, he passed with flying colours, and it was because of his perseverance that we could now regularly reassure our parents that we were still alive, not just in port but also underway. We received weather forecasts and sent our latitude and longitude to the Winlink website, where our position was displayed on a world map for anyone who was interested to see. The pain had been worth it, although whenever someone was foolish enough to ask about our e-mailing capabilities, Gjalt would complain to them at length of the trauma he had suffered at the hands of Mr. Morse.

Two days from landfall, a new cold front was forecast. To enter the Isla Mujeres anchorage from the north, we'd have to sail over a reef in a narrow and shallow passage. We didn't want to cross this hazard in the strong winds and rough seas generated by a cold front, so we had a choice of reefing the sails and waiting for the bad weather to pass, or we could ensure that we reached Isla Mujeres ahead of it. The idea of slowing down and turning *Stella Maris* into a sitting duck was not the least bit appealing, so despite being under full sail, we enlisted the help of the engine to keep our speed above six and a half knots.

Gjalt wanted to be at the helm when we reached the northeastern tip of the Yucatan Peninsula, where we were due to arrive at 1:00 am. From there, the final miles to Isla Mujeres were along the coast, so it was essential to take great care with the navigation.

In order for Gjalt to get enough sleep to keep him going until we made landfall, I remained on watch for seven hours. By this stage of the trip, the nights had become more friendly, so staying up was no trial. The clouds had dispersed, revealing an abundance of stars and allowing the half-moon to soften the blackness of the sea with a silvery sheen. *Stella Maris* glided across the water to the music on my MP3 player, which had been initiated into night watch service as soon as conditions eased. Billy Joel was sailing through Black Island Sound on his "Downeaster *Alexa*", and I was sailing towards the Yucatan Channel on my Westerly *Stella Maris*. I couldn't have stayed awake as easily, or enjoyed myself as much, without Billy to keep me company. Back in Texas, I'd been convinced that an MP3 player was a vital piece of boat equipment, and I was right. It transformed my watches from endurance tests to hours of listening pleasure, placing my entire music collection right in the palm of my hand. Without it, I might have gone crazy from boredom or fallen asleep at the wheel. With it I had no problem staying awake during any of the seventy nights we spent at sea during the following year. I often sang along, until a complaint from down below corrected my assumption that the wind was louder than I was.

I'd had some very vivid and colourful dreams as I sank into sleep on the Gulf crossing, and the final night was no exception. When Gjalt woke me up at sunrise to enjoy our first arrival in a foreign port onboard our own boat, he rescued me from a team meeting in which I was speaking my mind while my colleagues stared at me in shocked silence. I got dressed and climbed into the cockpit, where I slowly came to my senses. On seeing the palm trees and golden beaches of Isla Mujeres I was hugely relieved to discover that it had all just been a horrible nightmare about working folk.

Having safely crossed over the shallow reef that stretched from the northern tip of the island, we made our way into the anchorage. Marinas were now a thing of our past, and we moved between the dozen or so anchored yachts looking for the best place to drop the hook. Everything was perfect: the sun, the sand, the palm trees. We could even hear Mexican music drifting out to us from somewhere onshore.

"I don't think one year is going to be enough," I said.

Our first taste of yachtie camaraderie came within minutes of setting the anchor, when a couple came alongside in their dinghy, a small brown dog at the bow. John and Christine were British and had been lured over to *Stella Maris* by the pristine red of our brand new ensign. We learnt that the bright and cheerful early retirees had been sailing in the Caribbean for two years, their cruising experience evident from the duct tape holding John's glasses together.

"You're far too young to be enjoying yourselves," Christine

said, but soon afterwards endorsed my recent statement that one year of cruising wouldn't nearly be enough.

Having arrived on a Sunday, we had a day to get the boat tidied up and ready for any inspections the authorities might deem necessary. After five nights at sea, we were both looking forward to a long stretch of uninterrupted sleep, and by mid-morning, we'd crashed in the aft cabin. Afterwards I cheerfully dropped all our cold-weather gear into the laundry basket, ready to be washed and packed away for good. Sailing was about sun, blue skies, crystal-clear warm water, and beautiful tropical islands. I hadn't forgotten Gjalt's promise that the worst was now behind us.

The next morning, we retrieved our dinghy from the aft cabin, where it was stored during passages, inflated it on deck, and launched it into Mexican waters. With the outboard engine attached, Gjalt went onshore to clear us in. The port captain wasted no time ruining our slick plan by refusing to deal with him directly, citing newly introduced rules that required the use of an agent. The word 'agent' conjured up the image of an essentially useless middleman with a greedy grin and a desire to demand a fat fee for something we could easily do ourselves. At least in Isla Mujeres, an agent could be employed for twenty-five dollars; rumours were rife of fees up to ten times that amount being charged in other Mexican ports.

Having reluctantly hired the agent, the paper trail could begin. Gjalt returned to *Stella Maris* with Giovanni, a cordial quarantine officer dressed in a crisp white uniform. We filled out the forms he'd brought along, declaring the boat free of pestilence and the dead bodies of unfortunate crew members who'd perished underway. Giovanni checked the bilges just to be sure.

While the port captain didn't want to see either of us, the Immigration Department insisted on seeing us both. The officer was in Cancun for the morning ("He's always there," they told us when we enquired next door), so we awaited his return, idly sipping cold drinks in the beachside café opposite his locked office. Eventually he appeared and promptly dismissed us, directing us to the bank to pay our visa fees. A daunting queue snaked through the place, and progress was measured in centimetres as customers slowly shuffled forward. After a very long hour, we finally arrived at the counter, relieved that we'd made it before they closed for lunch.

The extensive formalities drifted on into the next day and consumed the better part of Gjalt's time. Before we could leave Isla Mujeres, we would have to clear out (practically the whole caper in reverse), and if we wanted to stop at any other Mexican ports on our trip south, we would be required to meander in and out of this bureaucratic labyrinth every time. This convinced us to head straight for Belize. The Panama Canal was 1,000 miles away, and we had two months to get there if we were to reach the Pacific by the start of the cruising season. There were better things to see in that time than Mexican paperwork.

The long-term resident yachties of Isla Mujeres had organised the Cruisers' Net, a daily broadcast on the VHF radio intended as a way of exchanging information. Members of the inner circle took turns acting as Net Controller, tasked with running through a fixed agenda of useful (check-in procedures) and less useful (joke of the day) items. Every morning at 7:30, we drank coffee and turned on the radio, as if tuning into *The Archers*.

Regular players included the Stranded Couple, who, having made it across from Florida a few months earlier, had been waiting ever since for the ideal weather window to sail south to Belize. They readily aired the finer points of discussions that would have been better kept private, the wife often seizing the microphone from her husband to publicly announce that she disagreed with him. She seemed to want it known that she was well aware she'd married a fool. Her voice occasionally wavered, as though she'd had a measure or two of rum at breakfast to steady her nerves. Both of them clearly viewed the ever-impending trip with extreme trepidation, but they were also desperate for a change of scenery. Every morning they looked to the self-appointed weatherman for good news and reassurance: *Couldn't he crack that magic weather window wide open? Was he sure there weren't any good anchorages en route to save them from having to sail overnight?*

Darrell the weatherman was, himself, a colourful character; as captain of a boat called *Nightmare,* this was not exactly a surprise. A wiry, middle-aged American, half-hippy/half-Vietnam veteran, with the distinctly wild air of a man who'd lived alone for far too long, he was the anchorage's jack of all trades. He offered to fix anything and every-thing for whomever was in need – engines, fridges, video recorders – and no job was too big or too complex. On the Net one morning, Darrell asked for someone to stand in as weatherman while he delivered a boat to Florida.

Astonished and horrified in equal measure, I watched Gjalt pick up the microphone and volunteer.

"Why did you do that?" I asked.

"I need to learn about the weather, and being put on the spot every morning will force me to do it."

I was relieved that he'd been motivated by self-reliance and not a desire to join the inner circle of the community. Personally, I preferred limited involvement.

It wasn't long before something of a friendship flow-ered between Darrell the weatherman and Gjalt, his keen apprentice. The two of them spent hours together on *Night-mare* talking about the weather and boat maintenance, veering onto paranormal sightings of human spirit clus-ters on foreign mountaintops, eventually landing some-where between fact and fiction along Guatemala's Rio Dulce, where they became embroiled in Darrell's shadowy adventures as a security guard. He even produced a bullet-wound scar to authenticate his stories.

When the Spanish arrived at Isla Mujeres in the sixteenth century, they found so many Mayan statues honour-ing the moon goddess Ixchel that they named it 'The Island of Women'. It was a mere half-mile wide, so even cruisers who hadn't used their legs for five days could easily cross to the eastern side and watch the Caribbean surf break on the rocky shore. The compact main town at the northern end of the four-mile-long island was a pleasant place for a stroll. Its atmospheric narrow streets were lined with low buildings painted in cheerful colours: hotels, restaurants, and many small shops, most of which sold paraphernalia for tourists. These potential customers were hoovered up from the enormous hotels that soared into the sky from the beaches of Cancun, whisked over on fast catamarans, and then released onto this charming island to sample a less modern, less crowded Mexico and hopefully part with a fair chunk of their holiday money. Around forty per cent of the 3,000,000 people who visit Cancun every year take the short trip to Isla Mujeres.

We ate good seafood at the no-frills cafés away from the more touristy quarters, bought bag-loads of cheap avocados from the supermarket, and steadfastly avoided souvenirs. I did this despite coveting one of the multicoloured blankets that brightened many of the shopfronts. There's always a love-hate relationship between natives and visitors in a place overrun by tourism, and there, with the whole town existing on tourist cash, I felt it was in full swing. Shopkeepers seemed aggressive as they tried to lure customers inside, whilst the customers remained on guard for the inevitable rip-off. I decided to wait until we reached a quieter corner of the Caribbean, where I could buy from someone who needed the business far more than an Isla Mujeres shopkeeper. It was a decision I came to regret, though, because we never saw such blankets again. So I learned a lesson: if you like it, you should just buy it.

Isla Mujeres was a wonderful destination after the cold, rough trip from the States, but we wanted to find quieter, more remote corners of the globe – those it was only possible to reach if you sailed there yourself. We were keen on heading south as soon as the weather allowed, but our plans were scuppered on Christmas Day, of all days.

On Christmas morning, Gjalt went for a swim, and I was seized by a desire to bake the first bread of the trip. It wasn't until the dough stubbornly refused to rise that it dawned on me I had doubled all the recipe ingredients except the yeast. Unwilling to admit defeat, I decided to bake the bread anyway; even if it didn't emerge light and fluffy, there was still a chance it would be edible. Well, at least that was what I thought.

When I took the two tins from the oven and turned them upside down, the loaves crashed onto the counter like pavement slabs. With a good aim and a strong arm, bakers could have used them as deadly weapons in a dawn duel. As the bread clearly stood the best chance in a duel with our teeth, I had no choice but to bury my maiden efforts at sea. I watched them sink to the depths, taking with them my premature pride at having been domestically self-sufficient.

My feelings of failure were soon swept away by a cold front that brought strong northwesterly winds into the anchorage from which there was no protection. Short, choppy waves were quickly whipped up, and the hostile conditions drew Gjalt on deck. He immediately saw that the boat directly upwind of us had broken off its anchor and was drifting in our direction, with no one onboard. It was a thirty-eight-foot Beneteau, a boat Gjalt thought would be light enough to catch and tie off behind ours. We got fenders and lines ready, but something – probably my inexperience – stopped me from suggesting we start the engine in case we needed to move out of the way, and this was a mistake I would soon come to regret.

As the boat, prophetically named *Driftwood*, approached us, it picked up speed and aimed straight for our bow. This messed up our plan. There was no time to rush back to the helm and start the engine, and suddenly Gjalt and I found ourselves manipulating fenders, frantically trying to keep *Stella Maris* from being damaged. In the mayhem, *Driftwood*'s rudder hooked on to our anchor chain, preventing the boat from drifting past. In the angry waves, it began relentlessly bucking up and down against *Stella Maris*.

Suddenly a dinghy appeared alongside *Driftwood*, and one of the two men in it climbed aboard her to try and start the engine. (We later learnt she'd been towed into the anchorage, as her engine was broken.) Then another cruiser appeared from nowhere on *Stella Maris* to help fend off the captainless attacker. After several minutes bearing the weight of two yachts heaving up and down on it, our anchor lost its grip on the seabed. As if things weren't already bad enough, we began drifting in tandem towards the nearby marina.

With the situation now desperate, a large catamaran miraculously arrived to offer assistance. Luckily for us, it had also dragged on its anchor and, having seen our predicament, the captain came over to help. We gave long lines to the man who'd boarded *Driftwood*, and he attached them to her cleats before passing the other ends to the catamaran. With the marina looming ever closer, we paid out our anchor chain so that it fell free of *Driftwood*'s rudder, and the unwelcome visitor was at last pulled free. With Gjalt at the helm, I winched up the anchor, which emerged from the water with a lobster trap clamped around it. Shrouded in this slippery wire cage, it hadn't been able to dig itself back into the mud.

We motored into the sheltered lagoon south of the main

anchorage and dropped the anchor, now freed from the trap; we were extremely thankful to be out of the fray. Few boats chose to stay in the lagoon because it was so far from town, but it was incredibly peaceful and well protected, a different world from the one we'd just left. When we inspected the damage, it was a relief to find that it had been mostly limited to the rub rail. A chunk of wood was missing, and there were several other dents and some chafing. Gjalt had wanted to save *Driftwood*, but that day we learned to protect *Stella Maris* first and worry about other boats later. Had we started the engine, as I should have suggested, we could at least have moved out of the way. We were immensely grateful to the people who'd rushed to help us, without whom we would have been in real trouble. Many other cruisers also worked together to prevent *Driftwood* from running aground, and more than once it turned out. Her captain had gone ashore to make Christmas phone calls, unaware that bad weather was on its way. In the sheltered streets of town, he hadn't even noticed the cold front and so didn't worry about his boat

We waited in vain for him to call us on the radio. On the Cruisers' Net the following morning, he thanked everyone who helped to save his boat, but he didn't utter one word of apology to us. It wasn't until late in the afternoon that he finally came over to ask if there'd been any damage to our boat, by which time our blood was almost boiling. "I thought there'd be a hole in it," he said calmly, as he inspected the hull.

We were shocked, because if he expected such serious damage, why on earth had he taken so long to show up? Fear of facing the music, probably. We managed to hold our tongues and invited him onboard, where we soon discovered that Al was a quiet, kindly man determined to do the right thing. He offered to pay for the damage immediately.

Al was a millwright at an oil refinery in Canada, but he also claimed to be a bushman. This brought to mind Grizzly Adams in a bearskin coat, surviving on rabbits during bitter winters, an image incongruous with clean-shaven, mild-mannered Al. He had been a contented, middle-aged landlubber until the evening he attended a talk given by a cruising couple who'd sailed around the world in their thirty-eight-foot Beneteau. Al was so inspired by their story that he promptly bought an identical boat himself, intent on emulating their achievement. Every winter for the previous five years, he'd sailed the waters around Florida, getting further afield each time. He and his wife had just completed the jump to Mexico. A few days later we met his wife, and she was as unassuming and endearing as Al, intrepid enough to share her husband's adventures without complaint. Their adult daughter was visiting them for Christmas, and like a wise mother aware that the time had come to let her children venture into the world alone, she refused to worry about her parents when they set off to sea.

The following morning the wind shifted, putting us too close to shore for comfort, but when we tried to up-anchor the electric winch refused to cooperate. Gjalt removed it from the deck and took it to Darrell for inspection. When they opened it up, they discovered that some of the magnets in the electromotor had been mangled into a jumble of useless pieces. Darrell knew of a workshop in Cancun that he thought might be able to replace the magnets, so Gjalt took the fast catamaran to the mainland and embarked on a thorough exploration of the sprawling city's commercial zone.

The men in the workshop couldn't fix the electromotor, but they suggested another place to try. From there, Gjalt was directed somewhere else. This chain of events continued until half a dozen workshops had failed to repair the electromotor, but they did succeed in leaving Gjalt with the feeling that he had been helped. During this tour through the industrial yards of Cancun, he managed to add a fresh layer of grease and grime to his clothing every time he took the electromotor apart. Eventually he was so filthy that even taxi drivers refused to stop for him; only when he turned his t-shirt inside out did he regain enough respectability to be picked up.

We were left with no option but to order a new electromotor from Florida. When *Driftwood* was pulled free of *Stella Maris* and I brought up the anchor, the winch must have jammed. Not noticing this in the chaos, I continued to operate it, causing the motor to overheat and the magnets to disintegrate.

The electromotor was quickly sent from Florida, but it fell straight into the hands of Customs in Mexico City, because the company hadn't used the courier we expressly asked for. Every day we went to the marina and asked the staff to help us get the package released. Every day they told us the wrong courier had been used. They made phone calls, they spoke to various people with encouraging gusto, but the head honcho was away for Christmas, and our electromotor wasn't going anywhere until he got back.

This carried on for six days. "Island time," people kept telling us. "Relax. Take it easy. Don't worry, be happy!" Wasn't it our goal to be like The Dude? Why hadn't we left our haste behind with the other possessions that weighed us down? It was proving hard to accept 'mañana' as a way of life.

We wandered around town, dinghyed to neighbouring islands, snorkelled, swam, and began to settle into the cruising community where everyone's 'back door' was always open and yachties nipped through the anchorage to exchange information over a beer. We became good friends with John and Christine, the welcoming Brits, as well as a retired Dutch couple in their sixties, Els and Henk. We held Henk in high regard for a number of reasons: firstly he had circumnavigated the globe in their thirty-three-foot boat; secondly, he sported one of those fantastic handle-bar moustaches that curl up spectacularly at each end, a rare and rather arresting sight in modern society; and thirdly, he had an enviable ability to emphatically refuse unwanted invitations whilst smiling so disarmingly that no feelings were hurt, a consideration normally conspicuously lacking in Dutchmen.

These wonderful people saved us from the dreaded 'potluck' dinners on the beach, a kind of communal picnic for which every cruiser had to provide a dish. Perhaps it was because my cooking repertoire was more or less limited to tuna and pasta, or maybe because I felt like a Women's Institute matron baking cakes for the village fete, but I never took to those functions; neither of us did. Instead, we celebrated the eves of Christmas and New Year with our equally potluck-phobic friends and realised that thanks to them, our enforced stay in Mexico had done us good.

The electromotor finally reached Cancun on a Monday morning. If we wanted it in Isla Mujeres before Saturday, we'd have to fetch it ourselves, so that was what we did.

The following day, Gjalt installed the fully operational anchor winch back on the bow, and the perfect weather window for sailing south miraculously opened up at that very same moment. The time had come to move on, and we prepared for an early morning departure to San Pedro, Belize, some 200 miles away.

We took *Stella Maris* to the fuel dock, which was rocked violently each time a catamaran launched away from the island to take tourists back to their hotels in Cancun. While we filled the tanks with diesel and water, I sat on deck pushing my feet against the dock to keep our boat clear of its rough wooden posts.

Once again, fellow cruisers came over to help, including the male half of the Stranded Couple, a slightly built man who we now met for the first time. "Don't you mind sailing at night?" he asked me.

"Not really. If the weather's nice and there's moonlight, I enjoy it."

"You should leave with us," Gjalt suggested.

"No, I don't think so. The conditions aren't right for heading south," he insisted and slowly toddled away. Evidently he thought us irresponsible, an opinion we later heard from our friends he'd freely aired over the radio once we'd departed.

For some time afterwards, we wondered if the Stranded Couple ever left Isla Mujeres.

# 3.

# *Negotiating the Shallows*

*Much of the 320 kilometres of Belize's coral reef has been 'bleached' in the last decade, and some scientists warn that it is likely to die, a victim of global warming.*

– Reuters news report, October 2006

We needed good northerly winds to push us south, but we also needed calm weather to navigate the pass through the reef at San Pedro. Without it, we'd have to continue on to Belize City, missing out on thirty miles of picturesque sailing in the protected waters behind the reef.

We used the best tactic for sailing south in the western Caribbean: timing our departure to coincide with the arrival of a cold front. After more than two weeks stranded in Mexico, it took a while to get used to being at sea again, not least because the swell beyond the shelter of Isla Mujeres generated impressively high waves. We got some welcome respite from these five hours later when we sailed through the passage between the large island of Cozumel and the mainland.

We were happy to be underway again. There had been too much drama too soon in Isla Mujeres, and we seemed to bleed money left, right, and centre sorting it out. Nevertheless, we were already taking to the cruising life and looked forward to exploring Belize, a country with dozens of anchorages and reportedly far less bureaucracy than its northern neighbour.

The north-flowing currents we were warned of didn't materialise, and we made excellent progress along the Mexican coast, sailing at over seven knots for much of the way. By the next day, it was clear we would arrive at San Pedro by 9 o'clock that evening. The entrance through the reef had to be negotiated with care at the best of times; at night it was impossible.

So we decided to spend a few hours at Chinchorro Bank, a large atoll situated off the south coast of Mexico. Lurking eighteen miles from the mainland, this twenty-six-mile-long, nine-mile-wide submerged reef had wrecked many an unsuspecting ship. It's one of only four atolls in the Northern Hemisphere, with the other three belonging to Belize. All the rest were waiting for us in the South Pacific.

We entered through a wide break in the reef at the northern end of Chinchorro Bank and instantly found ourselves in calm waters, protected from waves and swell. As soon as the anchor was down, we jumped over the side to snorkel, but it wasn't long before a Navy boat was heading in our direction. The atoll is an underwater national park, and the Navy was there to ensure that no one plundered it of fish or queen conch. We'd just seen many of these edible sea snails under our boat, the highly polished pink interior giving the large shells their distinctive beauty.

We climbed back onboard and had just enough time to get dressed before the Navy pulled alongside, brandishing machineguns and – even worse – yet more Mexican paperwork. The crew were more like nervous teenagers than elite Navy SEALs, so we weren't worried – which turned out to be a mistake. Not because they were more ferocious than they looked, but because they were as nervous as they looked. They'd only just arrived when one of them promptly dropped his gun. It struck the boat's metal floor with a worrying *clunk*, and we prepared to go down in a deadly hail of bullets. Thankfully it didn't go off, and every pair of relieved eyes watched the butterfingered teenager's face turn crimson as he scrambled to retrieve his weapon.

The youngsters stood guard in their boat while their commanding officer climbed onboard in his alarmingly sturdy boots. It wasn't hard to imagine the scuff marks they could leave behind. But the officer was pleasantly informal and perched in the cockpit as we patiently stumbled through the forms together, half in English, half in Spanish, neither side proficient but both well intentioned. He asked to have a quick look below, clearly more out of curiosity than suspicion of foul play, because he showed greater interest in the finer points of the woodwork than whether the bilges were stuffed with contraband. Satisfied with the tour, he gave us permission to stay, and we whiled away a few hours enjoying the tranquillity of that unique haven and catching up on some sleep.

The forecast was better for entering the pass at San Pedro the next day than the day after, and not wanting to risk losing the opportunity to sail in there, we headed out to sea again just before sunset. I took the first watch, as usual, and saw the sun melt into the horizon as we sailed along the western edge of the atoll. The peace wasn't to last, though, as the wind picked up steadily during the night, giving us a rough ride that a constant succession of rain squalls made even more wearing.

By daybreak, we'd arrived at San Pedro. While *Stella Maris* was rocked by waves of the darkest blue, we saw the steady masts of boats at anchor in a tantalising world of calm, turquoise water. We desperately wanted to enter that world; it would be painful to have to sail away from such serenity. The wind was blowing hard, and big waves were rolling onto the reef from the east, so we had to decide if it was safe for us to go through the pass. We headed in to take a closer look, and although I found it difficult to distinguish the white-capped waves over deep water from those crashing on the reef, Gjalt said he could see the pass clearly. We were going for it.

The gap in the reef was only 100 metres wide, and just to make the entry more challenging, a submerged coral patch lay in wait a stone's throw beyond the entrance. Almost immediately after passing through the gap, we had to make a sharp turn to the right to avoid ploughing straight into it.

A yellow buoy marked the centre of the pass, and Gjalt calmly steered *Stella Maris* towards it. I, meanwhile, being more red hot chilli pepper than cool cucumber, felt my heart bouncing between my stomach and my mouth and couldn't stop my hands from shaking. I kept one eye on the echo sounder and its ever-decreasing water depths and the other on the waves breaking on the reef beside us. Then, all of a sudden, we were behind the barrier reef, making the necessary handbrake turn, with the early morning light clearly illuminating the hazardous patch of coral ahead. This was good practice for all the atoll paradises waiting for us in the Pacific, but if I thought my nerves would be calmed by experience, I was going to be disappointed.

W e were extremely happy that we didn't have to sail on to Belize City, which had such a bad reputation for crime that checking in there was not recommended. We dropped anchor a mile north of the pass, but the seafloor consisted of a thin layer of sand over hard, flat limestone, so it took several attempts before it held. Gjalt dived down and found the anchor hooked behind a piece of dead coral; it would have to do for the time being.

The anchorage was even more tropical than Isla Mujeres, with colourful wooden buildings onshore and brilliant turquoise water all around us, thanks to the shallow water and sandy bottom. It felt wonderful to be protected from the sea by the reef; we were close enough to hear it breaking the waves. On the other side we'd been open to the full force of the wind and waves, but in the lagoon we'd found peaceful shelter.

Belize's Barrier Reef is a UNESCO World Heritage Site, part of the 1,000-kilometre Mesoamerican Reef that stretches from the northern end of the Yucatan Peninsula to the northern coast of Honduras, the second longest in the world after Australia's Great one. The 320-kilometre reef protects several hundred islands (called 'cays') from the Caribbean Sea, creating an ideal cruising ground, and is especially valuable during the hurricane season when it's capable of holding back tidal surges.

Gjalt went ashore to check in, and after all the hassles in Mexico, he was delighted to find that it was a breeze, a legacy from Belize's years as a British rather than a Spanish colony, I decided. We didn't need an agent, the paperwork was minimal, no one insisted on looking for rats or dead bodies in the bilges, and – best of all – we didn't have to pay a penny.

I was required to present myself to the immigration officer, so with Gjalt keeping an eye on *Stella Maris*, I had to dinghy solo for only the second time. The first trick was to go fast enough to make good progress without flipping the tender upside down with an overly ambitious twist of the throttle. After a sequence of stops and starts, like a learner-driver clumsily shifting gears, I found the perfect speed and headed for the landing jetty. Although I managed to reach it successfully any sailing instincts I might have had didn't kick in, and I promptly tied up on the windward side. As a result, the dinghy was forced under the jetty, her sides chafing against the rough wood. Naturally the prop of the outboard engine became entangled in a spiderweb of loose mooring lines, and it took me an embarrassing amount of time to manoeuvre free and relocate to the lee side. Every now and then, I checked to see if the people on the beach were laughing at me, but thankfully they were more interested in sunbathing than my inept nautical shenanigans.

As I strolled along the sandy streets of San Pedro the combination of two nights at sea and the oppressive afternoon heat left me feeling a little dazed and confused. I felt as if my feet weren't really touching the ground and my body was simply floating past the buildings, while my mind was caught up in a pleasantly surreal dream. The atmosphere was distinctly Caribbean, all brightly painted wooden houses, colourful bougainvilleas, and carefree barefooted backpackers. With many of the locals being of African descent and the main language spoken being English rather than Spanish, it felt as though we'd sailed far away from Central America.

Not wanting to look like a stranger in town, I marched confidently down the street, straight past the Immigration Office. After a haphazard detour through several side roads, I eventually spotted the sign and walked up the stairs to the second floor. I got another lesson in patience when I had to wait a good fifteen minutes for the officer to finish his telephone conversation, but then I was warmly welcomed to Belize with a stamp in my passport.

I wandered into an Internet café and snorted when I was told that the charge for five minutes on the Web was two dollars. I thought he was joking. For that amount of money, I could have surfed for an hour in Isla Mujeres. There were several people sitting behind computers, but it would have taken more than the free cup of coffee to persuade me to join them. From there on out, we abandoned the Internet and only returned to it when we were forced to take care of business that followed us from the world we'd left behind.

The wind continued to blow hard, and Gjalt spent a fitful night in the main cabin, acutely aware that the anchor's grip on the seabed was rather too precarious. We turned on the anchor alarm and the following day put out our second anchor.

By the time we arrived in San Pedro, it had been seven weeks since we stopped working. We'd been prepared for feelings of guilt to hit us at around the time when the trip progressed into something more than an extended holiday, but this didn't happen. We felt free and intrepid and were far too busy to feel like bums. We were constantly occupied with tasks of one kind or another and hadn't come close to being bored. It was becoming clear that the whole year would be like this: researching the next destination, planning the route, sailing there, exploring, and then planning the next destination in a perpetual cycle of adventure. I'd wanted time to slow down on the trip – I thought sailing could achieve such a miracle – but if anything, it seemed to have sped up. Both of us still felt the need to 'achieve' things and had so far resolutely failed to transform ourselves into The Dude. Many of my leaving presents had been books, because my colleagues imagined days, weeks, and months of languishing onboard with nothing to do. We did rediscover the joy of reading, but by the end of the trip, many of the books in our impressive library remained unopened because we just hadn't had enough time. We didn't miss television or the Internet, and we avoided listening to the news. We were in a different world now – a more peaceful and less troubled one – and we didn't want George Bush to bring his War on Terror into it.

We left the wind- and kite-surfers of San Pedro to seek out quieter anchorages further south. It was a short trip to Caye Caulker in water predominantly shallower than ten feet, something that made it increasingly difficult for me to relax, as I kept a constant lookout for coral heads. In spite of proceeding slowly and carefully, we did run aground off the northern tip of the island where we remained stuck for ten minutes. Luckily the bottom was soft sand, and Gjalt was able to wriggle *Stella Maris* free, but it was a good lesson in the need for caution, as hard reef wouldn't be so forgiving.

Caye Caulker was a laid-back island where young backpackers, old hippies, and Rastafarians ambled along the sandy streets slowly enough to avoid breaking a sweat. Beside the only beach, a big sign announced that, contrary to popular belief, it was, in fact, illegal to use drugs in Belize. Judging by the state of some people, not everyone had read it.

Wooden houses brightly painted with the cheerful palette of the Caribbean had further splashes of colour added by bougainvillea and hibiscus bushes trailing up to the balconies. Delightful as it was, the island did have tourism stamped all over it, and to us that meant high prices in the restaurants. We watched locals go to an open hatch in the side of an unassuming building, and from there we bought a takeaway lunch of chicken and rice, which we rounded off with two bottles of beer from Chan's grocery store. We took it to the end of a long jetty and ate while admiring the best sea view in town, which also happened to be free. To stretch our cruising budget, we needed to remember that we weren't on a two-week holiday from work. I kept a tight hold on the purse strings and allowed us five hundred dollars a month.

We received an e-mail from home telling us that Ellen MacArthur was four days and twenty-three hours ahead of the record for sailing solo around the world. We had moved some 900 miles in twenty-six days, while she'd sailed 18,362 miles in forty-three. I had absolutely no desire to trade our tropical anchorage for her impending jaunt around Cape Horn, but I guess she wouldn't have wanted to swap either. No one becomes a dame for cruising around the Caribbean.

As we headed south towards a channel running past the Drowned Cays, we were in danger of being drowned ourselves when it began raining so heavily we could barely see beyond the bow. In such conditions we wouldn't be able to distinguish the channel from the shallows, so we diverted to nearby St. George's Cay, where we spent the night. From this small island, British settlers fought and defeated an invading Spanish force during one week in September of 1798, and this battle is commemorated each year as a national holiday.

Onshore there was hardly a soul to be found, and all the houses were shuttered and abandoned. The eerie ghost-town-like atmosphere was accentuated by a leaden grey sky that prevented the sun from cheering the place up. The only life was at a British Army Rest and Recreation camp. We spoke to a female soldier who was there for an advanced diving course, her t-shirt emblazoned with 'Weapons of Mass Destruction' across her admittedly dangerously buxom chest. While we were chatting, a small dog called Dudley, who was apparently well known to the Army personnel, couldn't be dissuaded from his desire to fornicate with Gjalt's leg. The miniature canine was being driven mad by unrequited lust, and Gjalt's repeated rejections of his advances by means of swift jerks of the molested limb only seemed to further excite the fur-ball making him more determined than before. We had no choice but to return to *Stella Maris*, leaving poor, jilted Dudley whimpering sadly on the beach.

The following day, clear blue skies allowed the sun to throw its full light on the water making it easy for us to decipher the deep from the shallow. Dark blue was good, light blue required caution, and brown opened the door to a world of pain. An absence of wind left the sea incredibly flat, and I climbed onto the boom, where I would be able to see the water's secrets and have an excellent view of creatures splashing in the water. Dolphins and turtles were clearly identifiable, but there were larger, more mysterious disturbances to the surface that we attributed to the manatees reportedly living in the area. Learning to navigate around reefs and coral heads was a skill we would need in the Pacific as well, and I intended to learn fast. I didn't want to bump into anything.

Sailing behind Belize's Barrier Reef had so far tested my nerves, but as we crossed the azure beauty of The Flat, I relaxed for the first time. This large area of water was thirty feet deep, which seemed astronomical compared to the eight to ten feet we were used to seeing on the echo sounder. We passed four enormous cruise ships, their tenders scurrying back and forth like worker ants, transporting passengers on their daily excursions. I wouldn't have traded our way of seeing Belize for theirs, but I did envy the luxury of their overnight passages. I pictured people in fluffy bathrobes enjoying gin-and-tonics on their private balconies: no watches, no nights of broken sleep, and no concerns about colliding with anything deadly that was rendered invisible by the darkness.

We were welcomed to Colson Cays by a family of bottlenose dolphins. As soon as we had the anchor down, Gjalt slipped into the water, eager to fulfil his lifelong ambition of swimming with these endearing animals. In all his previous attempts, the dolphins had disappeared the moment he entered their world, but this group swam towards him, approaching to within metres. Gjalt was filled with a sense of magic at seeing dolphins in the wild for the first time, but also with a certain apprehension. The adults were big and unquestionably powerful as they swooped in front of him at high speed, stopping the young ones from getting too close.

Not wanting to miss out, I grabbed my diving mask and jumped in. The visibility was poor, but it wasn't long before the family came close enough for me to see them clearly. With their mouths curved into those famous smiles, they certainly had the appearance of friendly swimming companions. A playful trio dived around me, their stream-lined bodies making graceful arcs through the water. In a thrilling final encounter, one came to look me in the eye before they all vanished into the murk. They were even bigger than I'd expected, and only afterwards did Gjalt tell me they were quite capable of hurting us if they'd wanted to. But who ever heard of a dolphin attack? That reputation was reserved for the less adorable-looking sharks.

Cold fronts had been both friend and foe to us, and the latest of them to sweep overhead belonged in the foe category. Arriving at 3 o'clock, night's bleakest hour, it was twelve hours earlier than forecast, and the strong north-westerly winds it delivered turned our sheltered anchorage into a dangerous lee shore. It was pitch dark, and with coral heads scattered throughout the anchorage, we simply couldn't leave. Instead, with building waves buffeting *Stella Maris* menacingly, Gjalt went out in the dinghy to drop our second anchor. We remained on watch until dawn, when daylight revealed the full horror of the fierce white-capped waves that rolled towards us unabated. We wasted no time bringing up our anchors and escaped to Hutson Cay, a well-protected anchorage just ten miles south that offered an easy entrance through a deep channel.

Two hours later, we were in a different world. Tucked in snugly behind a mangrove forest, the change of conditions from wild and threatening to tranquil and cocooning seemed like a minor miracle. The wind instrument measured gale force winds at the top of the mast, whilst barely a breath drifted over deck.

In the afternoon, the sheltered anchorage even allowed us to try our hands at fishing, by trolling a lure behind the dinghy. We did get our first strikes of the trip, but the two big barracudas we hooked instantly launched from the water like Trident missiles and spat the hooks out with contempt. It was probably just as well, because barracuda are notorious for the high levels of ciguatoxin in their meat, which causes food poisoning known as 'ciguatera' in hapless human consumers. The early stages of ciguatera include nausea, vomiting, and diarrhoea, a miserable period spent running or shuffling between bed and toilet, depending on which way you're going. And while you're being thoroughly drained by all that, you need to brace yourself for the possible onslaught of headaches, hallucinations, muscle aches, and even coma. The symptoms can last from weeks (if you're lucky) to years (if you're not), so it's best to avoid the poisoning altogether, especially as there's no antidote. We did hear about a Caribbean remedy involving an enema of something rather dubiously called Guanabana juice, but apparently its effectiveness was open to some debate. People also told us that if flies refused to land on the fish, it was a sure sign of contamination, but it didn't seem appetising to wait and see if a fly was prepared to vomit on our dinner before we dared to eat it.

From a local sailing boat anchored off the east coast of the island came a wooden canoe paddled by three young fishermen. They must have witnessed our failure to hook a meal and decided we were sure bets to trade for lobsters. Suddenly, tinned tuna was off the menu and lobster thermidor was on. We exchanged a kilo of rice for eight delicious crustaceans. We'd sailed into a world where food was preferred over money, the nearest shops requiring a trip to the mainland. It was like stepping back in time.

Word must have spread that we were game for a spot of trading, because the next day, a family motored over to us in a battered old boat and asked for sugar in return for four large lobsters. Getting into the swing of things, we gladly agreed, but added some rice to our side of the bargain, as we thought the asking price was too low. The couple and their two small children lived on the island opposite the one we were anchored beside. The father fished for a living and sold his catch in Belize City. Ever keen on developing and honing his survival skills, Gjalt asked the man to teach him how to hunt lobsters, and it wasn't long before the two of them were free-diving together, searching nooks and crannies for tell-tale tentacles. The fisherman used a stick with a metal hook on the end to spear the lobsters and pull them from their hiding places. He could dive to great depths and hold his breath for minutes at a time.

"I love diving on the reef," he told Gjalt. "I have seen many, many beautiful things."

That a man who had to dive every day to ensure his family's survival spoke with such awe about the beauty of life in the sea made a lasting impression on Gjalt. The fisherman also gave us the first sign that too much burden was being placed on the reef by human need; finding large lobsters was becoming more and more difficult each year.

Whilst Gjalt dedicated himself to the manly pursuit of hunting, I felt it was about time I put an edible loaf of bread on the table. I'd chalked up two failures by this time, and having subsequently analysed the whole process, I concluded that the most critical step was getting the dough to rise properly. Understanding the yeast's need for warmth, I placed the bowl of dough on deck in full sunshine. After patiently waiting for a good half an hour, I cautiously lifted the tea towel with a mixture of trepidation and hope. Joy welled up in me when I discovered that the dough hadn't simply risen in the bowl, it was veritably launching out of it. I felt like Felicity Kendall in *The Good Life*; I *was* the Domestic Goddess. For the first time, we enjoyed freshly baked bread for lunch, and I sat proudly on my laurels, mistakenly convinced that a successful bread-baking future lay ahead of me now.

The strong winds lasted for the next few days, so we stayed in the pleasant protection of Hutson Cay and tried to take life at a slower pace. The wind dropped every afternoon, but always began to howl again right around midnight. Our sleep was constantly interrupted when we got up to check that the anchor was holding.

Gjalt hadn't had time to install a salt water pump in the galley before we left Houston, and now this chore had finally bubbled its way to the top of his to-do list. We didn't want to waste our precious fresh water on the washing-up, and savings could also be made by cooking rice and pasta in diluted seawater. The hand pump would put a limitless supply of this valuable resource at our disposal, delivering it to the sink a lot more easily than in buckets hauled up over the side and certainly a lot more safely when we were on passage.

After some effort, Gjalt succeeded in contorting his body into a shape that not only fit under the sink, but also allowed him to move his arms somewhat. Several hours went by, punctuated with disgruntled mutterings, numerous expletives, increasingly violent hammering, and interludes of prolonged stretching to realign his cramped muscles, before he announced that he had to remove the sink to complete the installation. It was at this point that I felt compelled to lend a hand. I eased Gjalt aside and squeezed my smaller, unbruised body into the tiny space, determined to avert disaster in the galley. Using a flexible ratchet and unexpected dexterity, I managed to tighten the inconveniently located plumbing component millimetre by millimetre, until it could move no more. The sink and I breathed a huge sigh of relief.

Fresh water was our most precious commodity onboard and we used it sparingly. Our tanks held 500 litres and after the seawater pump was up and running we utilised just 30 litres a week, somewhat less than the 2,100 litres a couple living in a British house gets through. We flushed our toilets with seawater, only did the laundry onshore and had a gigantic bath tub permanently filled with soothing sea salts just a short drop away. With a squirt of body wash on one of those odd sponges that resemble half a dozen sturdy hairnets meshed together, we were clean in no time. When conditions were too unpleasant for this outdoor option I was adept at washing my whole body with little more than a cupful of fresh water. This was rather more conservative than the 75 litres used by the average Briton when taking a five-minute shower, but then the time hasn't yet arrived when that average Brit is afraid he won't have any water left to drink afterwards.

Bathing in the sea was pleasantly invigorating, but the incessant exposure to seawater eventually caused the epidermis on our hands to disintegrate. Small patches of dead, flaking skin began to spread over them, making us look like highly contagious victims of white plague. I imagined scurvy to look something like that; not particularly appealing.

After three days in the same anchorage, we could no longer fight the urge to move, even if it was only a mile to neighbouring Garbutt Cay. But as we ventured beyond our cosy sanctuary, we suddenly found ourselves in a tumultuous world of choppy waves and shallow water. We knew from our excellent cruising guide that we needed to weave a path through a patch of scattered coral heads, but those obstacles were unnervingly invisible due to the overcast skies. Thinking we were sufficiently close to the island to avoid a reef marked on the chart, we were shocked when we felt an unpleasant thud as our keel hit something solid. With my nerves already twitching, as usual, I let out a pathetic girlish scream, but Gjalt remained calm. Pulling myself together, I rushed to the bow and peered into the sea, but the lack of sunlight made conning (the art and science of reading the colours of the water) impossible. Gjalt steered us slowly but surely towards the island without needing (or getting) any help from me, and we anchored without further bumps. He dived into the water to examine *Stella Maris*; thankfully she was unscathed. We hoped the same could be said of the coral we'd hit.

Our new anchorage was a rarity in the northern end of Belize's Barrier Reef; it had a sandy beach and palm trees instead of a muddy shoreline densely covered with mangroves. The scenery had the effect of transforming Gjalt into Robinson Crusoe, and he went onshore equipped for survival. Throwing a line into a palm tree until it hooked around a coconut, he proceeded to yank on it until the green fruit fell down beside him. A few hacks with his small axe and we were able to enjoy a refreshing, sweet beverage. He had harvested one of nature's wonders – water that grows on trees.

One afternoon, a Canadian boat invaded our quiet paradise and promptly anchored just upwind of us, setting our nerves instantly on edge. Within minutes the captain was in his dinghy and on his way over.

"Got any DVDs?" he asked, after he'd introduced himself as Gaston in a thick French accent.

A little taken aback by the effrontery of this stranger, we blurted out that we had not, even though we did have an unimpressive half-dozen or so onboard. We were still new to the cruisers' practice of lending each other DVDs and suspected that he wanted to make off with our collection. In hindsight, we would have done well to get shot of the *Beverly Hillbillies* and *The Dick Van Dyke Show*, farewell presents my boss had given me as fine examples of Americana (which we never were desperate enough to watch).

"It's not as nice here as in the San Blas islands," Gaston announced, standing in his dinghy as he held on to *Stella Maris*' guard rails. "There you have many islands with beaches and palm trees, all to yourself; no other boats."

*We had this wonderful island all to ourselves before you showed up,* we felt like saying, but instead we invited Gaston onboard. Another early retiree, he was cruising the Caribbean with his wife, and he had the lithe physique and deep tan to prove it. They had visited The Bay Islands of Honduras and Colombia's Isla Providencia, both of which were on our route, and he was happy to share their experiences. He also told us he didn't trade with the locals when the lobsters they offered were too small and therefore too immature to have reproduced. After the fisherman's comment about the growing scarcity of large lobsters, Gaston opened our eyes further to the danger of over-fishing and depleting stocks to a point from which they cannot recover. It was an issue we'd been largely oblivious to in the USA, where we filled our shopping trolleys with food from fully laden supermarket shelves without thinking too much about the ecological cost. Now that we were living within nature, the planet and her animals became increasingly important to us. We gradually became aware of the relentless damage being inflicted by mankind, but it had taken our escape from the sterile walls of the office environment and the hard concrete of civilisation for us to really take notice.

The following morning, Gaston came over to give us some information about Providencia and cheerfully announced that his boat had dragged past us in the night during a strong wind gust. Our prejudice against the ability of Canadians to anchor was growing.

We left Garbutt Cay in bright sunshine that fully uncovered the secrets the water had kept hidden during our arrival under overcast skies. We moved on to The Blue Ground Range, where we met Adolpho and Omar, cheerful Belizean tour guides who had the misfortune of being placed in charge of a sullen group of middle-aged Canadians on a kayaking holiday. Omar had just returned from a successful spear-fishing hunt and was skilfully preparing dinner for his charges, hurling the offal into the air for opportunistic frigate birds to catch on the wing.

Inspired by the bounty to be had in the waters around us, we returned to *Stella Maris* to get our speargun so we could also enjoy fresh grouper for dinner. (The speargun had been Gjalt's Christmas present to me, an only slightly less obvious gift to himself than the enormous heavy-duty bolt cutters he'd given me the year before.) *If we can't catch fish trolling a lure behind the boat, surely we can spear it,* we thought.

This sunset snorkel provided the best corals of our trip so far, and while I swam in peace through the beautiful underwater world, Gjalt prowled for victims. Just as the light was fading, he brought to the dinghy the ugliest crab I'd ever seen, its spider-like body run through with the spear. It wasn't anything we were ever going to eat, so the poor dead thing was put back into the water in the hope that it would become some other creature's dinner. It wasn't an impressive inaugural kill for the speargun or the hunter, and the fact that we didn't eat the innocent crustacean even turned it into a senseless killing – we never committed a crime like that again.

Returning to Placencia to check out of Belize, we saw signs of civilisation as we approached the mainland, something we'd all but forgotten about after two weeks of cruising around the cays. Onshore we met the largest congregation of yachties since Caye Caulker, all spending their last few days in Belize before sailing on, most of them to Guatemala's Rio Dulce.

As we ate in a simple restaurant beside the sea, we were joined by an engaging American couple in their sixties. Jim was every inch the captain, with his beard and peaked cap, and Sandra was his petite, unflappable crew. They had the perfect horror story to tell someone with a morbid fear of reefs and shallow water – i.e. me – and they seemed delighted to share it.

"Did you hear what happened to us over Christmas?" Sandra asked, leaning towards me conspiratorially. I told her I had not.

"We ran onto a reef," she said with near relish, staring into my eyes to draw full pleasure from the pained reaction of an easy victim.

"We were sailing south from Isla Mujeres and I felt so good on my night watch that when Jim came up to relieve me I told him to grab another half an hour of sleep. How I wish I hadn't been so generous," she said, leaning back in her chair.

"We were using the self-steering wind vane," Jim said, taking up the story. "I'm a retired merchant seaman, but Sandra's new to sailing and when the wind shifted during her watch she didn't notice. The shift altered the boat's course and sent her heading straight for a reef that extended out from the mainland. Sandra didn't recognise the sound of the breakers, but it was my fault; I'm the captain."

"Not long after I sent Jim back to bed there was a horrendous crash as we ran aground," Sandra continued. "The waves were so big and powerful that they lifted the boat right over the reef and into the shallow lagoon on the other side. She ended up stranded on her starboard side."

"She's a steel boat so she wasn't wrecked, but there were leaks in the hull," Jim said. "We plugged them with wood to save our things from being ruined by water seeping onboard. Some local guys came out at dawn the next morning; I think they thought they might have got lucky and were disappointed to find people on board, but over the next few days they did help us winch *Sirena* into deeper water inside the lagoon. Things turned sour when they demanded a lot of money from us, though. I guess they think all Americans are rich, but we're not," Jim said, shaking his head.

"An official even came along and accused us of damaging the reef," Sandra said with disbelief. "It wasn't as if we intended to run aground."

"A local fisherman showed us a channel that we could navigate if the conditions were right," Jim said. "So at high tide one day we took our chances and luckily made it back out to sea. We were so happy to get out of there."

"We were marooned for ten days. It was a Christmas and New Year we won't forget in a hurry," Sandra said, smiling. "Now we're going to the Rio Dulce to put it all behind us."

In hindsight, perhaps Jim and Sandra hadn't chosen the best name for their boat: according to legend, the Sirens lured mariners onto the rocks with their singing.

With the forecast promising a short window of northerly winds, Gjalt announced that we were leaving.

The prevailing winds in the Caribbean come from the east, a fact that makes easterly progress a challenge. If we missed this window we would have to fight headwinds to reach Honduras.

The minute Gjalt took the departure decision, he morphed into the captain from hell. He cracked the whip relentlessly, as if our lives depended on us being cleared out by the end of the day. We moved *Stella Maris* into Big Creek, dinghyed ashore, walked to Customs (deserted), hitched a lift to Immigration, paid an incredibly modest environment tax of eight dollars, hitched a lift back with the police (no crime committed), tried Customs again (occupied), got our clearance certificate, took *Stella Maris* to the fuel dock, filled her tanks with diesel and water, and anchored: mission accomplished.

I was looking forward to leaving Belize's nail-bitingly shallow waters, but first we had to exit the Barrier Reef through Queen Cays pass, one final jangle of my nerves. Once into the deep water of the Caribbean Sea, we would steer a course for Roatan, the largest of The Bay Islands of Honduras, just a ninety-mile sail away.

GARBUTT CAY, BELIZE

# 4.

# Diving in the Bay Islands

*The existence of the Caribbean or spiny lobster is threatened mainly because of over-fishing due to high demand for its meat. Statistics show a dangerous decline in lobster populations as a result of advances in diving technology and fishing boats that allow larger captures, added to the environmental degradation of their habitats, which has had an impact on their rates of reproduction.*

– WWF, October 2007

Having identified the break in the barrier reef that constituted Queen Cays pass, I went to the bow while Gjalt took the helm. As usual, he was calm and also as usual, I was not. I could see coral underneath us as we moved through the channel, the brilliantly clear water making it seem worryingly closer than the eighteen feet Gjalt assured me was indicated by the echo sounder. But there was no mistaking the lack of water over the barrier reef as the waves broke thunderously onto it, and I was glad we were centred squarely between the treacherous sides of the pass. Soon after we emerged into open water, the seafloor quickly fell away, dropping first in steps of tens of feet, then in hundreds, before becoming too deep for our echo sounder to measure. As the sea turned a nerve-soothing shade of dark blue, I relaxed and watched the palm trees of the Queen Cays fade on the horizon while we sailed away to Honduras.

Gjalt's decision to check out the previous day proved to be justified. At first, northerly winds allowed us to steer a course southeast towards our destination of Roatan, the largest of the three Bay Islands, some thirty miles north of mainland Honduras. The wind later shifted to the east-northeast, pushing us south and close to the most western island of Utila, from where we had to tack back to Roatan. Gjalt had been worried that we would have to motor for much of the trip, but we managed to sail most of it, which made the overnight passage a pleasant one.

I had an extended watch of five hours so Gjalt could get enough sleep before making landfall. I didn't mind at all, because Billy Joel and my other musical friends kept me entertained the whole time, and the dark sea was mesmerising as it shimmered magically beneath a full moon.

In the black hours of early morning, a brilliant orange glow appeared on the horizon. It was different from the sharp, focussed light of a freighter – more diffuse and more radiant. As we got closer, the glow began to flicker and change colour, a small aurora hovering above the sea, until finally I could make out an enormous cruise ship, decorated with a trillion blazing lights, give or take a few. I suppose the extravagant festive illuminations must have been essential to the wellbeing of the passengers, to lift their spirits should they fancy a turn around the deck at four in the morning. The ship was also heading for Roatan, and I watched it recede into the dying night, as we followed at our own, more stately pace.

In the soft light of a serene dawn, we sailed into the check-in port of Coxen Hole, Roatan's largest town. It owed its curious name to a seventeenth-century pirate called John Coxen who, I presume, holed up there.

A voice announcing itself as the harbour patrol boat called on the radio and welcomed us to Honduras. The voice belonged to Larry, and he led us past the cruise ship to a small anchorage close to town. The friendly welcome continued onshore with the port captain and then Immigration, the latter comprising a mother and her young daughter who earnestly filled out our arrival cards for us. Checking in was fast, simple, and cheap. The Bay Islands were making a very good first impression.

The port captain told us that the cruise ship had 1,114 crew tending to the needs of 3,076 passengers. This massive cargo of human beings swamped the small settlement for a few hours, nearly doubling its population, before returning like a well-trained herd to the floating hotel in order to be whisked to the next brief foreign encounter. The attraction of this kind of commercial cruising completely eluded us.

We wandered into the town which, apart from a super-market, offered little more than pasty cruise ship passengers in garish holiday clothes. We bought some fresh provisions and returned to *Stella Maris*. The anchorage at Coxen Hole provided scant protection from weather – or thieves apparently – so we departed for neighbouring French Harbour, a popular anchorage five miles away.

Without any wind to caress it, the sea was glassy as we motored along the steep coastal slopes, which were luxuriantly covered in a thick jungle of trees and bushes. It was a relaxing trip until we had to navigate our way into the anchorage. The Honduras cruising guide we'd bought before leaving the U.S. lacked any useful pilot instructions, and the afternoon light did nothing to reveal the whereabouts of a deep channel through the bank of coral that stretched across the entrance. We called the anchored boats on the radio but got no reply. A long metal stake marked the edge of a clearly visible reef patch to seaward, but other than that, there were no other clues about which course to take. Numerous coral heads reached towards the shore, an extensive patchwork of brown shapes disconcertingly embedded in a murky green background, giving the impression that there was no deep water at all. For a while, we wondered if the entrance was actually at the other end of the anchorage, further along the coast.

Cautiously we moved forward, with me on the bow staring desperately into the water like a novice fortune teller trying to read tealeaves. Noticing our predicament, a local man in a small fishing boat began to shout directions. Not only was it difficult to hear him, but the words I did catch were Spanish, which didn't help matters much. We tried to make sense of his accompanying hand signals and must have succeeded, because soon *Stella Maris* had made it into the anchorage without having bumped into anything. We carried on past the many yachts crowded near the entrance and nosed our way into a quiet, wonderfully sheltered spot close to the reef.

We had anchored opposite the Fantasy Island Dive Resort, and long-lost images of a little man in a tuxedo pointing to the sky and shouting "Ze plane! Ze plane!" surfaced from the deepest depths of my memory. Onshore there was no sign of him or his dapper boss, but we did find Roger, a sanguine, muscle-toned Honduran who foolishly agreed to take on the task of teaching me how to dive. Gjalt was an experienced diver and thought I should learn since our trip was going to take us to some of the world's best diving locations. I've been a keen swimmer since childhood, but I suffer from both claustrophobia and a fear of drowning, and diving always struck me as a potentially lethal combination of the two. But a large part of me didn't want to miss out on something that so many people rave about, so I decided to face my fears and go for it. The course would begin the next day, and I left armed with a book and a DVD, which Roger asked me to study beforehand. Being a bit nervous – and something of a swot – I did as I was told.

Gjalt dinghyed me to the resort in the morning, and I felt as though I was being dropped off at school. Roger gathered all the necessary equipment with an air of resignation that was almost insulting, as if nothing could be worse than having to teach me how to dive. He swaggered back and forth at a pace someone recently freed from the capitalist world might call slow, but which The Dude would undoubtedly have considered relaxed. Meanwhile, I hung around trying not to look out of place, or at my watch. Finally, with all the essential bits and pieces collected, Roger explained to me that novices sometimes feel choked by their wetsuits and are usually advised not to wear one the first time. Naturally, I deferred to his recommendation but was rather surprised – and felt somewhat duped – to see him emerge from his umpteenth visit to the changing room clad in a full suit himself.

Weighed down with various pieces of ungainly equipment, we lumbered over the sandy beach of the resort's pretty bay and waded into the shallow water. Roger instructed me to breathe deeply and slowly, and I stared at him thinking, *Yes, yes, I watched the film....let's get on with it!* I was eager to take my first breath underwater and experience the delight the DVD had promised. With great confidence, I mirrored his thumb-down signal and sank to my knees, fully expecting to instantly master this breathing-underwater malarkey.

So there we were, mask to mask, our heads just below the surface, with Roger's face reduced to a pair of brown eyes, framed by what looked like a hugely unattractive pair of safety goggles, and a protruding round mouth made of rubber. A fleeting urge to laugh vanished the second I took my first breath. I discovered that I was not at all delighted, I was positively horrified, and I immediately began sucking on my regulator as if I'd just run a marathon. It seemed impossible to draw in the requisite number of air molecules needed to stay alive. Roger gazed at me passively, as if regarding a creature he found rather dull, and leisurely moved his hand to and from his chest to indicate that it would be better if I breathed more slowly. *Wasn't it obvious that I was trying?*

This was not what I'd been promised by the DVD, with its teeth-whitened novices celebrating every easily achieved success with a triumphant high-five. There was no relaxing silence underwater for a start; each breath bubbled loudly in my ears, sounding near-fatal and eerily mechanical, like the piston of an iron lung shunting up and down to force oxygen into my system. It was just awful, and I indicated to Roger that I'd had enough and promptly stood up.

I couldn't have been underwater for more than fifteen seconds, placing me firmly in the wimp category. I just hadn't been prepared for that dreadful sound or all those air bubbles rushing past my head. Roger wore the look of someone all too familiar with that kind of hysteria and began a well-honed routine of patient encouragement that I swallowed like verbal Valium. I wasn't prepared to be the first person ever to give up before they'd even begun, so I steeled my nerves and we submerged again.

This time I stayed under until I gained control of my manic breathing, something that took quite a while. I wasn't over the moon about all the exercises Roger then proceeded to inflict on me, such as taking my regulator out of my mouth and purging it of water before returning it where it could do me some good, but I did them anyway. When the time came to flood my mask with water, just so I could purge it and regain my view of the world, I plunged back down to the frustrating depths of ineptitude. All I had to do was breathe out through my nose, something I'd been doing successfully for thirty-six years, but underwater I just couldn't stop exhaling through my mouth.

"How do you breathe out through your nose?" I actually asked Roger after minutes of embarrassing failure, a question that obviously had no answer and consequently received no more than a look of incredulity. Perhaps it took that look of his to trigger the necessary electrical signals in my waterlogged brain, because soon afterwards, I did finally master that basic skill.

By the end of all this palaver, the lack of a wetsuit left me mildly hypothermic. Roger placed me in the sun to raise my blood temperature back to normal and then disappeared on some unspecified errand, while passers-by stopped to ask me if I needed medical attention.

The sun's warmth had barely made an impression on my core temperature when Roger returned and made me jump into deeper water for my first open-water dive. He led me on a cruise through a world of tropical fish and coral so enchanting that I entirely forgot about being cold, getting the bends, or drowning. Suddenly, it was all worth it.

The diving course more or less consumed my life for the next few days. I left Fantasy Island with my PADI certification and a stinking cold. After the first day, Roger had declared me mentally stable enough to wear a wetsuit, but it was so baggy that it didn't leave me much better off. Luckily, the nearby CocoView Dive shop had a suit exactly my size, as well as all the gear I needed to go diving, gear that would become very hard to find the further we got from civilisation.

Ten miles east, in the grand bay of Port Royal, I recuperated from the ups and downs of my initiation into the world of diving, and Gjalt caught my cold. Dinghying along the shoreline one afternoon, we spotted a 'For Sale' sign swinging from a wooden post on the small beach of a grand mansion. We stopped at the private jetty, where a grey-haired Honduran caretaker was fishing, and expressed a polite interest in the property. Unexpectedly, the friendly old man asked us if we wanted to look around. "Does the Pope shit in the woods?" as The Dude would say. I would never turn down the opportunity to snoop around a rich person's house, so with barely disguised excitement, I hopped ashore.

The owner wasn't there, but his massive guard dog, all muscle and snarling teeth, certainly was. A reassuringly hefty chain prevented the slobbering beast from biting through our vital arteries, but Brutus made a convincing display of trying to rip it from the wall the instant he caught sight of us. It was clear from the furious barking, which only ceased for brief interludes of fierce growling, that our presence displeased him, and the caretaker's assurances that the dog wouldn't harm a fly couldn't persuade us to take another step forward. But we still got a good look around the grounds and managed to sneak a peek through the windows, glimpsing enough to declare its faux opulent interior too tacky a prize for giving up our cruising life. We bid farewell to the accommodating caretaker and the Hound of the Baskervilles, muttered something about being in touch, and dinghyed further along the shore.

We stopped at a neighbouring property, where a chatty Swiss retiree, who was up to his elbows in the innards of an outboard engine, told us that the asking price for the house we'd just looked at was two million dollars. It was just as well we hadn't fallen for it.

We watched the sun go down from a viewing platform built high above the water. Behind it onshore, a path led up the hillside to nowhere. Someone must have run out of money before they could even start building their dream house, but they understood the importance of a good sea view.

A local fisherman paddled by in a wooden canoe and stopped to sell us a freshly-speared grouper; there was no trading this time. He told us about the pirates who had once lived in Port Royal and said there were still treasures hidden beneath the water. He often found old bottles and beaded jewellery when he went spear-fishing, he said.

Henry Morgan (the laughing buccaneer on the labels of our favourite Captain Morgan rum bottles) had established a base there in the mid seventeenth century, when it was one of the best harbours in the Western Caribbean. English, French, and Spanish pirates all thought Roatan an excellent place from which to raid Spanish cargo vessels attempting to take home loot from the New World. More than 350 years later, there was only one small catamaran anchored with us on the opposite side of this wonderfully large bay, and as far as we knew, there were no pirates onboard.

The lure of treasure enticed us to swim over to a shipwreck stranded on the seabed close to the fringing reef. Unfortunately there was little to see amongst the rusting remains of a vessel far younger than the galleon of a privateer. The water was murky, which encouraged visions of sharks to flood into my mind, but the only creatures that feasted upon us were hundreds of minute, stinging jellyfish. Their relentless attack forced us into a rapid retreat, and with the help of my brand new flippers, I torpedoed back to *Stella Maris*.

We left Port Royal when winds were favourable for sailing to the neighbouring island of Guanaja, and we arrived a few hours later, in the early afternoon. Behind the fringing reef, one pretty palm tree-covered island after the other was set like a jewel in a pool of aquamarine. One of these was Josh's Cay, a gem that belonged to Graham, a retired multimillionaire from the Cayman Islands. Unlike others fortunate enough to have their own private paradise, Graham actively encouraged yachties to visit. He provided free moorings, water, ice, and that most precious of treasures lost to the humble seafarer: a washing machine.

In the evenings, cruisers gathered in the bar and grill, an enticing open-sided wooden building painted sky blue, with sweeping views across the water. No one we met there was planning on venturing into the Pacific; they were all happily settled in the Caribbean. An Italian couple in their thirties, nonchalant Bruno and strikingly Amazonian Mercedes, had been heading to the Panama Canal when they stopped at Josh's Cay and lost the will to carry on. Eight months later, they seemed to have all but moved in with the hospitable Graham. Whenever we met new cruisers, they invariably asked us why we were in such a hurry to be on our way. This did eventually make us question if we were moving too fast, but our goal was to sail across the Pacific, and we didn't want to get stuck in the Caribbean, no matter how beautiful the islands we visited there were.

I hadn't done any laundry since Isla Mujeres when, still fresh from a working, earning existence in the USA, I'd paid someone to do it for me. We had so many clothes, towels, and sheets onboard that we could have reached Australia without ever having to wash anything, but the laundry bag wasn't big enough or airtight enough to hold all the soiled items until then. Besides, freshly laundered clothes are one of life's simplest pleasures, and having a washing machine at my disposal was now the height of luxury. I'd taken this mundane household appliance for granted whilst living on land, but being parted from it had spawned a newfound appreciation. The sandy beaches and towering palm trees on Josh's Cay were heavenly, but it was hanging up the laundry in the tropical sunshine that I enjoyed the most.

As I left it there to dry, I walked along a path that circled the island with Suelita, a pretty young woman who came out to Josh's Cay every day to work in the restaurant.

"Were you here during Hurricane Mitch?" I asked.

"Yes. It was terrible, really terrible. We all sheltered in a concrete building on the island and just waited there until it was over. The hurricane stayed for three days. The noise was the worst thing. It was so loud and just went on and on. I thought we were all going to die. I hope I never have to live through something like that again."

"Did anybody die?"

"An old lady, after the hurricane finally left. When she went out of the house and saw how much damage there was, she just collapsed."

When Hurricane Mitch formed in October 1998, it was about to become the deadliest Atlantic storm for more than 200 years. The eye lingered over Guanaja for thirty-six hours, but miraculously only a few people on the island died. When the storm moved south to mainland Honduras, it caused floods and landslides that killed 7,000 people. In total, an estimated 11,000 people were killed by what was then the fourth most intense hurricane in Atlantic records; a further 7,000 people were recorded as missing. Mitch has since been pushed to seventh place by three hurricanes that occurred in 2005: Katrina, Rita, and Wilma – evidence of global warming, some scientists believe.

More lives were lost in the waters to the south of Guanaja than on the island itself. With Mitch gaining force in the Caribbean, the 282-foot-tall ship *Fantome* went to Belize City to drop off its passengers and some of the crew. Thirty-two-year-old Captain March called the owner of the Windjammer Barefoot Cruises schooner in Miami, Michael Burke, and with forecasters predicting that the hurricane would hit Belize, they decided Captain March should sail *Fantome* southeast and take shelter behind Roatan.

The ship arrived early the next morning and began to tack back and forth behind the twenty-five-mile-long island. The storm was just seventy-five miles away, winds were gusting to fifty knots, and the seas were rough. A few hours later, Hurricane Mitch defied all the computer models. Instead of tracking northwest, it moved southwest, towards Roatan and *Fantome*. Boxed in by coastline to the south and west, Captain March had no option but to sail east towards Guanaja. By this time, the wind had reached sixty knots, and fifteen-foot waves were rolling *Fantome* heavily. Mitch was now just forty-five miles away, with winds a terrifying 155 knots.

Three hours later, Burke spoke to Captain March on the satellite phone for the last time. *Fantome* was south of Guanaja, fighting forty-foot waves and heeling forty degrees in eighty-five-knot winds. The hurricane had moved southeast, right into the path of the tall ship, and that's where it stayed for the next thirty-six hours, its eye close to Guanaja. The *Fantome* found a destiny true to its name, disappearing into the sea with all thirty-one of her crew.

Far from the horror of hurricanes, I enjoyed watching our clothes dry in a gentle breeze, while Gjalt browsed through useful nautical files on a CD borrowed from a fellow cruiser. But his joy came to an abrupt end when our laptop suddenly crashed. The rest of the day evaporated as we tried everything to bring it back to life. After all else had failed, we finally resorted to reinstalling the operating system. The sight of the familiar welcome screen led to a rum-and-Coke celebration, but it wasn't until the end of the next day that we'd successfully reinstalled all our programs.

We could have survived without our computer, but it stored all our files and digital photos, and most importantly, it allowed us to e-mail our family and friends. It was this that really kept us below deck performing vital surgery on our laptop while others enjoyed the magic of Josh's Cay. We did use computer charts when making landfall, but as we also had paper charts and cruising guides for every destination, it wasn't essential for navigation.

Sailing far from civilisation forced us to be self-sufficient in every aspect of cruising life. There was no PC World to repair a crashed computer, we couldn't get a plumber to install our salt water pump, and if the engine needed attention, there was no maritime equivalent of the AA to call. The incident made us vow not to accept CDs from other cruisers again, but after we discovered that it wasn't his CD but our hard drive that was at fault, we began swapping discs again. Exchanging information is, after all, an important part of cruising.

I looked forward to a complete day of relaxation after the stressful intensity of the laptop scare, but yet again, the weather pushed us into an early departure. We had to leave the following day if we were to catch a ride east using the northerly wind of the latest cold front, which was forecast to last for two days. Now, it seemed everyone was right after all: we were moving too fast. Each time a weather window opened, we jumped straight through it, even if we would have preferred to stay put a little longer. I'd been marched around Placencia the minute Gjalt decided we had to check out, and two and a half weeks later, he was about to repeat the experience in Guanaja. The weather was his master, and he was mine. Suddenly I felt as if our trip really was just a mad dash from one anchorage to another, from one country to the next, and although my eyes were open, I wasn't really seeing anything. One of my aims of going cruising was to slow time down, but on that hectic schedule, it seemed to be running away from me as quickly as ever. Compared to Ellen MacArthur, though, who'd just circumnavigated the globe in a little over seventy-one and a half days, we were crawling along.

In order to check out, we had to swap the blinding white sands and swaying palm trees of Josh's Cay for Bonnaca, a town founded on a rubbish tip and amazingly transformed over 200 years into the little Venice of the Caribbean. In a bid to escape from the millions of ferocious 'no-see-ums' and mosquitoes on the main island, the original inhabitants moved onto two adjacent cays a few hundred feet offshore. They bridged the gap separating the cays by dumping refuse and debris into it, and the town was now the largest in Guanaja, home to around 10,000 people. The main island terrain consisted of slopes so steep and densely covered in jungle that it still remained largely uninhabited.

With *Stella Maris* safely anchored, we landed our dinghy beside the motorboats and dugout canoes that provided the transport around this town of small canals. We walked along the narrow walkway that meandered past painted wooden houses crammed side by side, some of them rising up from the sea on stilts. Despite the large population, the streets weren't overrun with people, and those we did meet were cheerful and friendly, helpfully redirecting us whenever we got lost in the fascinating labyrinth.

Our midday arrival meant the port captain had gone for lunch, so we decided to do the same. We found a restaurant with a clear view of *Stella Maris* and went up the stairs to the veranda that extended out over the water. Seeing just two tables, the possibility suddenly dawned on us that we'd walked into a private residence. But since no one asked us to leave, and because it was the nicest place to eat we'd seen so far, we asked for food anyway; thankfully, our hosts seemed happy to oblige.

We passed a leisurely hour waiting for lunch to arrive, intrigued as to what culinary delights could require such extensive preparations. At last, a smiling teenage girl brought out a plate and proudly placed it on the table. To say we were disappointed to see just four small pancakes would be an understatement, but they were stuffed with cheese and beans and turned out to be a mini-feast that set us back a mere dollar. If we'd had a second hour to spare, we'd have ordered another round.

On our way back to the port captain's office, we passed the town's single-cell prison. From inside, half-hidden in shadow, a man looked at us through the bars and then raised his fingers to his mouth in an apparent request for food. We'd seen enough movies to know we were best advised to ignore him and continued on to the port captain instead, a rotund man not so in need of food and less likely to seize us by the throat when we got within grabbing distance.

"Are you from Guanaja?" Gjalt asked the jolly official as he filled out our clearance certificate.

"No. I'm from a town on the Pacific coast," he said, mentioning a name we'd never heard of. Responding to our blank looks, he suddenly stood up, retrieved his wallet from the pocket of his trousers, and pulled out a two-Lempira bill. "This is the place," he said, pointing at the picture with pride.

We duly made some appropriate noises of admiration.

"Here... keep it," he insisted, thrusting the note at us.

How could we not love a place where they gave us money when we checked out?

We moved *Stella Maris* to a sheltered anchorage just south of the main island and went ashore to take a look at the wreck of a sailing boat that was lying on the beach

– a victim of Mitch's wrath, we decided. A family of human victims were living in a shipping container nearby, their house having been blown away by the hurricane.

Walking inland, we met a middle-aged German man and his young, pregnant wife. He'd bought some land on the island twenty years earlier and turned it into a cattle ranch and fruit farm. "Too many people live on Roatan now," he told us. "Guanaja is still unspoilt. It hasn't changed since I came here. There are no cars and hardly any tourist resorts. It's a wonderful place to live." He asked us where we were heading, and we told him our plans. "Why are you moving so fast?" he said. We just shrugged. We were no longer sure we had a good explanation and, besides, no one who'd asked us this question had understood our answer anyway.

We shared the anchorage with three yachts that had been moored at Josh's Cay with us that morning. We assumed they also intended to head east to the Vivarillo Cays, but when we left at dawn the next day, we left alone. It only occurred to us then that the other boats had moved to shelter from the cold front, not to sail out into it.

The front only reached us at 5 o'clock that afternoon, and until then we had a lovely sail. The sun was out, the seas were calm, and with the gennaker up, we glided along in the light breeze at a smooth five knots. It was nice to start off in gentle weather, it gave us the chance to get used to being at sea again before the conditions turned testing. When the front arrived, a squall gave us a quick drenching, and then the northerly winds increased steadily, with gale-force gusts lasting for several hours. The waves built up, too, making life onboard rather demanding, but at least we made fast progress, averaging seven and a half knots with reefs in both the mainsail and the genoa.

Soon after dawn the next morning, we arrived at the Vivarillo Cays, behind us another 150-mile stretch of the Caribbean that was difficult to cross from west to east. It had taken Christopher Columbus twenty-eight days to sail this distance on his final voyage in 1502. With his ship unable to sail close to the wind, he had to tack the entire distance, the painfully slow journey made worse by terrible storms. When Columbus finally made it past the cape at the easternmost edge of Central America, he said,

"Thank God we have come out from these depths", so the cape became known as Cabo Gracias a Dios (Cape Thanks (be) to God), and the country became Honduras, Spanish for 'depths'.

There were two yachts anchored at the Vivarillo Cays, together with eight fishing boats that had sought shelter from the cold front. A few years earlier, our Dutch friends Els and Henk had felt threatened by fishermen there and warned us to be careful, so we found the presence of the other yachts reassuring. Only fifty miles from the Honduran and Nicaraguan mainland, it seemed sensible to be on our guard.

Marooned in the Caribbean Sea, the Vivarillo Cays consist of reefs and a few sandy islands surrounding an area of shallow water a striking shade of turquoise. We anchored opposite an island that was the temporary home of two families, who were eking out a living catching fish. They were the only inhabitants of this remote spot.

In the evening, we went to the boat *Heavenly Girl* for sundowners. Canadians Peter and Vicky, a bubbly blonde with a touch of Marilyn Monroe breathlessness about her, had been exploring the Caribbean for six years, much of that time with Susanne and Bruce from *Skylark*, the other boat in the anchorage. They made us feel like speed-sailors yet again, as they had just spent six months in Panama's San Blas islands. Both couples returned to North America during the hurricane season, leaving their boats in marinas south of the hurricane belt. It seemed an enviable lifestyle: six months sailing, six months back on land. A seed had been planted that might take hold in our own future.

The next morning they invited us to go diving with them at a reef wall they'd heard about from other cruisers. I was keen to get a dive under my belt and test out my new equipment. All my gear fit perfectly, but I had to practically suck the air out of my tank through the regulator, which didn't exactly help me relax. A frantic complaint to Gjalt led him to turn a valve that controlled the airflow, and miraculously breathing had less of a life-or-death urgency about it.

The plan was for everyone to descend together, but while the others effortlessly drifted downwards, my body merely bobbed just below the surface. As time passed, my legs began to float upwards, but trying to point my feet back down just left me flapping and paddling like a drowning duck struggling to reach the surface, which was where I was heading. Exasperated and embarrassed, I looked to Gjalt for guidance. He indicated that I should swim down, head first instead of feet first, and that was how I finally made it to the seabed, where the others were waiting.

A quick look at my instruments showed that I was now at seventy-seven feet, and this filled me with fresh panic, because Roger had told me not to go deeper than sixty (and I *always* do as I'm told). Gjalt held out his hand, and taking it calmed me down. We swam along the reef wall together until our regulator hoses became entangled, at which point I decided it was safer to swim alone. When Gjalt disappeared into a hole in the reef, only to sneak up behind me and tap me on the shoulder, I wondered how we were ever going to be suitable dive partners for each other. I was permanently teetering on the brink of a panic attack, while he insisted on clowning around.

The visibility was poor, but out of the murk, a very aptly named Goliath grouper appeared, the highlight of the dive. I was quite happy to observe the grumpy-looking creature from a safe distance, but Gjalt just couldn't resist looking the man-sized fish right in the eye.

In the afternoon Peter, Bruce, Gjalt, and I went to see if the fishermen living on the island had a compressor that could be used to refill our dive tanks, but they didn't. It was a Sunday, and the families were playing cards and relaxing in the shade of their simple huts while their salted fish dried in the sun.

Afterwards we dinghyed over to a newly arrived fishing boat to see if we could buy lobsters from them, and we were promptly invited aboard by the captain. The all-male crew stood on the aft deck looking like extras in a pirate film, eyeing us up and down as if figuring out how many meals each of us was good for. They ranged in age from small boys to old men. Most wore tattered clothes, and some of the younger ones had long, unkempt hair and an unnervingly wild look in their eyes. I was acutely aware of their beady eyes upon me as I climbed up the ladder, the last to board. Mistakenly understanding that I intended to wait in the dinghy, Gjalt had already marched off to the foredeck without a backward glance, leaving me to fend for myself, but I'd decided against staying behind like a good little woman. I wasn't going to just sit there and be gawped at while the men enjoyed a leisurely tour of the boat; I wanted to see it too.

As I reached deck level the crew shuffled forwards, forming a semi-circular wall of dark skin, stained clothes, and black hair around the top of the ladder. Suddenly an older man with a kind face stepped forward and held out his hand to help me step onboard. This made me feel safe from his more savage-looking compatriots. The men spent up to eight months at a time at sea, so it was little wonder they appraised me so mercilessly. Thankfully I was modestly dressed in long shorts and a t-shirt, temptation was limited to those with a weakness for ankles or elbows. Even so, I would have felt more comfortable still in a pair of rig coveralls. I thanked the older man and quickly made my way to the bow, where the others were being entertained by Captain Arlie, his name embroidered on his baseball cap, and his first mate, Stephen. They were distinctly less wild than their crew, positively refined in comparison, and I felt quite relieved to have escaped the charged atmosphere on the aft deck.

From the high foredeck, the anchorage looked completely different than from our own cockpit, which was only a few feet above the water. It was like seeing the majestic panorama of a completed jigsaw puzzle after having admired one tantalising corner. A sweeping arc of shimmering turquoise was bounded by islands and reefs, and beyond that was the deep blue sea, stretching to the horizon, where it met a cloudless sky. It was quite something.

Captain Arlie, an affable man in his sixties, made us feel welcome onboard, even going so far as to show us his small personal cabin behind the wheelhouse and photos of his family. He and Stephen told us how they spent months at sea fishing for lobsters, all of which were exported to the United States. They'd come to the anchorage to rendezvous with a supply boat that would have enough provisions to keep them at sea for the last six weeks of the season.

The talk of lobster-hunting led to Stephen telling us about the scuba dives he'd made to depths so dangerous he'd nearly blacked out. His smile never faded while he spoke, and his eyes radiated such spirit they practically sparkled against his dark, Afro-Caribbean skin. He was so unwaveringly sunny it was hard to imagine him ever being glum. When I mentioned that I'd just completed a diving course on Roatan, Gjalt embarrassed me by asking, "Do you know Roger at Fantasy Island?", a question I felt certain was on a par with "Do you know John Smith from London?", but as was so often the case when I thought Gjalt had asked something ridiculous, he hadn't. Suddenly Stephen's shining eyes lit up even more, and he raised his hand to give Gjalt a high-five. "I worked with Roger for eight years, not at Fantasy Island, but another resort," he said and went on to tell stories of their time together.

*What are the odds?* I had to wonder. *Two hundred miles to the east of Roatan, on a fishing boat truly in the middle of nowhere, we meet a man who knows my diving instructor.* Suddenly we had the warm feeling of having friends even in the furthest reaches of Honduras, and we appreciated that cruising let us look at the world through a very special window.

When we left the boat, Captain Arlie presented each of his fellow captains with a bag filled with twelve large lobster tails, and he refused to accept any payment.

"Is there anything you want in return?" I asked him.

"Just friendship," he said.

Later Gjalt dinghyed back to the boat with some books and beer for the fishermen, and Peter and Bruce did the same.

We spent one more day in the Vivarillo Cays, snorkelling and exploring the uninhabited island where mysterious ruins hugged the shore and a strange, inland swamp was concealed by a forest of trees.

We held a farewell lobster feast onboard *Stella Maris*; *Heavenly Girl* and *Skylark* were heading west to Guanaja, and we were going to sail south to the Colombian island of Providencia. Once again, the weather was right for leaving all too soon.

Skylark anchored at the Vivarillo Cays

# 5.

## *Unmolested in Providencia*

*Queen conch is a highly valuable fishery for the San Andrés and Providencia Archipelago, but according to landing statistics, the fishery peaked in 1988 and has been in decline ever since because of over-fishing.*

*The most pervasive threat to Colombia's reefs is over-fishing, threatening nearly 40 percent of reefs.*

    – World Resources Institute, 2004

We left the Vivarillo Cays just as the sun rose above the horizon. We were grateful to be heading out into seas that were calm, because for the first few hours we had to motor into light easterlies. By afternoon, the wind had shifted to the northeast and was increasing steadily, giving us pleasant sailing conditions that lasted all through the night.

Out of the late afternoon haze, an undefined shape far in the distance materialised into a shockingly huge ship. Just fifteen minutes later, it stormed past us a few miles off our starboard side, which meant it must have been moving at well over twenty knots. The cheerful Dole logo emblazoned on the side did little to take the edge off the banana boat's monstrous presence, and we were reminded of the need to be diligent about our watch-keeping at all times.

From the Vivarillo Cays, we had to sail sixty miles southeast to steer around the treacherous shallows and reefs scattered east of Cabo Gracias a Dios. Shortly after sunset, we'd cleared them and were able to ease the sheets and sail south. Like Columbus 500 years before us, we were happy to be out of the crook of Central America's arm and have the prevailing winds in our favour at last. The most difficult part of our trip was now behind us, Gjalt assured me. There would be no more need to ride with the wild cold fronts; from there on out, we'd be pushed gently along by the trade winds. As if proving him right, we had moonlight and clear skies to sail by that night, and we glided onwards over a benign sea.

The next day, we hoisted the gennaker as soon as the wind became light to ensure we'd reach the island of Providencia before sunset. With the big sail harnessing the breeze, we maintained speeds of over six knots. As *Stella Maris* marched south, she was deftly raised and lowered by an enormous, long-period swell that rolled at her from the east across 1,000 miles of Caribbean Sea.

With the 350-metre-high volcanic peaks of Providencia rising up from the horizon ahead of us, the scream of the fishing reel announced the first bite of our trip, a full two months after setting off from Texas. We weren't sure if our lack of success was a sign of over-fishing in the Caribbean or an absence of skill; we preferred to think it was the latter. We dropped the gennaker to slow down *Stella Maris* so Gjalt could bring in the fish. As he reeled it towards the stern, it jumped out of the water, giving us a view of its vividly coloured body shimmering in the sunlight. It was a beautiful dorado.

After fifteen minutes of strenuous heaving and reeling, our catch was alongside the stern. I took the rod from Gjalt so he could lean over the side with the gaff and hook the fish through its gills. He killed it by pouring tequila into the gills and then lifted the fish onboard. In order to bleed it, he made strategic incisions into its body, tied a line around the tail and then trailed it behind the boat for ten minutes.

The dorado was the exact length of the four-foot filleting table Gjalt had lovingly installed on the aft deck in anticipation of moments such as that one, but the excitement of catching our very first fish was unexpectedly tainted by a feeling of guilt at having killed such a magnificent creature. Its vibrant green and gold markings faded to grey as soon as Gjalt poured tequila into the gills, as if beauty and life were leaving together. But death brought beauty of a different kind; the tender white meat was so delicious that it lived up to its reputation as 'the food of the gods'.

The Providencia anchorage nestled between the northern tip of the island and the southern shores of Santa Catalina, a smaller island that seemed to have broken free and drifted a stone's throw away to claim its independence. A well-marked channel led us past the thickly wooded slopes of Santa Catalina, their tropical provenance made obvious by haphazardly scattered clusters of palm trees. Our alcoholic travelling companion, the privateer Captain Morgan, had been there before. In 1671, he used the island as the base from which he carried out a murderous raid on Panama. As in Roatan, pirates were part of Providencia's history.

We anchored in the late afternoon sunshine amongst three other visiting yachts and brought out Captain Morgan's more jolly descendant to toast our arrival. Minutes later, Walter, a German cruiser from the boat *Lemuria,* was alongside in his dinghy. With his chubby cheeks and a distinctly mischievous glint in the eye, he bore more than a passing resemblance to Benny Hill. He filled us in on the local procedures and the delights of the island, his sentences punctuated by short, unexpected bursts of giggling. He was a bubbly, one-man welcoming committee.

The following morning, Gjalt was in the full throes of churning out crew lists for the authorities when, in a stealthy pre-emptive strike, representatives from all the interested departments quietly pulled up alongside, packed together in a small wooden boat. Mr. Bush, a dreaded agent – but at least a friendly and helpful one – was the man in charge. With his dark skin, greying goatee, and non-confrontational nature, the only thing he had in common with George W., thankfully, was his surname. We invited him and his delegation onboard, and all the necessary paperwork was completed in the comfort of our own cockpit, a convenience that did, however, cost us forty dollars. Mr. Bush appeared to be well aware of the speed with which cruisers share information and was keen on making us feel welcome and safe on his island. "If you don't molest anyone, no one will molest you," he assured us.

This seemed entirely reasonable to us, and refraining from any impropriety ourselves, we did indeed remain unmolested for the duration of our visit.

Officially free to venture ashore, we were dissuaded by

a sudden deluge of torrential rain. Soon, a heavy mist rose up from the hot earth, obscuring the green slopes and making the island strangely reminiscent of not-so-tropical Scotland.

By early afternoon, the sun had returned, and we walked through the main town. We were surprised at the number of well-stocked supermarkets and mini-markets there were to cater to a population of just 4,200. The town was awash with teenagers, including pretty girls in tight-fitting and revealing clothes that the puritan colonists who had travelled there from England in the seventeenth century would definitely not have approved of. More than 300 years of Anglo, Spanish, and African influences had apparently softened the hardest religious edges, and boys now swept these modern beauties off their feet on noisy motorbikes. No one seemed to notice the arrival of two new cruisers into their midst.

Before long, a fresh downpour began, and we got soaked on our way back to *Stella Maris*. The rain continued until the following afternoon, which was probably a good thing, since it gave us an excuse (which we seemed to need) to relax onboard instead of tearing around our new port-of-call ticking off the sights.

When the weather finally cleared, we walked on the island of Santa Catalina, where we found our jovial friend Walter and his dark-haired, mysteriously enigmatic wife Gisela collecting mangos. They invited us onboard *Lemuria* for sundowners, a sweet, tasty concoction of home-made mango juice and smooth rum.

Like most cruisers we met in the Caribbean, this German couple had retired early from their working lives. They'd bought their boat whilst working in Turkey and spent several years learning to sail before setting off on their circumnavigation. Unlike us, though, they were taking their time, having already spent five years cruising the Mediterranean and the Caribbean. With so many years under their belts, it wasn't surprising that they had a good tale to tell.

"Friends of ours had recommended an anchorage in Venezuela," Walter began. "When we arrived there late one afternoon we were the only yacht in the bay. There were locals in boats who appeared to be fishing, but they were acting strangely, as if they were just *pretending* to fish. We had a feeling something was wrong, but it was late and we didn't want to look for a new anchorage in the dark.

"That evening we were sitting down below when we heard footsteps on deck. I got the shotgun we kept onboard and suddenly a man appeared at the top of the stairs. Gisela rushed at him, pushing him back out of the cabin, while I threatened him with the gun. The man ran away and we both chased after him, hearing the water splash as he and two other men jumped over the side. I fired a shot into the air to make sure they kept swimming."

"Then one of the men started to head back to the boat and shouted that he couldn't swim," Gisela continued, "but there was no way we were going to let him climb onboard. I shouted to Walter, 'Kill him, kill him', and he swam off. I was really angry."

"We immediately pulled up our anchor and left," Walter said. "It was dark and the exit from the anchorage was narrow, but we had to leave. Looking back, we should never have stayed in the first place. We were the only yacht in the bay and we knew the locals were acting strangely. We won't make that mistake again."

Surprisingly, Walter said they'd thrown the gun into the sea afterwards. Even though it had probably helped them that night, they felt it had the potential to escalate violence to a point where it would do them more harm than good.

Most cruisers think about what kind of defensive weapons they should have onboard, and we didn't want to take any guns. For a start they have to be declared to Customs, and the paperwork was bad enough already. But worse than that, there was always the chance that a nervous finger on the trigger might lead to the death of an unarmed local. Not only would our consciences have to wrestle with that, but we would also have to wrestle with the legal system of a foreign country, possibly even face murder charges. If we were ever unfortunate enough to encounter serious pirates with serious weapons, we felt we'd be more likely to encourage them to use their weapons if we started waving ours around. Whatever we were waving, they would undoubtedly be waving something bigger and would be better practiced and more willing to use it. We weren't prepared to fight an all-out gun battle with pirates. Instead, we bought an industrial-sized canister of weapons-grade bear spray. It was banned in most corners of the USA, but it was, of course, perfectly legal in the Lone Star State. The heavy-duty pepper spray was capable of immobilising an intruder from a safe distance of thirty feet – as long as he was standing downwind. As our chosen cruising route avoided most known areas of piracy, there was thankfully scant chance of us coming across anyone scarier than Captain Jack Sparrow, but if we did, we were ready to spray them.

One morning, while we were innocently sitting in our cockpit, we happened to witness something bizarre, to put it mildly. Gisela was dispassionately dinghying through the anchorage, unmoved by the fate of her husband, who she was towing in her wake. Walter was being dragged underwater for long periods of time, his head resurfacing just long enough to snatch a breath before submerging again. It really was very odd. We wondered if it was a method of punishment, a cruisers' version of keelhauling we hadn't yet heard about. "Perhaps Walter refused to take the garbage onshore once too often," I joked to Gjalt.

A tentative enquiry when next we met revealed that it hadn't been a case of being made to walk the plank, but rather a voluntary desire to dive with it. Walter had traded an old boat battery for a device called a dive-glider (known in non-professional circles as a short wooden plank), and what we'd witnessed was him trying it out for the first time. Whilst Gisela drove the dinghy, he held on to the dive-glider, which was attached to a towing line. By tilting it forward, he was pulled underwater, where he was able to admire the sea life at greater speed than he could muster under his own steam. This was apparently the next big thing: snorkelling for the lazy, or for the cruiser who enjoyed diving in the fast lane. I doubted if being dragged underwater at high speed was likely to catch on. If anything was ever supposed to be done slowly and peacefully, it was surely snorkelling.

At thirty-two kilometres in length, Providencia's barrier reef is one of the largest in the Americas and forms part of the Seaflower Biosphere Reserve, home to some of the most diverse marine life in the Caribbean. Unfortunately, incessant strong winds prevented us from being able to dive on the reef, so we settled for the site of a World War II shipwreck close to the island instead. Walter and

Gisela took a break from the joys of dive-gliding so they could join us for the afternoon.

We arranged to go with the island's dive operator, Scuba Town, which was actually more of a house than a town but had all the necessary gear and credentials. It was there where we ran into Jack Sparrow sooner than we'd anticipated. The dive master, with the superbly theatrical moniker of Geronimo, was a dead ringer for Johnny Depp. As might be expected of someone who looked like a Hollywood heart-throb, he was quietly confident, and his careless long hair and evident wild streak were clear indications that the man had never seen the inside of an office. He gave every impression of living up to his legendary name.

We raced over to the site in a large, rigid, inflatable boat, and I tried to look serenely unfazed as we bounced over the sea, churned up by a wind that continued to blow unabated. At least I knew I wasn't alone in my apprehension; Walter and Gisela's last dive had been two years before. Walter was even wearing a BCD that looked as if it had come from an Army surplus store and was of the same vintage as the wreck we were about to explore. It did gain some respect for its built-in emergency tank, although Geronimo was afraid the ancient air inside it might be more life-ending than life-giving. When Walter discovered the tank was frozen shut, Geronimo couldn't hide his relief.

With the boat safely anchored, we tumbled over the side like professionals and prepared to go under. I pointed my feet downwards, emptied the air from my BCD, and felt my head sink beneath the choppy surface. And then, true to form, I stayed there while everyone else descended. Feeling my legs floating upwards, I began to flap through my drowning duck routine until Gjalt signalled me to swim down – which I managed. A graceful feet-first descent was simply beyond me. Closing the gap between my ineptitude and the 200 dives under Gjalt's belt was going to require a very long bridge.

The strong winds and choppy seas had created poor visibility, and I didn't find the wreck particularly exciting. A few corals had anchored themselves to its hull, and the odd fish swam effortlessly by, but for me, the dive was more about building my confidence and not allowing so much time between dives that I lost my courage altogether.

Back on the beach in front of Scuba Town, Geronimo told us about U.S. helicopters chasing drug-trafficking speedboats around the waters of Providencia, sometimes shooting at their engines. Some islanders secretly hoped to find a package of jettisoned cocaine washed up on the beach, a local version of winning the lottery, albeit with a few dangerous obstacles to cashing in the prize hidden in the small print.

We hadn't wanted to leave *Stella Maris* unattended while the strong winds raged, so it was only when conditions eased a few days later that we rented a moped to tour the island. At just seven kilometres long and three and a half wide, we'd whizzed around it on our nifty fifty-cc red devil in no time. In four hours, we were able to circumnavigate the island twice, doubling the fun and value eked out of the twenty-dollar rental charge.

We followed the winding road up to attractive houses with spectacular views and down again to sheltered bays with long stretches of golden beaches lined with palm trees. The sunshine lit up the reef patches surrounding the island, and the shallow water had been coloured using a palette of subtly varying shades of blue. After two months of looking at land from the detached viewpoint of the sea, it was wonderful to be close to plants and grass and flowers again.

We had lunch at a small outdoor restaurant beside a beach and feasted on tender conch, sadly oblivious to the fact that its numbers around the island were in serious decline due to over-fishing. At a nearby table, a young woman was flicking through a copy of *In Touch*, an American gossip magazine. I saw that the cover had photographs of Angelina Jolie, Brad Pitt, and Jennifer Aniston side by side, under a headline that declared, 'The Truth Is Out'. It made me realise that not only was I out of touch, but the truth was out there, and I had absolutely no idea what it was.

We stayed in Providencia for a week, and it felt good to be in the same place for more than a couple of nights. We spent some time on boat maintenance, enjoyed the odd cheap meal in town, tested the beer at various establishments, and exercised our underused leg muscles. I also regained my belief that our aim of reaching Australia by the end of the year was perfectly sound. Paradise on Earth was waiting in the Pacific, and to make sure we were there as soon as the cyclone season was over, we had to move quickly now. We were just not the kind of people who could hang around in the Caribbean for months that stretched into years. Most of the cruisers we'd met were early retirees, and that was not what we were – or if we were, we hadn't realised it yet. Time would tell if we would go back to work after we reached Australia, or if we would carry on around the world and complete a circumnavigation. We certainly weren't missing office life, and just the thought of going back to work created a tight knot in Gjalt's stomach. He felt he'd lost himself there and was only now coming back to his senses. But we didn't feel like bums either; we were sailing too much and experiencing too many new things to think that what we were achieving had no value.

We came to discover that the need for speed is a common addiction in yachties at the start of their cruising lives, even amongst those who told us we were moving too fast. Gisela admitted it had been hard work to persuade Walter to stay more than one night in an anchorage when they first started cruising. It was clear that it took time to subdue a driven person reared to thrive in the capitalist arena of the West.

When we heard on the Caribbean Cruisers' Net that yachts were having to wait three weeks to transit the Panama Canal, our feet began to itch so badly that we just had to scratch them. We'd had half an idea to visit the San Blas islands of Panama, but this flew right out the window without a second thought. We wanted to get to Colón, beside the Atlantic entrance of the Canal, and onto that waiting list.

We tracked down our friend, the agent Mr. Bush, and ruined the poor man's morning by insisting he had all the checking-out formalities completed before noon, by which time we needed to be underway. While we waited in his office, he made the rounds to Immigration, Customs, and the port captain on our behalf. Once all the paperwork had been signed and stamped, he bade us farewell, no doubt glad to see the back of us.

We weighed anchor on schedule, waved goodbye to Walter and Gisela, whose calmer pace would take them across the Pacific the following year, and headed out to sea.

GJALT FILLETING OUR FIRST DORADO

# 6.

# *Crossing to the Other Side*

*Approximately 100 million containers are shipped annually over the world's oceans. Shipping across the North Pacific Ocean from Asia to North America is along Great Circle Routes in the West Wind Drift current at the northern edge of the Central Pacific Gyre. Frequent severe storms along this route cause the loss of hundreds of containers each year contributing, among other plastics, tens of thousands of shoes and millions of plastic shopping bags made in Asia.*

– Algalita Marine Research Foundation, 2007

As soon as we were south of Providencia, we picked up good northeasterly winds, which gave us a steady start to the two-day trip. With the sails set for the Panamanian Isthmus, we settled down to enjoy a lavish lunch in the cockpit, with all manner of goodies laid out, ready to be piled on top of the freshly purchased Colombian bread. One bite, however, proved it to be utterly inedible. It had the familiar unpalatable taste of every mass-produced loaf we'd tried in Central America, accentuated by the almost certain use of rancid butter and curdled milk. Only the most committed contestants on *Fear Factor* would have been able to force down a slice without retching, and no one was offering us fifty thousand dollars to eat it. We had no option but to ditch every last crumb overboard; the fish could have a go at it, if they dared.

Having safely reached the realm of the trade winds, we enjoyed our first truly restful passage. The large waves rolled towards us like giant sheets of liquid corrugated iron, moving us gently up and down as they passed on their way. The period of the waves was so long that *Stella Maris* remained steady enough in the water for us to play chess in the cockpit.

On the second day of the passage, the wind gradually died, and the large rollers flattened out. We hoisted the gennaker and were able to maintain a speed that would get us to Colón by lunchtime. It had seemed almost rude of Gjalt to breathe down Mr. Bush's neck in order to get our clearance document in Providencia, but if we hadn't been able to leave that day, we would have had to motor for half of the 250-mile trip. Gjalt had frog-marched me through the check-out process in all the countries we'd been to, bar Mexico, his stone-cold determination spawning feelings of moderate resentment and moments of intense irritation at the time. Unfortunately, I could never lambaste his bully-ing ways afterwards, because his urgency was always justified in the end. He was, however, wise enough not to push his luck by crowing about his good judgment.

As we approached Colón, we saw our first ship of the passage loom out of the haze on the horizon. It was so enormous and such a strange shape that we wondered for some time if it was really a ship at all; it looked more like the headquarters of SPECTRE, surfaced by Blofeld to launch an attack that would bring him world domination at last. It was only when we got much closer that we saw it was something almost as scary as the hideout of a James Bond villain: a massive cargo ship loaded with thousands of containers, stack after stack, rising up from every square metre of the deck to the level of the bridge. It was frighten-ingly clear to us how difficult it would be for the crew of that massive vessel to spot a small yacht at sea.

Sailing through an armada of these monstrous beasts waiting at anchor for their turn to go through the Canal gave me the creeps. Each time we passed in front of a bow, I took perverse pleasure in imagining that we were mid-ocean and I had just come on deck in time to see the gigan-tic steel hulk bearing down on us. This horrific notion sent shudders down my spine, not least because yachts had been run over in just this way. Our watch system was all about preventing it from happening to us.

Having obtained permission from Cristobal Signal (Port Control) to enter the yacht anchorage, we followed a freighter between the breakwaters and into the deep channel that led to the Panama Canal's first set of locks. Gjalt and I had just concluded that every ship entering the area must be required to have a pilot onboard when the voice of the Port Controller burst out of our radio.

"Motor vessel entering the port, you are sailing out of the channel. The water is not deep enough for your ship there, Captain. You must turn to port immediately."

"Cristobal Signal, that is understood. I will turn to port," came a calm Indian voice, as if nothing was amiss. The ship, however, maintained its course.

"Please, Captain, you must turn to port immediately and wait in the channel," the controller insisted, beginning to lose his cool.

"That is understood, sir, I am turning to port," the unshakeable voice came over the radio again, still without a hint of stress.

The freighter had clearly proceeded between the breakwaters without a pilot onboard. Perhaps the captain thought he could jump the queue and was intending to go straight to the Canal locks. Suddenly the ship turned so hard to port that it ended up broadside to the channel.

Just as we passed in front of its bow to enter the yacht anchorage, Port Control came on the radio again. "Captain, you must stop your vessel please. I can see that you are still moving. Stop your engines. Please do what you can to stop your vessel."

"Yes, sir. I am stopping the ship now."

Whether the captain's coolness was commendable or the cause of the drama we will never know, but it seemed astonishing at the time. His ship finally came to a halt perpendicular to the channel, blocking the path of a ship heading out of the port, much to the incredulity and annoyance of the captain.

"What are your intentions?" he demanded.

A pilot boat sped across to the uninvited ship, and it was soon on its way back through the breakwaters to anchor with the patiently waiting armada. We imagined the furtive whispering the captain had to endure as he moved amongst his crew in the weeks that followed.

We hadn't expected that such a dramatic event could occur at the Panama Canal, where forty ships transit on any given day. Later, a Port Controller told us that after the wide expanses of the open ocean, some captains felt as if they were about to take their ship through the eye of a needle when they saw the gap between the breakwaters.

Thankfully, our arrival was unremarkable.

No sooner had we dropped the anchor than a lean man with straggly, greying hair rowed over in a small wooden dinghy, his quick, urgent strokes making it obvious that he was in a hurry. Keith, a seasoned English solo sailor, had been scheduled to go through the Canal in a week's time, but the date had been brought forward to the next day, so he now found himself in desperate need of crew. Every yacht required four people to handle the lines used to secure it to the sides of the lock, and cruisers preferred one another over the Panamanian line-handlers, who each charged fifty dollars for their services. Besides, most cruisers wanted to find out what to expect from the Canal on someone else's boat before they had to take their own through. Unfortunately, we couldn't help Keith out, because we still had to check in and start the process of getting ourselves on the waiting list. Before he rowed off into the anchorage to continue his quest, he told us that he'd sailed from Florida in eleven days. I felt better already: the very first sailor we met had deposed us as the fastest boat through the Caribbean by months; we'd positively crawled through it compared to him. It was the first sign that we'd become part of a different band of cruisers.

Flags from all over the world flew proudly from the sterns of about thirty yachts that were waiting to take the short cut through to the Pacific. There were many more young people taking a break from their careers than those who'd washed their hands of them forever, couples in their thirties rather than their fifties. We were excited to be amongst them all and felt that we were really on the cusp of our big adventure now.

There was plenty of entertainment to be enjoyed from the anchorage. Ships lined up to go through the Canal like planes on a runway, and every detail of the operation could be heard on the VHF radio. I found it endlessly fascinating. We had a ringside seat at one of mankind's greatest feats of engineering, one that had stood the test of time for over ninety years. But it had come at a price.

In all, 27,500 labourers lost their lives to the monumental undertaking that the French began in 1881 and the Americans completed in 1914, and the surrounding environment was changed forever. To eradicate the mosquitoes responsible for vast numbers of deaths from malaria and yellow fever, hundreds of square miles of wetlands were drained and filled, and vast expanses were poisoned or covered with oil. A massive trench was dug through the Continental Divide, man-made Gatun Lake submerged more than 160 square miles of tropical rainforest, and the North and South American continents became separated by water. The Panama Canal is a perfect example of man's duality: his unparalleled capacity to overcome immense challenges with technology and his unparalleled capacity to have a detrimental impact on the natural world.

In the early evening on the day of our arrival, we watched two yachts set off for the first set of locks. Following in the wake of a massive container ship, they looked very small and sweet as they disappeared around the headland. If only two yachts were transiting each day, we knew it would be another fortnight before our turn would come.

To get our names on the list, we had to venture into Colón, a city with a fearful reputation for violent crime. Beyond the guarded grounds of the Panama Canal Yacht Club (a place less fancy than its name, but a haven from the streets outside nonetheless), cruisers had to stay on red alert. A notorious block of flats opposite the club provided an excellent vantage point for the local thugs to spot their easiest prey: the bright-eyed and bushy-tailed, newly arrived cruiser. With the target identified, a gang could have their victim surrounded in no time, machete blades drawn to encourage a speedy transfer of funds. So, the golden rule was to take a taxi for even the shortest trips – easy enough to abide by since fares were only one dollar. Two people we knew were mugged in Colón while we were there, and both assaults took place opposite the flats, in broad daylight.

Fully psyched up to enter Panama's poorest and most dangerous city, we set off early in the morning. Our clothes had been carefully chosen to satisfy two requirements: unappealing enough to dissuade the muggers from wasting their time on us, but not so shabby that they showed disrespect to the officials. We left our watches and sunglasses onboard, carried our boat papers and money in concealed belts, and armed ourselves with handy pocket-sized canisters of pepper spray.

We approached the mafia of quietly intimidating taxi-drivers-in-residence at the Yacht Club gates and asked to be driven the short distance into town. A tall, scrawny man led us to his car and thankfully didn't try to persuade us to employ him as our agent, a commonly purchased and relatively expensive service that two young couples had assured us wasn't necessary. Ellington could undoubtedly have been very persuasive if he'd wanted to be. An ex-U.S. Marine, he may have looked old and frail, but he had the steely eyes of a man who'd served in Somalia in the early 1980s and lost four friends in action there. He was polite and friendly, but was doubtless still able to snap a neck like a twig, if the urge grabbed him.

The trail between the necessary departments proved to be straightforward. Having been dropped off by Ellington, we scurried into the faded colonial building that housed the Maritime Office and quickly obtained our compulsory cruising permit. A short scoot across the road took us to the secure perimeter of the Port Authority, where guards allowed us in to make an appointment to have *Stella Maris* measured for the transit. And so, the day's missions were accomplished. All that remained was to get safely back to the Yacht Club.

With our eyes perpetually scanning for unsavoury characters keen on demonstrating the finer attributes of their concealed weapons to us, we emerged from the safety of the port. After a period of nervous loitering, it became clear that this wasn't a place taxis ventured looking for a fare, so we had no choice but to search for one ourselves. It was only a short walk to the main road, but it took us past a row of men and women who appeared to be waiting for something, although exactly what they were waiting for was unclear. We kept our hands on the pepper sprays in our pockets, just in case that something was us. With great relief, we flagged down a taxi before any of them broke formation and were soon driving past the notorious flats in our impenetrable metal cocoon. Safely back behind the Yacht Club fence, we felt proud of having survived our first excursion into Colón without having hired any body-guards.

The day was also memorable in another way; it had been the first of my non-birthdays. Since I was born on February 29th I had no real birthday that year, so as usual, I compensated by celebrating the occasion on both

February 28th (in the month that I was born) and March 1st (the day it would have fallen on had Julius Caesar not added a leap day to the calandar every four years). The practice of turning no birthday into two seemed like a good idea when I was young, but as more and more years were added to my personal clock, it just meant an additional day of feeling depressed. Suitably distracted by the Canal paperwork, this year's depression didn't set in until the evening, and then I wasn't entirely sure if it was really due to my birthday or because I felt somewhat trapped by the cruising lifestyle.

Gjalt and I had lived together in a home little bigger than a garden shed for two and a half months by that time. We'd sailed some 1,800 miles as we raced our way to Panama at the beck and call of the wind. Gjalt was very much in charge, and I was still a complete novice. Although we hadn't sailed in any weather that frightened me, Belize had tested my nerves with its shallow waters, learning to dive had forced me to confront my phobias, and everywhere we went we attacked the obligatory paperwork as if our lives depended on it. It seemed as though we were on one long military exercise with enjoyment being snatched in between sorties behind enemy lines.

That night, I dreamt I was trapped under *Stella Maris'* hull. I woke up sweating profusely, frantically pushing my hands against the ceiling as I tried to stop myself from drowning. My side of the bed was right up against the stern in a spot I called 'the coffin' because the topsides stepped down above my head, leaving me just a few inches of breathing space. Gjalt pulled me out of the coffin to the hatch, where frantic inhalation of fresh air eventually succeeded in calming me down.

The next day, the admeasurer, Tony, a towering Panamanian who looked eminently capable of swatting a troublesome cruiser like a fly, arrived right on schedule. Easygoing but professional, he had *Stella Maris* measured in no time, and we became the happy recipients of the piece of paper that allowed us to get onto the waiting list – an invoice for the transit. Yachts less than fifty feet were charged six hundred dollars, a small price to pay to avoid the thrills of Cape Horn, in my opinion. Tony gave us an interesting leaflet explaining the history and operation of the Canal, and it was rather nauseating to see that the same terminology we'd grown so tired of at work had slipped into the lingo there as well. The Panama Canal Commission, which took over the operation from the USA on New Year's Eve in 1999, 'valued diversity' and recognised that 'people were its most important resource'. But of course they did.

We ate in the Yacht Club restaurant that evening and, with my depression miraculously gone, celebrated my second birthday with some other cruisers. A few had just returned from line-handling on yachts that had been through the Canal that day, and we eagerly listened to their reports.

Most yachts were tied together within the locks in order to move more through at one time. Every yacht had an advisor onboard, and that day the advisors hadn't seen eye to eye. In a childish bid for dominance, they issued conflicting instructions to the line-handlers, adding some unwelcome excitement to an already stressful event.

"If they'd had knives they would have tried to kill each other," one of the cruisers said.

The information pack we'd received from Tony told us that the advisor needed to be provided with food, shade in which to savour it, and a toilet in which to deposit its digested remains, should that prove necessary. We heard horror stories about advisors who remained miserable no matter what was offered to lift their spirits. It was just a matter of luck; you were stuck with whoever turned up on your boat, so all we could do was wish that our luck was good.

Gjalt agreed to act as line-handler on a Norwegian boat, and I stayed onboard *Stella Maris* to look after her while he was gone. I watched them leave shortly before sunset and was fascinated to see four enormous cruise ships emerging from the Canal, dwarfing the sailing boats that went past them in the opposite direction. I had no idea that cruise ships went through the Canal and thought it must be more pleasant to experience the operation as a carefree spectator on such a vessel than as a key player on your own precious home. But of course it wouldn't be nearly so adventurous or anywhere near as rewarding.

I'd looked forward to a rare evening alone, but soon after Gjalt left, I began to feel unwell and crawled miserably into bed. At midnight, I was awoken by painful intestinal cramps, and when I got up, I noticed that a newly arrived yacht had anchored right behind *Stella Maris*. This gave me no reaction time if she dragged on her anchor and the holding ground in the anchorage was quite poor, as it consisted of silty sludge. By this time, we'd been securely anchored for four days, but that fact did little to reassure me. For the first time, I realised how well I slept when Gjalt was onboard doing all the worrying on my behalf. I woke up repeatedly during the night feeling decidedly ill, until finally I rushed on deck and vomited over the side. I suspected the steak and shrimp birthday dinner, but I couldn't help wondering how much of my nausea was stress induced, now that I was fully responsible for *Stella Maris*' wellbeing.

After all the weeks living squashed together, I was sure I'd enjoy some solitude, but I missed Gjalt and was glad when he returned. His trip had gone well and proved to be vital preparation for our own transit through the Canal. He'd been surprised by the height of the lock walls and their roughness; even a gentle collision would damage a yacht's hull. And he'd been shocked by the violent turbulence of the water as it flooded into the lock chamber and the tremendous strain it placed on the lines, which creaked alarmingly. He'd even witnessed a tugboat crashing into a lock wall when it broke free of its mooring, sending a navigation light flying in a high arc over the yacht he was on. Keeping the lines secured was a serious business.

Supplies were going to be scarce and expensive in the Pacific, and Panama was the last place to replenish our provisions cheaply. The taxi ride to the hypermarkets on the outskirts of town weaved us through the streets of Colón. It was probably the poorest place we'd ever visited and certainly felt the most threatening. Walls were daubed in graffiti, and narrow staircases in dark alleys led up to shabby apartments in dilapidated housing blocks. Crumbling colonial buildings hinted at a former prosperity enjoyed while the USA constructed the Canal, but those times were long gone. With poverty levels in the city among the worst in Latin America and unemployment the highest in the country, it was hardly surprising that crime was rife. We couldn't understand why none of the money generated by the Canal went towards rejuvenating the city that was lying right beside its Atlantic entrance.

The gleaming supermarkets could have been on another planet, one we were relieved we'd been transported to. We filled the trolley with essentials: rice, pasta, tinned tuna, corned beef, and twenty-four cartons of attractively priced Chilean wine – wine we'd also see a lot of on other boats as we made our way across the Pacific.

After all the stories of yachts having to wait three weeks for their transit, we were pleasantly surprised to be given a date just one week later. I didn't mind waiting in Colón. The operation of the Canal never ceased to interest me, and I liked staying put for a while. Gjalt was less keen on the place. At night, rubbish was set ablaze in a nearby garbage dump, and when there was little wind, a stubborn cloud of acrid smoke hung over the anchorage, enveloping it in a dense haze. We had to close all the hatches so as not to breathe in minute particles of charcoaled garbage, opting to suffer a sweltering, hermetically sealed night onboard instead. The following morning, we'd find a film of black dust on the topsides that was incredibly hard to remove. At such times I wasn't that keen on Colón either.

Four days before our transit date, Gjalt had secured three line-handlers in addition to me. Americans Greg and Jeff seemed to be long-term residents of the Yacht Club marina and volunteered simply because they enjoyed going through the Canal. Richard was an upstanding British solo sailor who'd served in the SBS, a credential that qualified him to handle the bow line, which Gjalt's test-run through the Canal had shown to be the most crucial.

Richard introduced us to Gillian, an inspiring seventy-four-year-old Canadian with striking long white hair, and her current crew, twenty-five-year-old free-spirited American, James. They'd met in Gibraltar when James, who was backpacking around the world to avoid being 'one-dimensional', asked Gillian if he could sail with her. She agreed to give him a test-run in challenging conditions, and he managed to prove his mettle. Several months later, he joined her in the Caribbean, and the two of them were now both nearing the end of their sailing adventures. Once they were through the Canal, James planned to return to his job as a forest firefighter in Oregon, and Gillian aimed to complete the final 300 miles of a circumnavigation that had spanned seventeen adventurous years. Gillian's husband, who didn't like sailing and had just had a hip replacement operation, was driving a campervan from Canada to Central America, where he would meet his wife and travel overland with her. And afterwards, as if this wasn't enough for two people in their seventies, they planned to go to Holland, buy a barge, and explore the canals of Europe. Listening to Gillian made our ambitions seem positively tame.

Our first call to the scheduling office revealed that we were due to go through the Canal with a French-Canadian yacht. We located it in the anchorage and dinghyed over to introduce ourselves, only to encounter a man who made plain his revulsion of the English language.

"*Pas un mot,*" he announced, turning away in disgust whilst dismissing our enquiry as to his linguistic abilities with an irritated flick of the hand.

Our French was rusty at best, and we knew that if we couldn't communicate with the boat crew, our transit was bound to be stressful. Gjalt cast his eye over the yacht and was worried that its cleats weren't strong enough to take the strain when the water started gushing into the lock. If the cleats were pulled out of the deck, *Stella Maris* would be smashed into the lock wall.

Things looked up a few days later, when two more boats were scheduled to transit with us, one of which was a perfect match to *Stella Maris* in size and weight. We made our move and agreed with the captain (an American who was not averse to speaking English) that our boats should raft together.

The evening before the transit, we heard from other cruisers that Gary and Jeff had left us in the lurch by line-handling for friends of theirs that day. They wouldn't be back in time to crew for us. We'd seen Greg that very morning, and he actually said, "You can count on us." We didn't realise that meant we could count on them to let us down.

Gjalt wasn't fazed by the news and easily slipped back into the familiar territory of project management. A deadline was fast approaching, and he just had to do whatever was necessary to meet it. He headed out into the anchorage and quickly recruited replacement line-handlers: Gillian's new crew, Gary, a sociable American fresh from the airport, and Erik, an imperturbable Norwegian approached by

Gjalt simply because his yacht was a Swan, and anyone with judgement that admirable had to be good. They were serious, dependable, middle-aged men, and we actually felt fortunate to be rid of the other two.

With one problem solved, another one reared its head. A call to the scheduling office revealed a last-minute addition to our transit group. The less than appealing plan was to sandwich a sixty-six-foot, forty-ton steel yacht between two twelve-ton yachts, one of which was ours. Gjalt almost blew a gasket at the idea of *Stella Maris* having to withstand such tremendous strain, whilst acting as a huge fender for this hefty boat, and spent a long time attempting to change the scheduler's mind.

The phone call did nothing to help reduce the tension that had set in since Gary and Jeff deserted us. To make sure he got a good night's rest, Gjalt took a sleeping pill. Not wanting to lie awake worrying all by myself, I took one too.

The day of the transit got off to a good start, when a final call to the scheduler revealed that we wouldn't be rafted to the steel boat after all. We were back to our preferred plan, which alleviated a great deal of stress. We took a taxi to the Maritime Agency to check out and then bought enough fresh food to feed everyone during the transit. In the afternoon, Gjalt picked up the men and briefed us all on how he wanted the lines to be handled. The need to deal with people distracted us from worrying about the transit. Gjalt was particularly anxious about the locks that would raise *Stella Maris* up, because the stress on the lines was so great, but having an experienced and mature team – especially Richard on the bow – eased his nerves. I was unexpectedly relaxed; now I just looked forward to getting on with it and being safely on the other side.

Our Panamanian advisor, Ricky, arrived by pilot boat at five, and after all the horror stories we'd heard about difficult advisors, he instantly put us at ease; he couldn't have been more considerate or more professional. We motored around the headland we'd watched so many other boats disappear behind, and by 6 o'clock, we were at Gatun locks. These were going to raise us eighty-five feet in three stages, up to the level of Gatun Lake.

We rafted to the other yacht as planned and motored

into the first of the three lock chambers, in which a container ship was already waiting. Its lines were attached to small electric locomotives on the lock walls, which kept them taut and secure. With each lock 1,000 feet in length, yachts were usually lifted together with a ship to conserve water; each transit flushed fifty-two million gallons of fresh water from Gatun Lake into the sea. The other two rafted yachts in our group followed us in.

Canal workers standing on either side of the lock threw a bow and stern line to each yacht, a metal weight at the end ensuring the lines could cover the distance. Afraid our solar panels would get shattered, I put myself in the line of fire by holding cushions over them. I expect my backside made a tempting target, but the canal workers resisted hitting it (which, with all the practice they got, they surely could have) and left the solar panels intact too. We tied the strong 100-foot lines we'd hired for the transit onto the thrown lines, and they were then pulled onshore and attached to massive bollards. With all the yachts safely secured on both sides of the lock, the sixty-five-foot-wide doors were closed. These huge expanses of seven-foot-thick steel liberally covered in rounded metal studs, their hinges alone weighing seventeen tons, looked like enormous iron maidens slamming shut on us. There was no turning back now.

The three flight Gatun locks were the most difficult of our transit because of the strain inflicted on the lines as twenty-six million gallons of water flooded into the chamber in eight minutes, raising us twenty-eight feet at each stage. Giant culverts, eighteen feet in diameter and embedded within the lock walls, piped the fresh water from Gatun Lake into twenty smaller culverts that branched off at right angles underneath the lock floor. Five holes in each of these ensured an even distribution of water within the chamber, minimising turbulence yet still producing a matrix of wild, boiling pools that were alarmingly tumultuous.

Richard and I handled the line on the bow; Gary and Erik the one to the stern. Gjalt manned the helm, from where he had an overview of the operation. When the water level rose, the lines had to be pulled tight to keep the yachts centred in the lock, and Gjalt had learnt from his test-run that, due to the huge strains involved, the best way of accomplishing this was by using the winches.

STELLA MARIS RAFTED TO HER PARTNER BOAT IN THE
PEDRO MIGUEL LOCKS, PANAMA CANAL

YACHTS PREPARE TO EXIT THE MIRAFLORES LOCKS

He was nervous about the imminent rush of water, but he remained confident that *Stella Maris*' strong cleats and winches were up to the job.

As the water flooded in, bubbling in large, ominous circles around us, the tension on the lines quickly became immense. I kept the bow line taut by taking up the slack with the anchor windlass while Richard secured it to the cleat. Had it broken or not been properly secured, we would have been pulled towards the opposite side of the lock, possibly sending our partner boat crashing into the wall.

Fifteen minutes later, we were twenty-eight feet higher. Ricky radioed the ship in front of us and asked the captain to be gentle with the throttle, so as not to create a violent backwash for the yachts to contend with. We only signaled the Canal workers to release our lines once the freighter was on its way out of the lock and the water had settled. Still rafted together, we then moved into the second lock.

There, the whole operation was repeated, and again in the third lock. The procedure ran more smoothly each time, reaching a point where it actually became enjoyable. We marvelled at being in the heart of this immense engineering achievement, the technology involved still working as faultlessly as on the day of the Canal's inauguration in 1914. It was simply awe inspiring.

Gjalt and I were hugely relieved when the gates swung open for the last time that evening, one hour after we'd entered the first lock. We motored the short distance to the overnight mooring on Gatun Lake, and after Ricky had been picked up by a pilot boat, the rest of us celebrated our safe ascent with a round of drinks.

As we had an early start the next day, our line-handlers picked their spots for the night soon after dinner. Gary and Erik slept in the main cabin, while Richard chose the cockpit. In a no-nonsense style one would expect from a SBS officer, he rolled out his sleeping bag in one fluid motion, launched himself into it, and fell instantly asleep.

We were up before dawn in anticipation of our advisor's arrival, keen on getting the final day of our transit underway. By 7 o'clock, mild-mannered Angel had been delivered and thankfully lived up to his name; he was as supportive and professional as Ricky. After everything we'd heard, we were grateful not to have to expend any energy managing obstreperous advisors. Of course, bad stories do have a tendency to spread further than good ones and to become increasingly toxic along the way.

The thirty-mile trip to the Pedro Miguel locks took us along muddy waters that weaved around islands of tropical rainforest. *Stella Maris* was in fresh water for the first time, crossing Central America on what was once the largest artificial lake in the world, although it has since tumbled out of the top thirty. It was created by building the Gatun Dam (the world's largest earthen dam at the time) across the Chagres River and then flooding the river basin. All but the tops of the hills were submerged, creating several islands to which the wildlife was forced to retreat. Although we didn't see any animals, we certainly heard the loud cries of the howler monkeys as we motored through a cut separating adjacent islands.

As the convoy of small yachts headed towards their adventures in the Pacific, enormous merchant vessels passed on their way to the Atlantic. Richard and I relieved Gjalt from the helm so he could relax and savour the majesty of the occasion. He sat on the starboard side staring at the jungle through binoculars, the most stressful part of the transit behind him and the Pacific just a few hours away.

Meanwhile, when I wasn't behind the wheel, I was busy keeping everyone properly fed and watered. As I spent the day preparing breakfast, lunch, and tea, playing the role of waitress and dishwasher, I discovered just how little I enjoyed 'being mother'. Although no one was the slightest trouble, I felt reduced to a mere skivvy and couldn't wait be promoted back to first mate again.

As we left the wide expanses of Gatun Lake, we entered the Culebra Cut. This 500-foot-wide, 9-mile-long channel had been dug through the Continental Divide, a ridge consisting of rock and shale. It had been the most difficult part of the construction project, with unforeseen landslides almost doubling the estimated amount of rock that had to be excavated to 100 million cubic yards. Even with the latest machinery brought in by the Americans at the start of the twentieth century, this was a monumental undertaking. It was hardly surprising, then, that back in the 1880s, labourers on the French project only managed to shave seventeen feet off the summit with far more basic equipment.

By midday, we were in the Pedro Miguel locks, being lowered thirty-one feet to Miraflores Lake. An hour later, the Miraflores locks had lowered us the final fifty-four feet to the level of the Pacific. Both were much easier to transit than the Gatun locks, as there was hardly any tension on the lines during our descent. Going down didn't create the same forces as going up; the water swirled down the 100 plug holes more gently than it gushed out of them.

There was a webcam at the Miraflores locks, and during the day, I kept sending e-mails to friends and family with updated arrival times. Many of them actually bothered to sit behind their computers for the big event, some waiting so long that their backsides went numb. Angel arranged to have the camera turned towards us, and we waved at it with great enthusiasm, not realising that pictures were fed to the website as a series of stills rather than a continuous film. By this stage, though, we were elated at being almost through to the other side, and the thought that our friends and family could share this momentous occasion with us in such a way put us in a jubilant frame of mind.

Things went slightly wrong in the last lock during the final moments of the transit, when the advisor on our partner boat suddenly gave the order to release the lines that rafted us together. In the confusion that followed, some lines dangled dangerously in the water, but both captains maintained control of their boats, and the crew retrieved the lines. The last set of lock doors stood wide open, allowing us into the Pacific, where a new world waited.

We'd made it through unscathed, and one of the most stressful episodes of our trip was behind us. For Gjalt, this long-awaited moment was awesome: relief and exhilaration dancing on top of an underlying apprehension. The planet's largest ocean lay at our feet, and there was no turning back. We had to sail across it, all the way to Australia.

As we passed under the welcoming arch of the Bridge of the Americas, we cracked open the bottle of champagne we'd been given by friends back in Texas and toasted our arrival with Angel and our line-handlers. We dropped them off at the fuel dock and gave our crew the car tyre fenders we'd acquired in Colón, which they would need for their own upcoming transits.

After filling our fuel and water tanks, we carried on to the Flamenco anchorage at the end of a three-mile-long breakwater constructed using some of the spoil from the Culebra Cut. We celebrated our arrival in the Pacific by jumping into it. It felt exhilarating to be on the other side.

We soon discovered that the anchorage was intensely rolly, not least because it was fully exposed to the wakes created by pilot boats and ships moving in the channel leading to the Canal. Over the next two days, *Stella Maris* rocked wildly for hours on end, and this friskiness at anchor simply irritated the hell out of me. My complaints seemed to make Gjalt far more sick than the motion however, and he accused my negative attitude of ruining both his relief at having the transit behind us and his joy at being in the Pacific. I, in turn, accused him of being hypersensitive not only to what I said, but also to how I said it, so that I felt I had to walk on eggshells in order to avoid upsetting him. Venting our respective views sent sparks flying and soon ignited a blazing row. Suddenly the boat shrank to a tiny space that just wasn't big enough for both of us. I stormed to the aft cabin, slamming the door behind me, while Gjalt escaped on deck.

Not many couples spend twenty-four hours a day together, and even fewer do so on a forty-one-foot boat. The stress of the transit and the intensity of the trip since leaving Houston had formed an explosive mixture, and it hadn't taken much to set it off. In the heat of the argument, I even threatened to give up on the trip right there in Panama. I wasn't the least bit serious, but Gjalt, who would never say something unless he meant it, thought I was. We soon made up after the row, but while I remained downhearted merely because we'd clashed so unpleasantly, Gjalt was quietly and unhappily contemplating whether he would continue the trip alone if I actually left. It was a sad start to our Pacific adventure, but one that we did gradually put behind us. On a trip into town to buy provisions, we secretly bought each other gifts. What could possibly have said sorry more movingly than the jumbo-sized bag of sweets I gave to Gjalt and the packet of fishing hooks he gave to me? The dark cloud above us blew away, *Stella Maris* morphed back into *Doctor Who's* Tardis, and life became fun again.

Onshore, Balboa couldn't have been more different from Colón, its desperately poor sister city on the shores of the Caribbean. The area was new and not only pleasant to walk around, but safe to boot. There were restaurants, shops, and even ice-cream parlours. No one warned us to beware of machete-wielding muggers, and we gladly left our pepper spray onboard. From there, we could see the towering skyscrapers of Panama City gleaming in the distance, and we were mystified as to why poor Colón had been left to rot.

The Pacific stretched like a vast playground ahead of us, so we didn't linger any longer than we had to. With full fuel tanks and five extra jerry cans of diesel strapped to the stern to get us through the doldrums, we were almost ready to set sail for the fabled Galápagos Islands, but first we wanted to take advantage of the conveniently close duty-free establishment onshore.

To avoid the outrageous five-dollar dinghy dock landing fee, Gjalt dropped me off at the anchorage's small beach. I scrambled up the loose shingle to the road, where a swanky new shop offered a fine selection of spirits. Inside I took my time scanning the tantalising displays of attractively bottled beverages, determined to choose wisely. We knew that alcohol would cost a small fortune in the Pacific, so if we didn't stock up we'd have to do without, and we had no desire to do that. The nice lady boxed up my carefully selected bottles in a chic box, complete with a convenient carry handle, and I slid with it back down the loose shingle to the waiting dinghy. Now, we were ready to set sail.

A YACHT PASSES THROUGH MONKEY CUT,
GATUN LAKE, PANAMA CANAL

A YACHT AND MERCHANT SHIP PASS EACH OTHER
IN THE PANAMA CANAL

# 7.

# Into the South Pacific

*Invasion by large-scale tourism and unsustainable fishing by mainland fishermen financed by foreign companies supported by authority, is waging permanent opposition to the restrictions of the Galápagos National Park. The resulting growth in population, unplanned urbanisation, pollution, damaging invasion by exotic species and the resulting degradation of habitats is unplanned for and barely controlled at present.*

– United Nations Environment Programme, March 2003

We were both happy to be at sea again. It was much calmer than in the Flamenco anchorage, and I was over the moon at having escaped the incessant rocking and rolling. After motoring for the first few hours, we found steady winds and began to make tremendous progress, sailing at over nine knots with the gennaker.

In the Gulf of Panama, we sailed into a large area of strangely disturbed water. Suddenly, the depth went into a determined nosedive, falling from 300 feet to a heart-stopping 20 in a matter of seconds. Terrified that we were about to run aground, I dived down below to double-check the chart. Although it confirmed what I'd been certain of just minutes earlier – that we were in deep water – I still shook like a leaf as I hurried back to the cockpit. Perhaps some hitherto unknown subsea volcano had erupted and oozed enough lava to rise dangerously close to the surface.

I stared nervously at the oddly rippling sea and braced for impact, looking to Gjalt for reassurance, but when the echo sounder began to cycle repeatedly between deep and shallow depths, I slowly began to relax. The charts were still correct: there was no bubbling volcano beneath us after all. We'd simply sailed into an area where different

109

current streams intersected, causing the sea to become choppy and the echo sounder to take erroneous readings. Since this instrument was connected to others that we needed, we couldn't turn it off, and I had to accept the horror of seeing shallow depths every now and then – something I always hated and never quite got used to.

In the first 150 miles of the trip, we encountered a lot of shipping traffic heading to and from the Panama Canal, but after that, we pretty much had the world to ourselves. We passed a sailing boat with a family of four onboard, also heading to the Galápagos. They kept in touch twice daily with a group of yachts on the same route, and we began checking into that radio net as well.

Just before sunset, Gjalt reeled in a good-sized mackerel. It was our first day in the Pacific, and already we'd caught a fish, a feat that had taken us two months in the Caribbean. We took it to be a good omen.

Our first night was a pleasure, thanks to a clear star-filled sky, the smooth sailing powered by our perfectly filled gennaker, and the entertaining shenanigans of a school of dolphins swimming around *Stella Maris*. Their speed and agility was made visible by millions of bioluminescent life forms radiating green neon as the playful dolphins streaked through the black water. We could see them approaching at high speed, shooting towards the hull like torpedoes before turning away at the last second to ride the bow wave. We hadn't seen anything like it in the Caribbean, and it was a magical welcome to the Pacific. The bioluminescence stayed with us the next night as well, leaving a long, glowing trail behind *Stella Maris* and creating eerie, indeterminate outlines of worryingly large creatures that we weren't able to identify.

The radio net we'd joined was abuzz with talk of pirates in the vicinity of Malpelo Island, a small territory of Ecuador just thirty miles south of our route. Apparently, two yachts had been chased by fishing boats in the region the previous month but luckily had managed to outrun them. To remain hidden, yachts were sailing at night without navigation lights, and we decided it prudent to follow suit. Still, even though we kept good watch, neither of us felt comfortable about being invisible, so after two nights of covert sailing, we turned our lights back on again.

Although I thought the scare was probably overblown,

the incessant talk of pirates made me peer into the darkness so intently that my imagination sometimes got the better of me. One night I was watching the distinctive incandescent glow of distant fishing boats when the lights suddenly disappeared. I urgently grabbed the binoculars and trained them in that direction, fully expecting to see a speedboat materialising out of the pitch dark. We'd flicked through a book about piracy in a chandlery in Panama. The facts and figures of the previous year's attacks were detailed on its pages in stark black and white, but it was the chilling photograph on the front cover that had stuck in my mind. Hardly chosen to reassure someone about to set sail on the high seas, it showed an open speedboat packed with pirates brandishing machine guns and even rocket launchers. The menacing gang hadn't looked particularly open to negotiation, and although the canister of bear spray we had onboard was undoubtedly potent, it was no match for that kind of firepower. It was those ruthless and determined men I now expected to see emerge from the darkness and pull up alongside our boat at any minute. But the night passed, and the pirates never came. Such terrifying encounters were reserved for the coasts of countries like Somalia and Indonesia. We were surprised by the long arm of America, though, when a U.S. Coast Guard plane made a low-altitude pass over us, presumably on the lookout for drug traffickers. They didn't reply to our radio call and just soared on by.

As expected, the wind disappeared when we neared the doldrums, but thankfully we didn't encounter any thunderstorms. With the engine pushing us onwards, we lost the tranquillity of sailing, but the going was easy on an ocean as smooth as polished glass, and the world was serenely beautiful. The absence of wind allowed the full intensity of the sun to beat down upon us, but we found respite under bucket loads of cooling seawater. On some days, we had up to two knots of current against us, and on the worst days, we had wind against us as well.

This stretch of water from Panama to the Galápagos was notorious for such impediments to progress, so we'd set off prepared. We transferred diesel from the jerry cans into the fuel tanks and pushed through the windless zones, relishing the times when we were able to sail again. The peace that engulfed us when we switched off the engine was wonderful. We'd heard of a yacht that spent twenty-five days at sea on this route because it ran out of diesel. Any progress the crew made when they could sail was eroded by adverse current when they were next becalmed. Our trip took just one week, but we motored for a little over half of it.

Whole days passed when we saw no wildlife at all. After the glowing dolphins had streaked around us the first night, we were visited by a large school of their frisky cousins during the day. It was as though they couldn't contain their excitement at spotting *Stella Maris* in their mostly empty world, so they launched from the sea in jubilation as they swam over to greet her. They played in her bow wave and leapt into the air alongside us, taking time to observe the strange two-legged creatures who were peering back at them from the deck.

On another windless day, we saw a pod of pilot whales, but these were far more aloof than the dolphins and soon disappeared when we turned the boat towards them for a closer look. Some nonchalant turtles drifted by, and a brown booby hitched a ride for a few hours before flying off again. As for fish, they stayed in the ocean; the mackerel turned out to have been beginner's luck. And there was little sign of creatures of our own kind either. We saw just one container ship and sailed within sight of a yacht for a day. It was nice to see the crisp, white sails of another boat at sea, but we preferred being in a world of our own.

Six days after leaving Panama, we reached the Equator, another dream conjured up by Gjalt's boyhood imagination. It was a lovely afternoon with flat seas, finally a nice wind to sail by and no current against us. Following tradition, we offered gifts to Neptune, hoping some cheese and white wine would make him more inclined to grant us fair weather during our stay in the Pacific. We made the mistake of indulging in a tipple ourselves as we celebrated this special occasion, and it left us feeling groggy for the rest of the afternoon.

As we closed in on the Galápagos Islands, we got an early taste of its famous wildlife when a pod of pilot whales swam directly towards us and dived under the boat. We weren't even there yet, and already the animals were living up to their reputation of fearlessness.

There was now so much wind that we were unable to slow *Stella Maris* down enough to avoid making landfall at San Cristóbal Island during the night. We decided to tack out to sea for three hours, which resulted in a very bumpy sail close to the wind, and then sail back towards the island for a dawn arrival.

At first light, we headed for the unappealingly named Wreck Bay. There'd been rumours of check-in costs being double the standard rates for boats arriving at the weekend, so some cruisers announced on the radio net that they planned to anchor and hide out until Monday morning. Relative to other ports-of-call, the cost of visiting the Galápagos was high, but even double those rates wouldn't come close to the cost of flying in on a package deal. Besides, arriving by yacht after a week-long passage and then exploring the islands alone was far more preferable than being herded around in a compulsory life jacket by a tour operator, and it was definitely worth paying for. Without a permit, it was forbidden to anchor anywhere other than one of the three designated bays, and we didn't want to violate the rules in one of the most unique places on Earth. There is precious little left on the planet that hasn't been damaged by humans, and the last thing we wanted to do was leave our mark on one of the precious remaining untouched places.

We were surprised at how green the island of San Cristóbal was. We'd read several accounts describing the Galápagos as 'barren and unwelcoming', but what lay in front of our eyes as we arrived was positively luxuriant. It was a wonderful, inviting sight after a week at sea and our longest passage so far of 900 miles. Wildlife abounded from the start; the fins of whitetip sharks sliced menacingly through the water behind our stern, while frolicking groups of sea lions greeted us in a manner that seemed altogether more cordial.

Tired from the rough night of killing time before making landfall, we snapped at each other as we approached the anchorage. The tension increased when incorrect coordinates on our computer chart put us on course for the rocks instead of Wreck Bay and consequently pushed our already strained nerves closer to the edge. We steered towards the anchored yachts and found a spot on the outer rim of the bay, harbour to the town of Puerto Baquerizo Moreno, capital of the Galápagos. With the anchor securely dug into the seabed, our moods quickly improved.

Twenty minutes later, a bright yellow water taxi appeared alongside and delivered a Naval officer in a uniform so dazzlingly white we needed sunglasses to look at it. Jorge climbed aboard, and after some preliminary greetings, he asked to go down below to carry out a quick inspection. I'd only just had enough time to get things vaguely organised, but he didn't trail his fingers over surfaces to check for dust or anything, and the interior seemed to meet with his approval. He asked us to report to the port captain two hours later and then removed his glorious whiteness back onto the waiting taxi.

We met some of the cruisers we'd heard on the daily radio net outside the port captain's office. They were all families with children of roughly the same age (between eight and twelve), travelling in a convoy known as the 'kiddie boats'. We hadn't expected so many parents would be prepared to undertake such an adventure, but it certainly seemed to do their offspring a world of good. Without exception, every child we met in the Pacific was polite and mature for their age.

Ricardo, the stocky, square-shouldered port captain, did not speak English. Gjalt spoke no Spanish, and to say mine was limited would be an understatement. In order to comprehend what was being explained to us, my brain had to jump on every word it recognised and translate it at lightning speed. The process was no doubt very similar to Gjalt's deciphering of Morse code. Seemingly oblivious to our ignorance, and in any case unperturbed by our blank faces, Ricardo relentlessly bombarded us with his quick-silver Spanish words. By the time he stopped talking, I thought I'd caught enough of them to understand that we could do all the necessary paperwork on Monday. The best news was that we were allowed to anchor at two of the three permissible islands for a total of twenty days. In previous years, cruisers had only been allowed to stay for a woefully short seventy-two hours, so we were overjoyed by our good fortune.

At the end of our meeting, with the formalities over, Ricardo relaxed and leant back in his chair. His eyes acquired a mischievous sparkle, and as his hands made flourishing sweeps through the air, he announced that he was a connoisseur of world beer. He collected ales from the nations of all visiting cruisers, he explained, and said he would be extremely grateful if we could bring him a Dutch beer and a British one 'for his collection'. There'd been no mention of the dreaded overtime charge, but if that was it, we were more than happy to cough up.

The quiet streets of Puerto Baquerizo Moreno were clean and safe to walk, a refreshing improvement on Colón. The only danger came from getting too close to the enormous sea lions that sprawled on the low walls lining the seafront, like cantankerous drunkards recovering from a wild night on the town. The males weigh up to a hefty 250 kilos, so we gave them a respectfully wide berth.

People were friendly, and there were many small restaurants selling tasty, cheap food, but we worried about the effect all this human activity was having on the environment. Ecuadorians were moving to the islands in droves to cash in on the burgeoning tourist industry, which accounted for forty per cent of Ecuador's income in the sector. When organised tourism began there in the late 1960s, around 2,000 people visited the islands, and some 3,500 called them home. By 2005, the population had risen to 20,000, and visitor numbers had exploded to almost 125,000. By 2007, just two years later, the threats to wildlife and plant species from this dramatic human invasion were so great that UNESCO declared the world heritage site 'in danger'.

We followed a long trail through a black volcanic landscape that was softened by patches of green plants and reached a bay heaving with massive sea lions that barked at our intrusion. An affectionate ginger cat accompanied us all the way to the bay and back again, stopping and miaowing whenever it wanted to be carried, which was often. It was difficult to leave the sociable feline behind, and in retrospect, perhaps we should have taken it with us, because cats are just one introduced species known to have a detrimental effect on the archipelago's endemic wildlife. They prey on birds that have never known predators, as well as young iguanas, snakes, and lava lizards. The locals are fond of their cats, but the Galápagos would be better off without them, and the ultimate aim of the Charles Darwin Foundation is to remove all of these domestic creatures from the islands.

Several shops in town sold DVDs. We had been without television for three months and hadn't missed it at all, but the chance to buy some recent films for a little over a dollar each was too good an opportunity to miss. They were all pirated, naturally, and the quality of some was, quite frankly, desperate. They'd clearly been made by someone who'd smuggled a camcorder into the cinema inside a bucket of popcorn and hadn't got a clue how to set it up. Sometimes the film was at an angle, often it was out of focus, and every now and then, a human silhouette would move across it, presumably on the way to the toilet.

A young Brazilian couple we'd met in Colón, who were as averse to joining tour groups as we were, invited us to go snorkelling with them in a bay of the small island of Isla Lobos. Mariana, a pretty twenty-four-year-old, and her ever-helpful husband Caju, some ten years her senior, had set out from Florida, where they'd been working. They were both so full of energy that they made everyone else look lazy; they always seemed to be rushing around.

That morning, they sped us three miles along the coast in their fifteen-horsepower-driven dinghy to reach a shallow bay. We'd expected to snorkel with fish, but as frisky sea lions jumped into the air around us, we realised we'd come to play with them. We slipped into the clear water, and at least a dozen sea lions swam around us, turning over and over as they dived down to the seabed, then sneaking up behind us to nibble our flippers. They would swim towards us at full speed and only veer off at the last second; the sea lion version of playing chicken. Neither side tired of playing with the other, and it was only when a tour bus arrived and deposited a crowd of people into the bay that we exited the liquid playground.

We warmed up while exploring small and tranquil Isla Lobos. Entire nurseries of furry baby sea lions sunned themselves on the rocks and gazed at us with those huge, black eyes that seduce everyone except Norwegian and Canadians hunters. Male frigate birds sat in the trees, puffing out their impressive red throats to attract the ladies, while yellow canaries hopped from branch to branch and boobies behaved as if having bright blue feet was perfectly normal. I bent down to investigate a small lava lizard and, by way of indicating my friendly intentions, offered my hand, from which it delicately licked the salt. After about half an hour, the tour group was herded back onto their bus, and we returned to the water to play with our friends the sea lions again.

These creatures were hunted back in the eighteenth century and are still at risk today from poachers. In 2001, thirty-five males were clubbed to death, and their teeth and genital organs were removed, presumably to make aphrodisiacs for the Asian market. In 2008, fifty-three sea lions were found with their heads caved in; the motive remains a mystery, but the culprits were undeniably human. The population is listed as 'vulnerable' and is threatened by El Niño events, which raise water temperatures and consequently diminish the sea lions' food supply.

Flush from the success of this encounter, Mariana and Caju took swimming with wild animals several steps further by suggesting we join them on a shark dive. It seemed unwise, to me, to seek out an encounter with known man-eaters, and I was surprised to discover that some believe it's a totally sane and harmless thing to do, even fun. This would only be my third dive since qualifying, so even without the sharks I would have been apprehensive. However, I was more afraid that if I did not keep at it, I'd lose my newly acquired and not very finely honed skills altogether.

The dive took us through a wide crack that bisected a massive rock lying a few miles off the San Cristóbal coast called Lion Dormida, 'the sleeping lion'. It combined pretty much all the elements guaranteed to freak me out: cold water, strong currents, and, of course, sharks. The only positive thing was that it wasn't deep, so at least I didn't have to worry about getting the bends, which was something I worried about quite a lot whilst diving. In the event I was inexplicably relaxed and calm enough to operate the underwater camera; there wasn't much to photograph, though, because the visibility was dreadful, revealing just a hint of a shark somewhere in the distant murk. For this, I was secretly grateful.

For a few days, we dedicated most of our time to boat maintenance. Gjalt performed all the technical chores while I busied myself with general housekeeping efforts. Our domestic tasks divided naturally along common gender lines, which suited us both. I had no interest in changing engine oil or replacing anodes below the water-line, and Gjalt had no desire to understand how the dirty clothes he threw into the magic laundry basket reappeared in his cupboard neatly folded and smelling of Persil. As our workloads balanced evenly, there were never any indignant accusations of people not pulling their weight.

After a morning of steady industry, Gjalt suggested we reward ourselves with a swim to a small bay along the coast. As he always did whenever he proposed a new adventure, he assured me that what he had in mind was perfectly safe. Since it was quite a long swim, my main concern was that I would get cold, but getting cold turned out to be the least of my problems.

As I approached the head of the bay, I got caught in the wild surf that crashed onto the sandy beach, and was sucked back and thrust forward like a piece of insignificant flotsam. Terrifyingly jagged volcanic boulders were scattered everywhere, and in my desperate struggle to avoid them, I swallowed copious quantities of water. I stretched out my arms and pushed against the stony obstacles with my hands, eventually steering a clear path between them after surviving several oceanic surges. When I was at last spat out onto solid ground, I stumbled to a sandy spot, where I gradually recuperated from my ordeal and cursed Gjalt and his bright ideas.

Looking along the pretty beach, I saw several sea lions enjoying an afternoon nap, completely oblivious to my presence. I was about as enthusiastic about plunging back into the turbulent washing machine in the bay as they appeared about joining me. Gjalt emerged from the water unfazed – invigorated even – and altogether too perky to give my bitter complaints any credence. I vowed (and not for the first time) never to listen to him again.

Before long, we began to sizzle in the heat and were forced to return to the water. Having spent a good amount of time surveying the scene for the best point of entry, I plunged in and swam out of the surf zone as if a great white was on my tail. Somehow, the waves were more merciful now that I was leaving, and I was soon clear of the treacherous boulders, paddling contentedly with two large green turtles. That was the thing about Gjalt's schemes; they usually turned out well in the end, making the horrible episodes seem worth it.

Back at *Stella Maris*, I levered myself up the side of our dinghy, only to find it already occupied. In our absence, a sea lion had decided it was an ideal spot for a siesta. He was not best pleased by my interruption, and his angry barking forced me to retreat. Afraid that sooner or later the creature would deposit something steamy and unpleasant in our dinghy, Gjalt persuaded it to find an alternative resting place.

After a week at San Cristóbal, we sailed overnight to Isabela Island, the largest in the archipelago. It was an easy, short trip in the silvery light of a nearly full moon. Early the next morning, we hoisted the gennaker, harnessing the fading wind to cover the final miles.

The Isabela anchorage was very different from that at San Cristóbal, with a long, sandy beach and majestic palm trees to give it a distinctly tropical feel. This made the sighting of a small penguin on a rocky islet beside the anchorage all the more bizarre. Galápagos penguins can survive on the Equator because the Humboldt Current sweeps cold water and nutrients up from Antarctica. Like the sea lions, though, their survival is threatened by a lack of food during El Niño events. The strong El Niño of 1998 reduced the population by sixty-five per cent, and the remaining 2,100 penguins are now listed as 'endangered'.

The town of Puerto Villamil was much quieter and more laid-back than bustling Puerto Baquerizo Moreno. The streets were unpaved, traffic was scarce, and tourists were nowhere to be seen. There were a few restaurants scattered about town, some more inviting than others, as well as a handful of small shops, from which we acquired several bottles of very fine and modestly priced Bacardi Oro. Puerto Villamil was not quite a ghost town, but it was at least a century behind Baquerizo Moreno. Naturally, this made it all the more appealing.

Walking along the road out of town, we came across a trail that was simply begging to be followed. It led to a giant tortoise breeding centre, set up to ensure the survival of the species after which the Galápagos Islands were named.

The unrestrained hunting of tortoises for their meat and oil began with pirates in the seventeenth century and continued unabated throughout the eighteenth and nineteenth centuries with the arrival of whalers and colonists.

Whenever a whaling ship visited the Islands, hundreds of the easily harvested creatures were loaded onboard where, stored upside down, they could survive without food or water for up to a year before the cooking pot beckoned. The original tortoise population, estimated at a quarter of a million, was simply decimated, and current numbers stand at around 20,000. Three of the fourteen species were hunted to extinction. These impressively oversized reptiles, which can weigh up to 300 kilos, continue to be threatened by the animals introduced to the Islands by humans; pigs dig up the eggs; dogs and rats eat the hatchlings; and goats ravage the vegetation which the tortoises rely on for food. Mankind really does have a lot to answer for.

Five tortoise species remain on Isabela, each existing in isolation on one of the large volcanoes, separated by wide lava fields they are unable to cross. Even the smaller adult tortoises at the centre were 60 years old, but the coffee table-sized ones were up to 150 – and they certainly looked it. Scaly, wrinkled skin hung from their necks in loose folds, and their faces were decidedly grumpy, like those of ancient men who while away their final days on shady benches in sleepy French villages. Several of the males seemed intent on fornication (here, they probably differed from the old Frenchmen, but you never know), heaving their weighty bodies onto the backs of utterly indifferent females. Once the food came, though, the males lost all interest in mating as well.

We followed an intriguing trail that stretched inland and branched off in numerous directions, every single one of which we explored without seeing another person. One side trail led to the shore, home to teeming masses of marine iguanas. These dragon-like creatures, with horny plates of armour crowning their heads and lethal spikes running the length of their spines to the tip of their long tails, blended into the black volcanic landscape so well that we only noticed them when the lava up ahead appeared to become molten. When lumps of this shifting rock proceeded to spit a disagreeable white spray in our general direction, it became obvious that they were, in fact, iguanas. The spray was a kind of salty snot the creatures ejected through their nostrils after filtering water from the sea. It was a very useful survival trick, if somewhat offensive. Darwin didn't seem to be particularly enamoured of the iguana, considering it 'a hideous-looking creature, of a dirty black colour, stupid and sluggish in its movements.'

Unlike the great man, I didn't find the iguanas hideous at all and observed them to be nimble both on land and in the sea. Few allowed us to get as close as Darwin had, as he actually grabbed them and hurled them into the water to study their reaction (which was annoyed, I would guess), and apart from the sea lions at Isla Lobos and a finch that sat on Gjalt's knee one day, all the animals fled as soon as they caught sight of us. Darwin might have considered them stupid and sluggish, but one thing they quickly learned from the recent human invasion was to be afraid of the planet's most lethal predator.

At the end of the main trail, a massive barrier of shaped volcanic blocks loomed up abruptly from the dry earth. Known as the Wall of Tears, it was a sinister construction some six metres wide at the base, tapering gradually to a height of nine metres, and one hundred and seventy metres long. It was the only remaining evidence of Ecuador's most infamous penal colony and was conceived as a brutal punishment that ultimately cost the lives of a dozen inmates. Some convicts died from exhaustion or dehydration, others from beatings by guards, and a few simply fell to their deaths. In 1958, twenty-one convicts escaped to the Ecuadorian mainland in the commandeered yacht of an American millionaire, an incident that brought twelve years of inhumane treatment to the world's attention. As a result, the penal colony was closed in 1959, and the Galápagos Islands were promptly declared a National Park.

We knew about the Islands' fabled animals and reputation as the catalyst for Darwin's *Origin of Species*, but we were oblivious to its history as a dumping ground for unwanted citizens. Of course, the idea of a country removing its undesirables to far-flung outposts of the empire was hardly new, and although the Galápagos Islands weren't as far from Ecuador as Australia was from England, it would still be a hell of a swim to get home. As early as 1832, when Ecuador took formal possession of the archipelago, troublesome political prisoners were sent to the Islands to reconsider their opinions. With the benefits of exile immediately apparent to the authorities, they soon deported felons whose crimes had been altogether more violent. Prisoners were put to work on various ventures initiated to support settlement of the Islands, but working alongside free settlers inevitably sowed discontent. In time, there were uprisings on Floreana, followed by San Cristóbal, and finally Isabela.

One morning, our computer committed a rebellion of its own, refusing to work yet again. Adept at performing brain surgery on it by that time, I wiped the memory clean, then reinstalled the operating system and all our programs for the umpteenth time. We were concerned that the laptop would crash beyond resurrection while we were on the long passage to the Marquesas Islands, leaving us unable to download weather information or reassure our families that we were still alive. I knew that our parents would not enjoy three weeks of silence while they waited to hear we had safely crossed 3,000 miles of open ocean.

After two weeks in the Galápagos, Gjalt was keen to embark on the epic journey looming ahead of us, and once again I felt as though I was being dragged along in his slipstream. Departure decisions seemed to be thrust upon me without warning, and I was upset that we were leaving the Islands almost a week before we had to. In truth, though, we had already seen what we could, and there was so much more to come and so little time to fit it all in. Then, an influx of yachts into the small anchorage swelled the total number from six to a tightly packed twenty, convincing me that it was, in fact, time for us to be on our way.

For our last meal onshore, Gjalt wanted to go to a dodgy restaurant buried down a charmless side street because he'd seen locals eating there, always a ringing endorsement in his book. He was averse to places that had even a hint of the tourist industry about them, so my desire to dine at one of the more pleasant establishments on the main road (with an outdoor veranda, festive tablecloths, pot plants, and a pleasant view) was blithely dismissed. Instead, we sat at a table so close to the road it was quite possibly in it; our food acquired a light sprinkling of dust whenever a car drove past, which was often. The tablecloth consisted of an easy-to-clean plastic sheet, dropping a big hint about the dining etiquette of the restaurant's regular clientele. To add to the already unique ambience, a loudspeaker so enormous it had probably seen active service at a Rolling Stones concert loomed over us, blasting out the greatest 'hits' from *Now That's What I Call Garbage*. Had the food at least compensated in some way for all this, lunch would have seemed less of a disaster but, being partial to chicken that both looks and tastes better than road kill, it did not.

The crowning moment of the whole experience came when we left the restaurant. "It was a bit of a dive, wasn't it?" Gjalt said cheerily, as if the Changing Rooms team had sneaked in just after we'd sat down and turned a Michelin-starred restaurant into a greasy spoon. I just looked at him, speechless.

We went into the main grocery store to buy some fresh provisions, and saw on the television behind the counter that the Pope had died. It was April Fool's Day, but it turned out that it was no joke. When the shopkeeper saw us gazing at the screen he said, "*El Papa ha muerto*," and drew his finger across his neck to make certain the gringos understood. This unexpected gesture did make us wonder, for a moment, if Pope John Paul II had in fact been murdered.

The next morning saw the first yacht depart for the Marquesas, and there was nothing like watching a boat set out to sea to make me want to follow. I don't know why, but I've always hated being left behind.

Having survived the seven-day sail from Panama to the Galápagos without any adverse mental effects, I was not at all daunted by the long journey ahead. In my case, ignorance was bliss. With his greater experience, Gjalt viewed the 3,000-mile passage with much more respect. The distance was equivalent to the length of the Sahara, and it stretched through an ocean that was just as much of a desert. The Pacific is vast, covering about one-third of the Earth's surface, an area larger than all the land combined. Gjalt estimated that we'd be at sea for around three weeks, away from everything and everyone, away from any help. In case of emergency, we were well equipped and prepared: we had our medical kit, a life raft, EPIRB, and the ditch bag ready by the steps.

We weighed anchor soon after the first boat, hoisted the gennaker to catch the light southeasterly trade winds, and sailed out into the awesome expanse of the Pacific Ocean.

CORINNA ATTEMPTS TO BEFRIEND A MARINE IGUANA, GALÁPAGOS
ISLANDS

A SEA LION HAS A SIESTA IN OUR DINGHY, GALÁPAGOS ISLANDS

# 8.

## The Longest Passage

*Over forty-six thousand pieces of plastic litter are float-ing on every square mile of ocean today. In the Central Pacific, there are up to six pounds of marine litter to every pound of plankton. Plastic waste kills up to one million seabirds, one hundred thousand sea mammals and countless fish each year.*

– United Nations Environment Programme, 2006

We had light winds for the first three days of the passage, but managed to keep up a good speed thanks to the gennaker. Gjalt found it infuriating when this large sail wasn't adequately filled by the vari-able, weak wind, and he often stared at it darkly, mutter-ing grumpily to himself when it flapped. For my part, I was happy to start the trip in gentle conditions, as it made settling into life offshore a lot easier. I didn't feel seasick and could help with all the routine chores, such as cooking and washing-up, right from the beginning.

It still took us three days to adjust to the broken nights, to fall asleep quickly and deeply enough that we didn't need to steal extra hours the following day. Sometimes we would have to be practically dragged out of bed for our turn on watch. Then, even the waiting mug of coffee, a hando-ver gift from the person gratefully slipping into the freshly vacated bed, did little to help wake us up. Although the calm nights made it more bearable to sit out in the cockpit, they also made it harder not to doze off. We had to move around, purposely inflicting bursts of activity on ourselves, to keep our extreme fatigue at bay. We rummaged in the galley for food, hoping a sugar boost from a Mars bar and a can of Coke could see us through the shift. Time on these watches passed awfully slowly.

In the light winds, we felt every breath the ocean took. With the wind not strong enough to keep *Stella Maris* heeled over, we rocked from side to side each time a wave rolled on its way. The unpredictable periodicity of this motion infuriated me whenever I had to walk below deck. In the head, I inevitably lost my balance when removing or pulling up clothing, and in the galley, the dinner plates sometimes skidded across the counter, splattering half our meal around the point of impact.

We always placed cushions inside the cupboards when we were underway to try and keep things from shifting, but now the contents had to be completely wedged together, or they would *clink* and *chink* me to the outer edge of sanity. If I latched on to a repetitive sound when trying to sleep, I couldn't rest until I'd tracked it down and silenced it. I took to using earplugs, but the most irritating noises still penetrated those defences.

Back when promises were being made on the rough waters of the Gulf of Mexico, I hadn't been told about this tendency of the Pacific to roll yachts from side to side. Gjalt had painted me a picture of idyllic sailing, *Stella Maris* gliding across an oceanic canvas like a curling stone on highly polished ice. But we weren't sailing close-hauled in gale force winds with thunderstorms exploding overhead, so I couldn't really complain.

One calm afternoon early in the trip, I cut Gjalt's hair with a kit I'd bought at a Walgreens drugstore in Texas. It resembled the shavers used by sheep shearers in the Australian outback and, funnily enough, produced similar results. I admit I've never been a talented hairdresser, but although things invariably looked bleak for Gjalt at the start of a session, with perseverance on my part and faith on his, they usually turned out okay in the end. I never drew blood, his scalp always remained firmly attached to his skull, and not once did it look as if a pudding bowl had been used during any stage of the procedure. Nevertheless, there were skinheads who looked friendlier than he did after I'd finished with him, so it seemed prudent to allow three weeks of regrowth at sea before parading him in polite company again.

We kept up a twice-daily radio schedule with the other boats en route to the Marquesas Islands. We discussed the weather and the strength and direction of the ocean current, and enjoyed a little social contact with other human beings. It was strangely comforting to know that we weren't the only small yacht crossing that vast ocean. If we had embarked on a mad journey, at least we had company. Mealtimes broke up the days and became occasions to look forward to. Breakfast usually consisted of cereal and milk that I'd prepared from powder the day before so it had time to chill; I found it inedible if it was lukewarm, but Gjalt was less fussy. When the bread ran out a few days after leaving the Galápagos, we resorted to instant noodles or mashed potatoes for lunch, mixing in some kind of chunky soup to bulk it up. When there was no fresh fish (which was more often than not), we ate tinned tuna, which we never tired of, or corned beef, which we quickly did.

Our intake of vegetables was woefully inadequate, dangerously below recommended daily requirements The actual peas filling the tins from Sam's Club were a far cry from the crisp, tantalisingly green ones shown on the label, so it was difficult to knowingly ruin a meal with them just for the sake of our health. Aside from tinned sweet corn and fresh onions (of which we always maintained a comfortably large stock), the peas were the only vegetable we had onboard. We were a little better at sharing a tin of peaches or mandarins after dinner, but we doubtless suffered deficiencies in a whole host of essential vitamins and minerals during long passages. Whenever this dawned on Gjalt, he insisted we take one of the unpalatable multivitamins we'd brought along. I always tried to resist his prescription, because the disturbingly large pills both looked and tasted as though they should be inserted into the body at the other end; it always took tremendous effort on my part to swallow the things.

In the late afternoons, we washed away the heat of the day with buckets of refreshing seawater that we hauled up over the side. Soon afterwards came dinner, and once the washing-up was finished, Gjalt would go to bed and I would take the first watch. Sunset was my favourite time of the day. I could write my diary and read a little before it got too dark, and the gradual transformation into night was a pleasure in good weather. I watched the sun sink to the horizon, turning a burnished orange and spreading its dying glow across the boundless sky. It was easy to settle

CORINNA WEYRETER

into this watch and certainly a lot more enjoyable than starting the next one, which began at midnight after just three hours of sleep.

We hadn't had fresh fish for weeks and longed for the taste of sashimi. Gjalt trolled two lines behind the boat, and although he soon had three strikes, all of the fish got away. One escaped with the lure, while another managed to bend a stainless steel hook. The third strike had been an appetising dorado, which Gjalt reeled all the way to the stern, only for it to slip to freedom at the last moment. I suppose the sight of two salivating sailors with starved looks in their eyes encouraged the fish to find one last burst of energy and leg it (or 'fin' it, as it were). I was cooking dinner at the time, and the dorado could have gone straight into the frying pan, but alas, another tin of tuna bit the dust. It was a good job we'd bought a lot of it.

We discovered that the most successful method of catching sea life was to just let it jump onto the boat by itself. Every morning, two dozen flying fish and the odd squid lay dehydrated on deck, a look of horror frozen in their lifeless eyes. When they'd launched from the water the previous night, scared out of their wits by an encounter with *Stella Maris*, they surely didn't expect to find themselves flapping helplessly on her hard, unforgiving deck. The odds of a flying fish coming to grief in this way must be about the same as a yak herder being run over by a car in the middle of the Gobi Desert. Two of these unlucky creatures actually flew clean through the hatch of the main cabin and landed on me while I was asleep. Now the odds of that simply boggle the mind. Another night, a squid had also been making a beeline for my bed when it came to a sticky end, entangled in the hinge of the hatch. When I got up for my watch, I saw something strange and unfamiliar dangling in front of my face. I fetched the torch and shone the light along the length of a long, slimy tentacle until I could see two large black eyes regarding me predatorily. It was like a scene from *Alien*, although thankfully without the acidic drooling and being eaten part.

The flying fish smelt atrocious. The instant one landed in the near vicinity, a distinctive, shockingly pungent scent hit the nose like a punch. We did meet cruisers who ate them (the majority being male solo sailors given to eccentricity), but we weren't desperate enough to mess with the small, malodorous, bony creatures ourselves. In any case, by the time we found most of them, they were as stiff as boards and had to be prised from the deck. Gjalt did see an opportunity to improve his fishing results, however, by using them as bait. After much intricate preparation involving thin wires and a level of dexterity normally associated with neurosurgery, the flying fish lure was paid out behind the boat. Unfortunately, the bait was too delicately constructed to withstand the turbulence for long enough to tempt a passing predator and, discouraged, Gjalt soon returned to his less labour-intensive man-made lures.

Four days into the trip, we picked up strong trade winds and their increased strength brought increased seas. It was inconvenient, then, that the fridge waited for conditions to worsen before it packed up, because to fix it we had to empty out the cockpit locker and then squeeze Gjalt inside. So, while *Stella Maris* coursed through steep waves, Gjalt got bashed around in a space the size of a household airing cupboard. Thankfully, being charged with repairing everything that went wrong onboard (which over time extended to a rather long list) was turning Gjalt into a handyman skilled enough to fix almost anything. It took time and patience in equal measure to track the fault to a burnt-out power wire, but when his repair brought the fridge back to life again, he was justly proud.

A full week after setting off, having tried every possible lure in his extensive collection, Gjalt at last achieved success in the fishing department; and like waiting forever for a bus to arrive, two came along at once. We must have sailed through a school of dorados on the hunt. The final tally of fish landed, filleted, and deposited in the fridge dropped to fifty per cent of those hooked when one lucky victim wriggled itself free from the devil and back into the deep blue sea. The filleted dorado only provided enough meat for one square meal, so feeling as if we had the sashimi gods on our side, we paid out the lure again.

Sure enough, within minutes, the reel let out its distinctive scream once more. This time, the fish was much stronger, so I furled in the genoa and turned *Stella Maris* into the wind to reduce her speed from eight knots to four to make it easier for Gjalt to reel in the catch. But to our great surprise, the fish swam *towards* the boat, as if giving itself up. Only when it was right behind the stern did it appear to comprehend the severity of its predicament and begin to fight for its life. Having helped the enemy so much, though, it was far too late for any struggling to pay off. Gjalt passed me the rod and I held it firmly, while he wielded the gaff. Unfortunately the hook went through the body instead of the gills, and it fell to me to deliver the fatal blow while Gjalt held the large, heavy fish within striking distance.

With *Stella Maris* lurching up and down in the choppy waves, the final and deadly act was reminiscent of the shower scene in *Psycho*, as I desperately tried to kill the poor creature with a sharp knife. Some of my stabs were so off target that I pierced an eye, causing blood to flow from it like crimson tears. It was awful. When the fish finally succumbed, I felt as bad as a mediaeval executioner who'd made a hash of it on his first day at work. The deranged Norman Bates had killed with less ferocity than I had. It was not a hunting experience either Gjalt or I was proud of.

We hauled the fish onboard, and only then did we see just how magnificent it was. We were overcome with guilt at having pulled such a wonderful animal from the ocean and ended its life in such a frenzied and disrespectful way. It deserved better. We guessed it to be about five feet long, and using our various sea life and fish books, we identified it as a shortbill spearfish. It was clearly designed for speed and agility through the water, with a bright blue sail-like dorsal fin, two long pelvic fins that fit perfectly into thin slots on its underside, and a powerful curved tail. There was so much meat on it that we didn't need to pay out another lure for a week. It was the most tender, delicious fish we had ever eaten.

The strong trade winds continued, and we kept up speeds between seven and eight knots using the mainsail combined with the genoa poled out to windward: our trade wind rig. We made fantastic progress, covering over 180 miles a day, but the steep, choppy waves and incessant rolling was tiring. I didn't send a position report for three days because typing on the computer at the navigation table

GJALT WITH THE MAJESTIC SHORTBILL SPEARFISH

made me nauseous. It was also hard to keep watch during the day, because we had to constantly stand up to properly see the horizon and then wait until we had been raised onto crests enough times to fully scan 360 degrees. It was easier to keep watch at night, when the bright lights of ships could be easily seen up to twelve miles away. During the haze of the day, it was much harder to discern the white bridge of a ship in the distance, and it was rarely possible to spot it from more than eight miles. But we hadn't seen a single boat since leaving the Galápagos Islands a week earlier.

When we weren't even halfway, each passing day seemed to last longer than the one before. Apart from the odd school of jubilant dolphins swimming along with us once in a while and the rare visit of a seabird, there was nothing to see but waves, endlessly flowing towards us like liquid volcanic glass. Large rollers lifted us up to considerable heights. From the crests, we could see for miles, as though we were standing on a hill in the middle of a vast plain, but when we were lowered into a trough, we couldn't see beyond the sides of the nearest waves.

We whiled away the hours between mealtimes gazing at the sea, always looking out for ships that rarely materialised. We got the chance to dig into our library, and I read book after book, studying the art of writing and becoming increasingly inspired to write more myself. On calm nights I read, but I could only concentrate for a page or two before imagining a huge tanker steaming up behind me. Then I immediately switched off the headlamp and quickly turned around to make sure we were still alone out there. Even though we saw just two ships during the entire passage, I never stopped swivelling my head like the girl in *The Exorcist*. It led to severe muscle strain, an injury that couldn't be eased by swivelling my head in the other direction.

The moon slowly waned to nothing, but it was remarkable how brightly the stars illuminated the nights. The Milky Way stretched overhead in a dramatic cloudy band, and every now and then, a meteorite streaked across the black sky. I made a wish each time, usually the selfish one that we would reach land safely. And by this time, land really was something I was beginning to long for. I wished I could see my family and best friend and have a full night of sleep in a bed that didn't move. I fantasised about all kinds of food that I couldn't have: my mum's cooking, fresh fruit, salads, ice-cream, even Big Macs and French fries. Such thoughts were small, perverse acts of self-torture.

My MP3 player continued to help me through my watches, but we had spent thirty nights at sea since leaving Texas, and I was beginning to tire of my music collection. An annoying side effect of our computer crashes was that my Walkman, convinced I wanted to load it with albums pirated from a different computer, simply refused to accept any new songs. This was utterly infuriating for the honest music purchaser already suffering a faulty hard drive.

Gjalt rarely listened to music, not wanting to be isolated from the sounds of the elements and the boat. He identified the source of each noise and kept his hand on a hard surface to feel for vibrations, always ensuring that everything was in order aboard our small oasis in the desert of the surrounding ocean.

The nights gave both of us uninterrupted periods of solitude, a chance to think. I looked back at my life, digging up memories from school, then university, and finally from my time in the oil industry. I had to stop my mind from wandering as I attempted to step through each year in turn, trying to remember all the significant things I'd done and the people I'd known. It felt as if I was opening cupboards in my mind that I hadn't looked in for years, finding things I'd forgotten all about. I tried to sort through it all and put everything back in better order.

Two weeks after setting off, and just a few days from making landfall, something of a race developed between several yachts within a day's sail of each other. Twice daily, we all announced our positions on the radio, so everyone knew who was where. The racer in Gjalt burst to the surface and made us replace the wholly adequate mainsail and genoa combination with the mighty gennaker. We stormed along like that for twenty-four hours, with my intermittent reminders that we were cruising, not racing, falling on deaf ears.

Finally a strong gust of wind put a stop to the madness, when we were overtaken by a sudden squall. It caused *Stella Maris* to broach and the gennaker halyard somehow became stuck in the block at the top of the mast. Nothing we tried got it free. We were at least able to pull the sock over the huge sail, but we couldn't just leave it hanging there for the last days of the passage. There was only one thing for it: Gjalt had to go up the mast. Although he thought this was all part of our adventure, he knew he had to be extremely careful; we were in the middle of nowhere, a long way from help if he fell.

First, he tried to go up with *Stella Maris* moving slowly forward under a small section of mainsail. He was only a few metres off the deck when the rolling waves started to swing him relentlessly from side to side, making progress impossible. He came back down, and we let out the genoa and hove to, so that *Stella Maris* would remain heeled over to one side.

The ocean was fairly calm, but still rolly enough to make the ascent a challenge. With the mainsail out, Gjalt couldn't clasp his hands around the mast, and he lost his grip on it several times, suddenly swinging free, dangling above the ocean that was waiting for him far below. For a second he would hang motionless in free air, suspended until the waves sent him back where he came from, smashing him into the waiting mast and adding more bruises to his growing collection. The ocean toyed with him, moving him from side to side like a human pendulum.

Eventually he made it to the top of the mast, where he saw that the halyard had been yanked into the block with such force that it had bent it open and become firmly wedged. He had no option but to cut it in order to lower the sail. In the process, his expensive, multipurpose Leatherman slipped out of his hand and sank to a watery grave several thousand feet deep. By the time Gjalt was back on deck he was utterly exhausted, and even the skin on the most tender parts of his body was black and blue. To add to his pain, the broken block meant we couldn't fly the gennaker again, a serious racing handicap if light winds returned.

I was immensely relieved when he was safely down again. Witnessing him crashing onto the deck in a crumpled heap would have been horrendous enough, but having to deal with the aftermath would have made things even worse. Even if he survived the fall, he would have broken a good number of his bones, not to mention suffered serious internal bleeding that could have proven fatal without emergency surgery. If he didn't survive, I would have had to bury him at sea; being six-foot-four, it would have been impossible to wedge him into the fridge in one piece. Either way I would have had to sail the last few hundred miles alone, bereaved, distressed, and severely traumatised. That was just not the kind of trip I'd signed up for.

Afterwards, we still managed to sail between six and seven knots with the genoa and mainsail, but Gjalt remained disgruntled by the loss of the gennaker from our sailing arsenal. I was beginning to feel less than content myself. The incessant rolling from side to side had worn wafer thin, and I longed to have the anchor down in a sheltered bay. My backside was permanently numb from so much sitting down, and no matter how often I shifted, it never recovered for long. My legs itched from lack of exercise and, despite doing aerobics to the music on my Walkman during my night watches, I felt the muscles steadily atrophying. I was a woman on the edge of a nervous breakdown, and had Gjalt seen the signs, he would not have pushed me over it.

At two in the morning, he woke me up an hour ahead of schedule to help him pole out the genoa following a wind shift. While he worked on deck, I handled lines in the cockpit. We were still relatively inexperienced at this operation, and Gjalt made a mistake rigging up the pole – a mistake that took ages to correct. It was fifty minutes before everything was set up in the right way and I was able to go back down below. Grumpily, I fell into bed and even more grumpily crawled out again a little over an hour later, when Gjalt woke me up for my watch.

Four o'clock is the worst time of the night. It seems darker than normal at that hour, and dawn takes forever to arrive. A person is meant to be cocooned in the depths of revitalising slumber; this is what the brain expects and so it directs all body heat into the core, leaving the limbs shivering. That night I was so incredibly exhausted that I had no defence against my first attack of insanity. I was sick and tired of not getting a full night of sleep, maddened by being constantly rolled from side to side, and bored of seeing nothing but water. The more I dwelt on my predicament, the more angry I became. I was trapped on a small rocking boat in the middle of the ocean, and I wanted to get off.

I began to kick my foot hard against the opposite seat in the cockpit, like an animal in a zoo repeatedly striking at the bars of its cage, hopelessly unhinged by its imprisonment.

It wasn't long before Gjalt appeared at the top of the companionway to find out the cause of the strange banging noise and he was more than a little disturbed to discover that it was me. Feeling helpless and not sure what to do, he just kept quiet while I ranted and raved, allowing me to blow off steam. It turned out to be the right thing to do, because gradually I calmed down, and Gjalt managed to talk me back to a state of mind verging on normal. I sat out my watch without kicking anything and without hurling myself over the side, something that had seemed tempting for the nanosecond or two when I desperately wanted the passage to end.

The next day, I caught up on my lost sleep and felt happy again. The fact that land was only two days away, and flatter seas made sailing more pleasant, undoubtedly had a lot to do with it.

Then the toilet in the forward head got blocked. I had foolishly tried to pump out a fibrous wet wipe, but at a certain point, it simply refused to move any further through the pipe. Knowing he would have to tackle the repair as soon as we reached the Marquesas, Gjalt was not impressed. When we bought *Stella Maris*, I thought that having two toilets onboard was an excessive luxury, but now I was mighty glad we had a backup in the aft cabin. Without it, 'Homer's All-Purpose Bucket' would have had to be pressed into service.

The night before making landfall, Gjalt's watch was enlivened by a series of loud explosions just a few boat lengths away on the port side. He couldn't see anything in the dark, but the noise receded as we sailed by and so became less alarming. He thought it must have been a whale slamming its tail on the water, perhaps warning the large intruder entering its territory to keep moving. We did just that, and were thankful the whale didn't follow up its threat with a physical challenge.

At first light, eighteen days after leaving the Galápagos, we saw something on the horizon that ended the familiar monotony of sea and sky: land! It stretched like a long, dark wall ahead of us, still too far away to make out any features but close enough to choke us with unanticipated emotion. It was the island of Hiva Oa, its exotic name ringing with a promise of adventure befitting the enchanting world of the fabled South Seas.

By the time we got closer, the sun had risen enough to bathe Hiva Oa in a warm glow. The island acquired detail: light defined ridges and shadows revealed valleys, steep cliffs could be seen plunging down into the ocean. As we sailed closer inshore, heading for the anchorage of Atuona on the south coast, the dull orange of barren volcanic rock faces yielded to slopes covered in patchwork blankets of bushes, trees, and grass. With our eyes now accustomed to a canvas dominated by blue, they could barely cope with all the striking shades of green. It was like being blinded by bright emerald and jade lights.

The slopes became steeper as they stretched inland, growing into dramatic mountains, their summits shrouded by the misty underbelly of thick clouds that hung over the island. It was a magical sight, not least because we had crossed 3,000 miles of open ocean in our small boat to see it. And although we had dipped our toes into the odd puddle of madness, we'd arrived with our sanity intact.

ARRIVING AT HIVA OA, MARQUESAS ISLANDS, AFTER
EIGHTEEN DAYS AT SEA

STELLA MARIS ANCHORED IN ATUONA BAY, HIVA OA,
MARQUESAS ISLANDS

# 9.

# The Garden Warriors

*Pirate fishing is a very lucrative business worth about seven billion euros per year. As the tuna populations decrease rapidly worldwide, pirate fishing in national waters is increasing. In fact, each year about 300,000 tons of tuna are caught illegally in the Pacific, with small island-states like the Cook Islands, French Polynesia, Micronesia and Kiribati being the most affected since they are not able to sufficiently control their territorial waters.*

– Greenpeace International, September 2007

The entry port of Atuona was the wonderful haven of flat, calm water I'd dreamt about on the passage. It was quite small and crowded with other yachts, but we found space near the sheer volcanic shore and put out a stern anchor to keep *Stella Maris* from swinging into her neighbours. A dense jungle of trees and tropical plants crowned the steep wall of black rock that hugged the edge of the bay, the foliage a spectacular contrast to the blue ocean we were used to. We heard the leaves rustling in the wind, accompanied by a chorus of singing birds. Rich greenery covered the gently sloping hills surrounding the bay, and in the distance, the magnificent bulk of Mount Temetiu reached to the sky, its peak veiled by mist. At times, this newfound beauty was so overwhelming that we just had to look away.

We quickly turned *Stella Maris* from a seaworthy yacht into a cosy, comfortable home. She'd done a fantastic job keeping us safe and earned a reputation for being fast amongst the other yachts. The constant trade winds had allowed us to sail the whole way, leaving our tanks full of diesel that had cost a mere dollar a gallon in the Galápagos and not thirsty for the French Polynesian diesel that cost five times as much. We felt a tremendous sense of achievement at having completed our longest passage. The office dweller in Gjalt had been replaced by a man entirely at home on the ocean; he felt fit, strong, and headily free. The suburbanite who took out the garbage was long gone. We slept like corpses that night, a wonderful eight-hour stretch of uninterrupted pleasure that I had so craved in recent days.

When we dinghyed ashore the following morning, the tide was out, and the only way to reach solid ground was to scale an enormous tyre hanging against the concrete wharf. Gjalt lifted me up half the distance, and I managed to scramble the rest of the way, but his solo ascent was less successful. He launched onto the unconventional rubber ladder, relying on sheer momentum to carry him to the top. Unfortunately, momentum just sent awkward rubbery spasms through the tyre that promptly sent him tumbling into the water. Having carefully selected clean clothes suitable for an audience with the port captain, he now either had to go back to the boat and change or risk a sodden appearance. He chose the latter and clambered onshore, hoping to dry out on the walk over the ridge to the town in the neighbouring valley.

The sky was a rich blue, the sun shone brightly, and we were relieved that our leg muscles were still capable of taking us further than a stretch of a few metres. Strolling along the winding road and smelling the fragrant flowers that lined it was pure joy. It was as if we'd landed on another planet after spending years in the vacuum of hyperspace to get there. Everything looked more vivid and smelt more intense than on planet Earth.

The heart of Atuona consisted of a few buildings scattered around a main road that was pleasingly devoid of cars. An abundance of trees and plants softened the hard concrete surfaces, and brilliant sunshine bathed everything in an uplifting, warm glow.

At the gendarmerie, the policeman didn't seem to notice Gjalt's damp clothes, but we certainly noticed his uniform. A tall, muscular Frenchman, he wore a shirt so tight the buttons strained to contain him, and he'd somehow managed to squeeze himself into a pair of shorts several sizes too small. Consequently, there was a distinct whiff of deviant Boy Scout leader about him. Still, checking in was painless and cost us next to nothing, so he could wear whatever he wanted as far as we were concerned, provided he left the Scouts alone.

Officially at liberty to enjoy French Polynesia for three months, we extracted French Polynesian Francs by the thousands from an unexpected cash point machine in the bank and began our explorations by finding out just how expensive everything was.

There was a fair selection of merchandise in the town's few shops, but a dozen eggs would set us back six dollars, as would one kilo of tomatoes. At seven dollars for a two-litre bottle of Coca-Cola, it was immediately clear that we were going to have to find a new mixer for our rum. The good news was that the essentials of everyday living, which for the French meant baguettes and pâté, were subsidised – the perfect surprise for yachties on a budget. We could afford to supplement our ever plentiful onboard stores with a few local delicacies after all. As for restaurants, we heard of cruisers who'd paid fifty dollars for a two-person meal of hamburgers, fries, and beer, so we realised it would be a while before we ate out again.

With a freshly bought aromatic baguette and a small tin of pâté, we set off to have lunch with Paul Gauguin. It was a hot day, so we were glad when the driver of a telephone company pickup truck stopped at the bottom of a steep hill and offered us a lift. We slid onto the wide front seat beside a Frenchman whose ample girth implied that he wasn't as concerned about the high price of food as we were. I resurrected enough 'O' level French to convey how wonderful we thought his island was, but he just shrugged in that nonchalant manner peculiar to the Gallic race. Apparently, he didn't share our enthusiasm, his disillusion having something to do with the fact that he'd lived on Hiva Oa for thirty years. This tropical island was normal to him, and how could anything he saw every day be special? Perhaps this inability of humans to appreciate familiar things, to no longer see their beauty, was what drove Gjalt and me to keep sailing on, always looking for the next paradise.

Wanting to escape Europe and 'everything that is artificial and conventional', Paul Gauguin had also come to the South Pacific in search of paradise. Ultimately, the famous painter would spend eternity there, having been laid to rest in the Calvary Cemetery in 1903. We enjoyed a pleasant lunch in the shade of a frangipani tree beside his grave, a substantial construction of volcanic blocks with his name and year of death simply written in white paint on a round stone at the foot. At the head stood a cast of the sculpture he considered his finest work of art; the woman was called *Oviri,* meaning 'wild or savage' in Tahitian.

From the cemetery, we had a wonderful view of the Atuona anchorage, its calm waters hugged by the protective green arms of the surrounding hills. As final resting places go, it was up there. It was a peaceful spot to reflect on how far we'd come in just four months. Houston and the oil business seemed a long way away, mere memories fading into a past that felt very distant. We had taken a risk leaving our comfortable lives behind, but we'd been rewarded by sailing into parts of the planet that were hidden from most of the world. Beyond sight of land, the ocean offered us a world to ourselves; on remote islands, the land offered us unspoilt nature and people untarnished by the desire for perpetual economic growth. We had jumped off the capitalist treadmill and discovered precious secrets.

Back on *Stella Maris*, the rather less precious secret of the blocked toilet awaited its own discovery. With every more preferable avenue to re-establish free flow exhausted, Gjalt had no option but to remove all the pipes to clear the blockage. Thankfully, as he was the onboard plumber, this decidedly unpleasant job fell squarely on his shoulders, even though I was responsible for the calamity. Once all the pipes were out, though, we saw that they were encrusted with hard calcium carbonate. This had drastically reduced their internal diameters, making it impossible for the fibrous wet-wipe to squeeze its way through. There was nothing for it but to go ashore and knock the plastic pipes against the dock to dislodge all the calcium carbonate. Not wanting to be associated with this embarrassing, antisocial activity, I disappeared to the open-air sinks with an immense pile of washing and busied myself with the laundry.

As I prepared to wrestle with the first batch of dirty clothes, a young girl from one of the kiddie boats approached me. "Are you going to do all that washing on your own?" she asked, her eyes wide with disbelief. Her family, it transpired, had a built-in washing machine on their catamaran.

"Yes – unless you want to help me."

Needless to say she did not, and she skipped away to tell her mother about the unfortunate people who had to wash their clothes in a bucket.

And how many bucketloads it took! Sometimes the soapy water turned such a disturbing colour that I felt sure dye was bleeding out of a dark t-shirt, only there wasn't always a dark t-shirt in the bucket. I would quickly slop the dirty water down the sink before a passer-by caught sight of it, then give the load a second pounding in fresh suds. Despite putting my back into it, I failed to get things thoroughly clean; the best I could hope for was the removal of the worst grime and an improved aroma. I was surprised at how much water was needed to rinse out the soap, and by the time I'd worked my way through the whole load, a good few hours and a lot of fresh water had flowed away. Still, it was a pleasant location for such a chore, and at least I kept clear of the toilet pipe operation, which was all over by the time I finished.

I was joined at the sinks by Dana, an outgoing American in her twenties who was crewing on one of the kiddie boats. Without a man's clothes to clean, her washing required considerably less effort than mine. I eyed her modest pile of laundry with envy, but her single status wasn't without its challenges. Wanting to sail across the Pacific, she'd taken a training course to qualify as crew, then flown to Panama in search of a position. There, she was taken on by a family with four young children. Two months later, life onboard the catamaran had become strained, and both sides were now looking to end the arrangement. Dana feared the inevitability of an expensive flight home, but a few days later, she joined two young American brothers on their mission to sail around the world in two years. While I admired her intrepid nature, I also thought she was crazy: going to sea with men I barely knew was adventure I could do without. For all she knew, they might have been totally inept sailors or – even worse – homicidal maniacs. How could she tell? Women had thought Ted Bundy was charming; it could prove fatal to be too trusting. Trapped on a yacht in the middle of the ocean, no one can hear you scream.

With the dirty laundry transformed into a fragrantly damp mass, it was my turn for a wash. Thankfully I didn't need to climb into 'Homer's All-Purpose Bucket', because beside the sinks was a single, secluded open-air shower. For the first time in months I stood under fresh running water, and it felt absolutely wonderful.

After a few days in Atuona working on boat maintenance, we replenished our water tanks, stocked up on pâté, and sailed to Hiva Oa's north coast. A family of dolphins escorted us for a while, and the joy of seeing these playful creatures was still as fresh as the first time they'd swum around *Stella Maris*' bow.

We made our way into the large, scenic bay of Hanaiapa, skirting an enormous rock that from a distance looked like a man's head in profile rising from the water. There were only three boats in an anchorage far more spacious than that of Atuona. One was about to sail for Hawaii, and afterwards home to Canada, while the others would continue west to Australia or New Zealand, just like most yachts in the Pacific.

We went onshore to loosen the leg muscles that had become stiff and mildly painful after our first exuberant excursion on land. We walked along a dirt trail that tracked the path of a narrow, meandering creek and led to a paved road at the start of Hanaiapa village. The village had been invisible from the boat, hidden like a well-kept secret by a wide forest of palm trees lining the beach.

It felt as if we were walking into the Garden of Eden after Adam and Eve had just left. There was freshly mown grass on either side of the road, bordered by flowering plants and trees laden with bananas, papayas, limes, and all kinds of exotic fruits we'd never even seen before. Only the apple tree was missing; that and the inhabitants. There was an eerie absence of humans in a village that was supposedly home to two hundred.

We passed modest homes made of wood and corrugated iron that would have seemed abandoned were it not for the exceptionally well-tended gardens surrounding them, full of tropical flora: purple bougainvilleas, pink bromeliads, white jasmine, red hibiscus. A pretty white church with a steeply sloping, tiled roof was the most expensive building in the village. A sneak peak through the open windows revealed a highly polished tiled floor and rows of wooden pews inside.

Just as we were beginning to think there were no people to fill those pews, we came across a few inhabitants engrossed in the upkeep of their gardens, watering and weeding as if they were expecting Alan Titchmarsh for tea. One man, his bare chest adorned with impressive Marquesan warrior tattoos, was picking small dead leaves out of his hedge and placing them one by one into a wheelbarrow brimming with the shrivelled brown rejects. Not long ago, the ancestors of these people had practised cannibalism, and now their descendants were dedicating themselves to winning the Garden of the Month Competition.

At first sight, the Marquesan men had an intense, warlike manner about them, which the symbolic tattoos adorning their bodies enhanced with a certain menace. Their eyes shot a hostile look in our direction, as if swiftly appraising how tasty our flesh might be after a slow roasting over an open fire. We defended ourselves with our only weapons: a friendly smile and a cheerful 'Bonjour', immediately followed by a compliment about their garden. Every time, to our great relief, the ferocity melted away as quickly as it had appeared, replaced with wide smiles and genuine hospitality. They were always extremely generous, offering us as much of their luscious fruit as we could carry. We were still struggling to dredge up the school French buried twenty years deep in our brains, and what we did manage to drag to the surface had to be perfectly enunciated since the Marquesans seemed to have acquired the pedantic French need for precise pronunciation in order to comprehend what we were saying.

The Spanish navigator Alvaro de Mendaña was the first European to sight the Islands back in 1595. He named them after his patron, the Viceroy of Peru, who was a marquis. Nearly two centuries later, in 1774, a visit by Captain Cook spread word of the Marquesas, and by the early nineteenth century, merchants and whalers sought adventure and fortune there. When the Islands were annexed by France in 1842, an initial trickle of Protestant and Catholic missionaries soon swelled to a flood. Thinking the natives 'defective in morals', they brought their religious zeal to the task of destroying traditional customs, forbidding singing and dancing, native dress, tattooing, and the elaborate system of *tapu* (taboos).

Worse still, along with their Bibles and self-righteousness, the Europeans brought infectious diseases, against which the natives had no immunity. Estimates of the pre-European population vary greatly, from 40,000 up to 100,000, but what is not in doubt is the number left alive less than 100 years later. By the 1920s, only 2,000 Marquesans remained. They had been decimated by such killers as typhoid, tuberculosis, influenza, and smallpox, the number of births plummeting in tandem with the escalating death toll. British novelist Robert Louis Stevenson, author of *Treasure Island,* visited the Marquesas in 1888 and observed the effect this devastation had on the remaining population. He found it peculiar that there was widespread depression and acceptance of the eradication of their race, but with people suddenly dying in the thousands, it doesn't seem so strange to me. He claimed that some Marquesans chose suicide over the unbearable anticipation of death's inevitable arrival. One old man, infected with smallpox, was said to have dug his own grave and lived in it for a fortnight before finally succumbing to the disease.

Beneath a group of trees near Hanaiapa's dinghy jetty, dozens of wind-fallen limes lay neglected, and so we chanced upon the ideal replacement mixer for our rum sundowners, now that Coca-Cola was prohibitively expensive. I spent several meditative hours squeezing limes and decanting the juice into our forlornly empty Coke bottles. We spent many more hours imbibing it, after it had been infused with the rum I'd stowed in various compartments around the boat. (The discovery of new bottles in unexpected places was always a pleasure.) Gjalt tried his hand at spearfishing while I baked bread, and so slowly but surely, we edged our way towards a life of satisfying self-sufficiency.

Late in the afternoon of one of those rewarding days, the *Aranui,* a 386-foot supply ship with capacity for 200 passengers, entered the anchorage. She proceeded to head aggressively for *Stella Maris*, the captain blasting the horn and calling us on the radio to demand we move out of the way. This abrupt invasion into our peaceful world brought forward our plan to sail on to a neighbouring anchorage, and we weighed anchor, leaving the bullying Goliath to it.

We had a wonderful cruise eastward along the rugged north coast of Hiva Oa. We usually set sail early in the morning to ensure that we were safely anchored well before sunset, so seeing the cliffs and inlets of the island in the burnished glow of the late afternoon sun was a rare pleasure.

We arrived in the Puamau anchorage just as the sun disappeared below the horizon. The lack of a protective headland exposed the large bay to the might of the Pacific, and the waves rolled into it unchecked. We anchored in a small area between the shore and two small *motus* (islands), hoping these would protect us from the swell, but we soon realised that the proximity of land around us would undoubtedly lead to a stressful night. Therefore, we promptly moved further out into the open water of the anchorage, preferring to be rocked to sleep rather than kept awake by worry.

The next morning, the sun lifted the veil that the previous day's twilight had lowered over the enormous bay. A steep and jagged hillside rose to the west, an incomplete carpet of green exposing scattered patches of barren rock. To the east, a ridge stretched to the ocean, a pinnacle of bare rock resembling a gloved hand soaring into the sky like a warning from the gods. Between them curved a long, wide, golden beach as deserted as the bay. We were alone, cut down to size by the grandeur of nature surrounding us, new arrivals in the land that time forgot.

*Stella Maris* danced around behind her anchor, but the motion was gentle and not unpleasant. The rollers responsible made landing the dinghy on the beach a tricky business, because they tended to crash exuberantly onto the sandy shore. With a dunking almost guaranteed, we left the outboard engine on *Stella Maris* and rowed instead. As we progressed into shallower water, we kept glancing over our shoulders with increasing trepidation. The arrival of a wave with our names on it was just a matter of time.

We both saw it coming, watched it surge up behind us for the attack. I quickly slid from the rim of the dinghy onto its floor, hoping to use my weight to stop it from being flipped upside down. Gjalt chose to hurl himself into the water, preferring to jump rather than be thrown out so he at least had some control over the situation. The wave curled over the top of me as it surged us forward, but it failed to overturn the dinghy. Thoroughly drenched, I remained seated on the floor and allowed Gjalt to tow me ashore as if I was some bedraggled Victorian lady.

Laughing at our inelegant landing and grateful for the absence of an audience, we dragged the dinghy onto a patch of grass in the shade of a palm tree. We spotted a tap beside the paved road running parallel to the beach and asked a passing local man for permission to use it to rinse the salt water from our skin.

We walked through the village, another heavenly place filled with lovingly kept gardens, and on to the archaeological site on the hillside at Iipona. It was the largest in the Marquesas and reportedly harboured the Islands' best stone statues, called *tikis*. The road led us past overgrown jungles of tropical plants, and in their midst, huge bunches of bananas and ripening papayas grew wild. The air was hot and steamy, causing sweaty rivulets to trickle down our skin as we climbed the hill.

The site had been reclaimed from the encroaching tentacles of the surrounding rainforest. Exquisitely manicured gardens sought to impose order and control, but they failed to quell the raw power of the stones that had been placed there by some lost civilisation. Ceremonial platforms constructed from roughly hewn boulders stood mysteriously amidst the remaining walls of vanished sacred buildings, the function of which can now never be fully understood. The Marquesan culture was passed on orally, and most of the secrets were buried with the dead during the nineteenth century. The missionaries endeavoured to make the living forget the rest.

Scattered around the site were the carved stone tiki statues, all different shapes and sizes, but each one exuding an aura of power from its squat, heavy body and inscrutable expression. The largest, Takaii, stood eight feet tall, smaller only to the statues on Easter Island. Tikis are thought to represent revered ancestors or tribal gods, and Polynesians believe they have special powers. It wasn't difficult to see why; they might have been made of stone, but it seemed unwise to anger them.

In Mexico, such a place would have been crowded with tourists deposited by the coachload, but at Iipona we could wander around alone and unhurried, able to absorb the atmosphere, its magic unspoilt. Cruising rewarded us with experiences like that.

On the way back to the anchorage, we followed a path that wound through a valley thick with palm trees and emerged into a remote corner of the village.

As we walked downhill towards the bay, a pickup truck came to a stop next to us, and we suddenly found ourselves being appraised by a disconcertingly intense pair of Marquesan eyes. "Have you eaten pamplemousse?" he demanded, pointing to the fruit hanging in the trees beside the road.

For an alarming second, we thought he was accusing us of having stolen fruit from his orchard. We quickly flashed him our brightest smiles, looked at the pamplemousses as if noticing them for the first time, and said, "*Non.*"

Suddenly he shot out of his truck and straight up the nearest tree, where he began pulling down these large cousins of the grapefruit as if it were a matter of life and death. Soon there were eight of them spread out by our feet. "Wait here," he said and drove off up the road, disappearing around a bend. Some minutes later he returned, his truck loaded with a bag of mangos, two huge bunches of bananas, and his wife and young son.

Sébastien earned a good living growing nonis, a foul-smelling fruit the size of a pear that was the miracle elixir of the moment for those seeking eternal youth. Copra (dried coconut meat from which oil is extracted) was no longer economically viable and heavily subsidised by the French, but noni fruit grew quickly and required little attention. Sébastien's harvest was shipped to Salt Lake City, where drinks and creams were produced from the fermented fruits. Having smelt the stench emanating from plastic drums full of rotting nonis on more than one occasion, we intended to steer well clear of the stuff.

Still, the American desire for this miracle drink enabled Sébastien and many other Marquesans to afford brand new four-wheel drive vehicles, irresistible even on islands with only a few paved roads. Having given us far too much to carry, he insisted on driving us back to the beach in his pickup. We were experiencing the full force of Marquesan hospitality, untainted by tourism and kept intact by the scarcity of visiting cruisers. Having gone onshore prepared for just such an encounter, I pulled a small soft toy from my backpack for Sébastien's son. It wasn't much, but it was something more than our words of thanks.

To get beyond the surf that had assaulted us when we came onshore, we had to swim out through it. We loaded the dinghy with our fruity bounty, and Gjalt guided it over the incoming waves, while I worried about sharks biting my legs as I waded out. Once we were safely into the deep surf-free zone, we hauled ourselves into the dinghy and rowed back to *Stella Maris*.

Onboard, we devoured our first pamplemousse, something we hadn't even known existed before we arrived in the Marquesas. It was the most delicious fruit we'd ever tasted. Peeling away the outer green skin revealed the grapefruit-like citrus encased within. The yellow segments separated easily, and each harboured hundreds of tightly packed teardrop-shaped sacks bursting with juice of the most divine sweetness. It was the start of an addiction.

At daybreak, we left for Fatu Hiva, the island made famous by Thor Heyerdahl. Like Gauguin, the explorer had wanted to escape civilisation and return to nature, so the day after his wedding in 1936, he set off for the island with his young bride. Although their adventure started well, they were gradually worn down by tropical diseases and an inability to live happily among the locals. They began to long for home, and one and a half years after their arrival, the young couple returned to Norway.

Just south of Hiva Oa, we changed course to reach a flock of seabirds in a feeding frenzy and soon reeled in a four-foot wahoo. We hoisted the gennaker to harness the morning's light wind, but there wasn't enough to fill the sail, and we needed the engine's assistance to complete the forty-mile trip. Along the way, we were visited by a school of dolphins, a small baby sticking like glue to its mother's side as she rode the bow wave.

The barren cliff faces on the northern shores of Fatu Hiva formed sheer edges to the sloping green hills that rose gently inland. The now familiar patchwork of light green grass and dark green trees and bushes covered the volcanic island, its peaks hidden by mist.

We sailed south along the steep cliffs of the west coast until we reached Hanevave Bay, a small indent cutting in between soaring hillsides. As we headed for the anchorage, we were disappointed to find that Fatu Hiva's fame and beauty had made it very popular. We carefully sought out a good location between the yachts that were crowded together in the small bay, but it took several attempts before our anchor set. When Gjalt dived down to check it, he saw that the seabed consisted of flat, cracked rock, with nothing for the anchor to hook on but the odd loose boulder. He spent time wedging it behind the nearest one as best he could. It was no wonder yachts often dragged on their anchors there.

It was certainly a beautiful spot, as long as we mentally blocked out the ugly goal posts onshore, starkly white behind the black shingle beach at the head of the bay. On either side of the anchorage, palm trees clung confidently to the base of the near-vertical cliffs; higher up, the hard rock was softened by a carpet of soft grass and a smattering of lush bushes. Standing like sentinels at the entrance to an inland valley, huge rock formations reminiscent of virgins (if you were a Catholic missionary), phalluses (if your leanings were more carnal), or just strangely shaped rocks (if you were neither) stood guard. (Rumour has it that the bay was originally called Baie des Verges (Bay of the Phalli) and renamed Baie des Vierges (Bay of the Virgins) by disapproving missionaries. How convenient that one small letter could so easily remedy a problem of lewd immorality!) A transient mist, alternately veiling and revealing the serrated edges of the inland ridges, completed the mystical atmosphere.

By the end of the day, twelve yachts were huddled together in the small anchorage. That, combined with the poor holding ground, made it difficult for us to relax. We'd been spoilt by the uncrowded bays on the north coast of Hiva Oa and could barely see the beauty surrounding us while we were hemmed in between other boats. To us, sailing meant freedom, the opportunity to experience unique, far-flung corners of the globe without being overrun by other people.

The next morning, we awoke to find a rusty Dutch boat anchored so close to our stern that we could practically reach out and touch it. Knowing the precarious hold its anchor must have had on the seafloor, we were irritated and concerned by this incursion into *Stella Maris'* swing room. I was all for telling the old couple onboard to get lost, but Gjalt decided on a different tack and, much to my horror, invited the grizzled captain onboard for coffee. His wife remained elusive below deck. After some sociable chit-chat that seemed interminable to me, Gjalt casually pointed out the proximity of his compatriot's boat to ours and asked if he would make sure that the two didn't bump into each other while we were onshore. The man readily agreed to stay on his boat until we got back and anchored further from us when other yachts left the bay. Gjalt had been right to choose diplomacy over confrontation.

A morning of rain and grey skies did not help improve my melancholy mood, but by the afternoon, we were discovering the island's fabled beauty for ourselves, as we followed a trail to a 200-foot waterfall. We were mere specks in a grand landscape that was richly coloured by the greens, yellows, and browns of tropical plants, its splendour accentuated by the gem-like flowers scattered all around. Fruit trees bearing bananas, limes, and papayas grew by the side of the path, as did small bushes laden with red and green chilli peppers. The razor-sharp ridges atop the towering peaks rose like spines on the backs of giant dinosaurs. It was the kind of landscape that could easily have been home to such long-lost beasts.

The trail led us into a steamy forest that gradually became so overgrown we had to scramble our way past fallen trees and rampant bushes. At the end, we emerged into a clearing, where a broad veil of water streamed down a sheer rock face, filling a deep pool below. The falling water sparkled in the sunshine and gave the smooth rock a glistening sheen. The chance to cool off was irresistible, and we jumped right in.

Back in the village, we wandered through the side streets and fell quietly victim to the tourist industry that had sprung up on the island due to the large number of visiting yachts. An unassuming man lured us to his house with polite conversation, but once we were there, his wife subtly laid an entire collection of his carvings at our feet. By then, it was too late to just walk away. We hadn't yet bought a single souvenir on our trip - we'd rarely even been tempted - but the mystical tiki gods, wonderfully carved from dark wood, enticed us. The artist who had skilfully ensnared us now hovered silently in the background, unwilling to tarnish his creative soul with vulgar commercial exploits. Meanwhile, his significantly more robust wife, elegantly dressed in a yellow sarong, with a red hibiscus flower tucked behind her ear, sat cross-legged in the doorway of the house and encouraged us to choose something.

After considerable humming and ha-ing, we selected the best tiki: a head shaped like an aerodynamic bicycle helmet, a large mouth as broad as the face, and hands that rested contentedly on a distended belly. She said it cost fifty dollars, which we took as our cue to suggest an alternative to money. We'd heard of the locals' desire to trade for things that were expensive or hard to come by on the island, so I had come somewhat prepared. Hesitantly, I asked if she might consider trading. She nodded immediately. With a touch of embarrassment, I produced a small collection of toiletries from my backpack, certain that such humble cosmetics would be dismissed as an insult.

To my great surprise, though, she wasted no time seizing the perfume bottles and removed the stoppers to judge the fragrances within. An offer was made: the tiki in return for two miniatures of eau de toilette. Having been asked for fifty dollars in the first place, this trade seemed totally unbalanced, and I proceeded to give her lipstick and eyeshadow as well. She now felt it necessary to reciprocate with gifts of a carved turtle and a hair ornament and sent her artist husband to fetch bananas, bread, and limes for us. Clearly, each side thought it had short-changed the other, but adding more goods to the scales certainly felt better than making a deal that seemed unfair.

Back on the main street, we were badgered by less friendly and more insistent locals who wanted us to look at their wares. Suddenly, Fatu Hiva had the unpleasant air of tourism about it, something we hadn't encountered on Hiva Oa at all. This atmosphere, together with the crowded anchorage, led us to set sail at daybreak the next morning for the island of Tahuata, some forty miles to the northwest.

Skirting the rugged southern tip of the island, we entered Hanatefau Bay on the west coast. It was enormous, and when we saw there were only two other boats anchored there, we were glad we hadn't stayed any longer at Fatu Hiva. This was one of the best places to snorkel in the Marquesas, with crystal-clear water and a myriad of multicoloured reef fish living amongst the corals growing on the steep sides of the bay. When a young American couple showed us the beautiful cowry shells they'd found there, we instantly became avid collectors ourselves. The thick, sturdy shells were a few centimetres long, decorated with incredibly intricate patterns and so highly polished they looked as though they'd been glazed in a kiln. Having so far been content to snorkel at the surface, with a reassuringly inexhaustible supply of oxygen at my disposal, I suddenly began diving twenty feet down to search the seabed for these elusive, well-camouflaged treasures. We spent hours at a time in the water, only giving up when we were too cold to carry on.

With no shops from which to buy tasty French bread, I resorted to baking my own again. The dough rose up out of the bowl as God intended, and I divided it into two tins that went straight in the oven. I was so into this homely domesticity that I promptly set about making a chocolate cake as well. (A quirky side note here is that I used cocoa powder that had been bought in Oman, shipped to Norway, then to Houston, and had now been sailed across the Pacific to the Marquesas. It was undoubtedly the most travelled cocoa powder in the world, and at about ten years old, it was still perfectly good.)

While I was in the main cabin, diligently stirring the chocolate mixture, there was suddenly a tremendous explosion in the galley, accompanied by the sound of breaking glass. I went to investigate and found that the inner window of the oven had shattered. After sweeping up the shards, I decided to continue baking with just the one pane of glass left in the oven door, keeping well clear of the galley in case that one shattered as well. The bread turned out edible, albeit a little pale, but it was not the masterpiece it surely would have been had the process not been violently interrupted halfway through.

With the oven still intact, I was determined to bake the chocolate cake as well. The metal grill on which I placed the tin sat at an angle, however, so the finished cake emerged with a distinct gravity-defying slope to it. All things considered, I felt proud of my efforts and, flush with success, created a pretty good banana cobbler the next day. I was encouraged to use the fruit creatively, as about forty had ripened simultaneously on the enormous stalk hanging on the stern.

We left Tahuata three hours before sunrise so we would arrive at the kite-shaped island of Ua Pou (pronounced Wa Poo), sixty miles to the northwest, before sunset. Continuing the tried and tested method of changing the boat's course to follow frenzied seabird activity, we reeled in a skipjack tuna. By now, we'd caught enough fish that Gjalt had the gaffing, killing, and especially the filleting procedures down to a fine art. I did worry when he started to remove the skin with his teeth rather than the knife, though, and I found it mildly disturbing to watch him slurp flesh from the fish's head to assess its quality as sashimi. He'd often return to the cockpit from the filleting table on the aft deck with blood smeared around his mouth and a maniacal look in his eye. At these times, there seemed little chance of him ever putting on a tie and calmly sitting behind a computer in an air-conditioned office again.

We sailed along the east coast of the eight-mile-long island and joined several other yachts in Hakahau Bay, near the northern tip. This bay was so small that bow and stern anchors were needed to stop the boats from swinging into each other. From the anchorage, we had a breathtaking view of the island's famous basalt rock spires, standing like the sharpened flint tips of the spears of the gods. Oave, the highest, soared 1,200 majestic metres into the sky, its pinnacle often floating above the surrounding ridge, cut off by a scarf of white clouds wrapped around its base.

Onshore the following morning, we heard melodious singing coming from the Eglise Saint-Etienne and wondered why people were in church on a Thursday. A notice board outside informed us that it was Ascension Day. It was a pretty building constructed from rounded beach boulders, and its steeply sloping tiled roof gave it a distinctly Nordic air. We'd arrived at the end of the service, and the congregation filed out dressed in their Sunday best; some of the women sported large, flamboyant hats that wouldn't have been out of place at Ascot.

Once the church had emptied, we went inside. Two rows of closely spaced wooden benches stretched the length of the large room, reaching forward over the tiled floor to the altar. Above this was a life-sized wooden carving of Jesus on the cross, the suffering of his spirit etched into his face, the suffering of his body shown by straining muscles and an emaciated stomach. The wooden ceiling rose in a peak above the statue, a wide set of windows below making it the lightest part of the room and drawing eyes to the Son of God. The pulpit had been finely carved from a single piece of tou wood and depicted the prow of a ship atop a sea of symbolic marine creatures; religion was linked to the islanders' everyday lives. On either side of the altar stood two more statues, a peaceful one of Mary with the baby Jesus in her arms and a harrowing one of a saint in spiritual agony, looking skyward for help. The craftsmanship of all the carvings was superb. On one side of the church, a broad, triangular window open to the elements framed Ua Pou's towering rock spires, bringing the beauty of the natural world inside, uniting it with the worshippers' spirituality.

During our walk around the village, which was home to half the island's 2,000 inhabitants, our keen eyes spotted some pamplemousses lying on the ground of a neglected garden. As we were down to our last one of these delicious anti-scurvy fruits, we looked around for someone we could ask for permission to take them. We attracted the attention of a Frenchman on a small scooter, and he directed us to the neighbouring house of Hubert and Katrin. Hubert, a grey-haired man of advanced years, regarded us with a confused look, possibly due to our appalling French, or maybe because of our strange desire for wind-fallen fruit. In any case, he ignored us. Katrin, on the other hand, graciously walked with us back to the garden. A petite lady, considerably younger than Hubert, she firmly declared the pamplemousses on the ground to be no good and proceeded to pick fruit from the tree instead. She refused to accept any money, so I asked her if she would like a gift.

"*Oui*," she replied shyly.

Out came my trusty make-up case, and she seemed happy with the Estée Lauder lipstick I selected for her – so happy, in fact, that her teenage son, who had since arrived on the scene, was promptly sent up the tree to harvest the largest pamplemousse of all for our collection.

The trading and gift-giving was working well for us, and we had the pleasant feeling that it was working well for our hosts too. When we later investigated the prices of toiletries in the shops, we understood why. A small perfume bottle of unknown origin, and no doubt dubious fragrance, cost around thirty to forty dollars. We also discovered that rum was a particularly scarce commodity and that spirits sold for fifty dollars. The question was: would we come across anything we wanted so badly that we'd be prepared to exchange Captain Morgan for it? It did seem highly unlikely.

We moved some five miles around the rounded northern coast of Ua Pou to Hakahetau Bay, which was large enough for us to anchor away from the other two boats already there. We had to row ashore so we could pull the dinghy out of the water, as the landing jetty was not protected from the swell rolling into the bay.

We went for a long walk through a forest and collected more wind-fallen limes. The trail ended at a house that announced itself as Manfred's Place, and a quick, illicit sortie into the grounds showed that Manfred had it pretty good.

Back in the village, a barefoot old man wearing rolled-up trousers picked freesias from the roadside and presented them to both of us with an enigmatic smile. We imitated his style and placed the sweet-smelling flowers behind our ears before carrying on to the pretty village church. We sat beside it for a while, soaking up the tranquillity and soothing influence of the surrounding tropical flora.

Seeing us there, a villager abandoned the watering of his finely landscaped garden to bring us a bottle of orange juice and two plastic cups. "It is very hot," he said, after our surprised looks asked him to explain his kind gesture. Perhaps he thought the heat had affected our sanity, with those freesias sprouting out of our ears.

First flowers, then orange juice! We were again utterly charmed by the Marquesas and their hospitable people. Even in the twenty-first century, the Islands retained their reputation as paradise on Earth.

The next day, we sailed north to Nuku Hiva, the group's largest island and our final destination. Racing along at seven and a half knots in good wind, we reached the south coast in just three and a half hours. We passed between two large, rocky islets guarding the entrance to Taiohae Bay and moved in one and a half miles to the head of it. There were nearly thirty yachts anchored between the protective land to the east and west, but the bay was enormous, formed by the remains of a volcanic crater, and we had plenty of space around us.

For some elusive reason known only to Gjalt, he decided on a different tack for getting ashore than everyone else in the anchorage: we would not put the outboard engine on the dinghy and whiz to the jetty with its convenient landing steps, but instead row a shorter distance to the rock-strewn beach opposite us. Rowing was the easy part; it was getting onto dry land that was the challenge. With waves lapping at our ankles, we slipped and stumbled across smooth, irregularly shaped boulders, as we lugged the unwieldy dinghy ashore. Being forced into this unnecessary and infuriating exercise left me not only wet, but grumpy as well. I failed to understand why we couldn't just do things the easy way, like everyone else.

We strolled through the largest town in the Marquesas, passing the grand Notre Dame Cathedral on our way to the gendarmerie. There we completed the paperwork with yet another policeman in eyebrow-raisingly tight and tiny shorts, our communication limited by our annoyingly faltering French. In the grocery store, Gjalt at last found the brie he'd been dreaming of for months, and we finally threw caution to the wind and splashed out on eggs, tomatoes, cucumbers, onions, and other luxury goods, such as a four-dollar cabbage. (Surprisingly, even cabbage becomes appealing after months without fresh vegetables.)

With our tasks back in civilisation completed, we headed five miles east to Controleur Bay. After crowded Taiohae Bay, we were amazed to find it utterly devoid of yachts. It seemed that even cruisers, surely some of the most independent people on the planet, liked to hang out together when they got the chance.

Gjalt dropped the anchor, and I reversed *Stella Maris* in order to dig it into the seabed. Suddenly I noticed the dinghy sidling up alongside and immediately threw the engine into neutral, just at the very moment there was a mini-explosion. I was certain that the entire dinghy had burst. In fact, its line had been pulled so tight that the metal ring it was threaded through ripped the thick PVC tube attached to the dinghy's bow, causing the terrible noise. The line had wrapped around the prop, and if I hadn't put the engine into neutral quickly enough, we might well have had a ruined gear box. Thankfully, everything remained intact, apart from our wounded dinghy. It was a reminder that all aspects of cruising required care and attention; we were a long way from spare parts.

We enjoyed lunch in the cockpit with an uninterrupted view of the surrounding steep slopes, every square metre of which was covered with green trees and bushes. A manta ray circled the boat in water that had been turned muddy by recent heavy rain, the tips of its wings piercing the surface as it swam. Then it leapt into the air and disappeared from sight.

Onshore, more ancient tikis hid in the forest close to the village of Taipivae, and we set out to find them. We dinghyed past the beach at the head of the bay and as far up the small river leading to the village as we could get before the water became too shallow. We stopped beside an extensive coconut grove that seemed a good place to make landfall and tied the dinghy to a fallen palm tree. Once we were onshore, though, we discovered that what had appeared to be solid ground was, in fact, gelatinous mud, home to a seething mass of crabs. We trudged on, trying to identify the firmest patches, but before long, I found myself knee deep in mud – so completely stuck in the thick mire that Gjalt literally had to pull me out. After prolonged heaving, I came free with a slurpy *pop*, but my sandals had been left behind. I reached in and rescued them before they sank into oblivion.

At last, we emerged into the garden of a woman who looked especially clean in a cheerful, bright orange sarong patterned with large white flowers. She smiled at the sight of our mud-caked legs and instructed her children to take us to the neighbour's house, which had an outdoor tap we could use to make ourselves decent again.

The woman's thirteen-year-old daughter walked with us to the village, and I was better able to speak French to the friendly teenager than to the Boy Scout-uniformed gendarme. It felt good to communicate at least a little with one of the exotic inhabitants of these Polynesian Islands.

After crossing a bridge, she turned right to go to her dance class, and we went left in search of the tikis, but not before we had indulged in an ice-cream at the grocery shop. I'd been dreaming of ice-cream for weeks, and there it was, an irresistible treat in the sticky heat of the afternoon, and only one dollar at that.

Despite asking everyone we passed on the main road for directions, we still managed to overshoot the path leading to the Paeke archaeological site. A sympathetic local told us to jump in the back of his pickup truck and drove us down the hill to the start of the trail, which we'd walked past because it seemed to stop at a house. In fact, it continued on behind it, snaking up a forested hillside to a ridge, where stone tikis and large ceremonial platforms built with huge basalt blocks had been cleared from the creeping jungle. Although it was less impressive than the expansive Iipona site on Hiva Oa, it had the same mysterious atmosphere of a lost civilisation that had once worshipped its gods there and presented them with human sacrifices. We stayed long enough to explore everything, and made sure we left before someone turned up and decided we'd make a good offering.

Back beside the muddy coconut grove, the kind woman in the bright orange sarong had filled bags with limes, oranges, and pamplemousses for us. And as if that wasn't generous enough, her husband emerged from the house and cut down a fresh stalk of bananas to add to the bounty. Thanks to the kindness of the locals, we were getting much healthier than we'd been in Houston, where we rarely ate any fruit at all.

As we approached the river, smeared in gooey mud yet again, we clearly heard someone singing. When we drew nearer, we saw a young man standing beside our dinghy, one foot raised onto a fallen palm tree, like a conqueror celebrating the defeat of his slain enemy. He was staring off into the distance, lost in his chanting, and looked quite the wild warrior with his muscular bare chest decorated with tattoos and his sleek black hair pulled back in a ponytail. I thought we'd stumbled into some ancient religious ritual, in which our dinghy was playing a central, mystical role, and I was afraid to interrupt it. Before we could turn and quietly steal away, though, he noticed us and brought our escape to an instant stop with a typically aggressive look.

I responded with a hasty '*Bonjour*', and the ferocious look dissolved into friendliness which, as always, was a tremendous relief.

We were lucky to find our dinghy where we left it. The tide had come in, and the massive palm tree we'd secured it to had just begun to float. We'd learnt yet another lesson: only tie the dinghy to objects that can't drift away.

On the north coast of Nuku Hiva is an anchorage reputed to be the calmest in the Marquesas: Anaho Bay. It is also one of the most picturesque, with beaches of fine golden sand and abundant coral, a rarity in the Islands. Having such a good reputation, of course, meant it was popular, and we arrived to find six boats tucked behind the headland in the calmest corner. Accustomed to the luxury of solitude by this time, we chose to anchor in the centre of the bay, away from the other boats. Lacking the protection of the small hook of headland, we put out a stern anchor to keep *Stella Maris'* bow perpendicular to the swell and so stop her rolling from side to side. We were perfectly happy in our solitary spot opposite the longest beach, with its breathtaking views of the jagged volcanic peaks cloaked in green.

It didn't last, though. The next morning, we awoke to find we had an enormous neighbour breathing down our necks - the *Aranui*. She had chased us out of one bay and was now imposing herself on us in another; she dominated our view and spoilt the tranquillity with her rumbling engines. We tried to be grateful for small mercies, though; at least the captain hadn't blasted his horn in the middle of the night and demanded that we move.

We rowed ashore and walked over a ridge to the neighbouring bay, passing some overgrown ruins along the way. Grass covered the sand dunes at the head of the broad east coast bay, and a family of nine wild horses grazed on it happily. We sat down, and they trotted over to us after a while. Having never been terribly confident around large animals, I asked Gjalt if I was in any danger. I knew horses weren't known for spontaneously trampling people to death, but these were big animals up close, and they were wild, after all. Thankfully they didn't attack but tiny, vicious 'no-see-ums' did, something we only discovered after they had feasted on our blood.

STELLA MARIS ANCHORED IN THE CALM CORNER OF NUKU HIVA'S ANAHO BAY, MARQUESAS ISLANDS

When the *Aranui* and several of the yachts left the following day, we moved to the sheltered part of the bay and discovered why the others had nestled so closely together in this nook: it was flat calm. Not only was there no need for a stern anchor, but the water was an inviting aquamarine, and a short distance away, coral heads waited to be explored.

We wanted to give our legs a stiff workout before sailing off to the low-lying atolls of the Tuamotu Archipelago, so we embarked on a long walk over a high ridge to Hatiheu Bay. It was a good, strenuous hike, with panoramic vistas along the way and some exciting slipping and sliding in mud created during a downpour the previous day.

The bay was huge and offered no protection from the ocean rollers. It looked uninviting compared to tranquil Anaho Bay, but the shoreline had been beautified with some small stone tikis and was a pleasant place to sit before trekking back.

Robert Louis Stevenson had the exciting honour of meeting Chief Kooamua of Hatiheu during his visit in 1888, a man he described as 'the last eater of long-pig in Nuku Hiva'. Just as interesting as Kooamua's cannibalistic reputation for taking a bite from the raw flesh of an enemy's arm was his awareness that the island's resources had to be properly managed. When devil-fish became scarce on the reef, he imposed a *tapu*, forbidding the removal of that type of fish until its numbers had recovered; and when the coconut palms began to suffer from the over-harvesting of green nuts, he *tapued* his own section of forest, knowing that his example would be quickly copied by others. If only we could be as sensible with worldwide tuna stocks, these fish would not be facing extinction.

The next day, we decided to leave for the Tuamotus. Although we had good fortune in the fishing stakes soon after setting off, catching a five-foot wahoo off the northeastern corner of Nuku Hiva, we had worse luck with the weather. By the time we reached the south coast, it was clear that the forecast wind had simply not materialised. We didn't intend to motor the 450 miles to the atoll of Raroia, so we pulled into Controleur Bay, where we spent a peaceful final night in the Marquesas Islands.

TIKI STATUE AND STELLA MARIS, TAIOHAE BAY,
NUKU HIVA, MARQUESAS ISLANDS

# 10.

## *Paradise Found*

*Even in the most optimistic scenarios, climate change
will continue well into the present century. If the more
extreme predictions occur, then most of the atoll nations
will disappear beneath the ocean, and coastal strips
and communities around the high islands will be inun-
dated within the next 50 years.*

> – European Commission, Overseas Countries and
> Territories Environmental Profiles, Pacific Region,
> January 2007

We left Controleur Bay the following morning and set
sail for Raroia. It was on this atoll that, in 1947,
Thor Heyerdahl's famous voyage on his balsa
raft, the *Kon-Tiki*, came to an end. Intending to prove that
native South Americans could have migrated to islands
in the Pacific, Heyerdahl set off from Peru with five crew
and sailed across 3,800 miles of ocean for 101 days before
crash-landing onto the atoll's outer reef.

The Tuamotu Archipelago is a group of seventy-eight
atolls, which formed on drowned sea mountains and volcanoes. It extends almost 1,000 miles in a northwest-south-
east direction, but has a combined land area of just 885
square kilometres. This land consists of flat, hard reef and
coral islands rarely higher than three metres above sea
level, with palm trees adding just another twenty metres
to some. This makes them difficult to sight from more than
a few miles away. Often, the southern edges of the atolls
have no islands at all and consist solely of barren, partly
submerged reefs, only made visible by the breakers crashing onto them. Before the existence of GPS, very few cruisers
dared to visit what early explorers nicknamed 'The Dangerous Archipelago', due to the alarming number of ships

that were wrecked as they negotiated their way through it. With only a sextant to navigate by and strong, unpredictable currents able to push ships off course, the chances of running aground were enormous. Even today, these waters remain hazardous and still claim boats.

We had good wind from the start and hoisted the gennaker to catch as much of it as we could. Unfortunately, the line holding the new block at the top of the forestay broke in the first strong gust. Gjalt had rigged this line to reduce the strain on the block and prevent it from breaking, as the previous one had done on the crossing from the Galápagos, but it wasn't strong enough to withstand the gust. We could have sailed the three-day passage without the gennaker, but as we'd just left a calm anchorage, we decided to go back so Gjalt could climb up the mast and make a quick repair. Within an hour of our return, we were heading out to sea again, grateful to be able to use the gennaker during a few hours of light winds in the early afternoon.

With three-quarters of a full moon shining brightly in a near-cloudless sky, we were gently reintroduced to night watches after a month's respite in the Marquesas. My first off-watch was interrupted, however, when the wind died and we had to roll in the genoa, remove the pole, and hoist the gennaker once more. Due to the changeable conditions, Gjalt hadn't slept much during his first off-watch either, and after I went back to bed, he woke me up early because he could no longer keep his eyes open. This lack of sleep, and sleep interrupted, made us both incredibly grumpy.

When a squall passed overhead the next morning, we didn't take the gennaker down quickly enough, and a powerful gust broke the repaired line. But with the winds now blowing steadily, our trade wind combination of the genoa poled to windward and the mainsail to leeward kept us moving swiftly along. The day brightened, and the ocean was calm with waves of less than three feet, so the sailing was extremely pleasant, allowing us both to catch up on much-needed sleep.

The wonderful conditions didn't last through the night, though, as we sailed into the Intertropical Convergence Zone (a belt of low pressure around the Equator) and the skies clouded over bringing rain and lightning. The bright moon kept us from being plunged into total darkness, but the world wasn't as friendly and idyllic as it had been the night before.

By the third day, we'd got into the rhythm of our watches, and both of us felt better rested. The skies remained overcast and brought more rain, but the seas were calm, and we were sailing fast. By evening the clouds had moved on, allowing the near-full moon to shine down on us in all its glory. In the dark early hours, we sailed past the small island of Tepoto, and the twinkling lights made me wonder about the people living on that small pinnacle of land marooned in the vastness of the Pacific Ocean.

By morning, our progress was such that we would reach Raroia just after nightfall. Our timing could not have been worse. We needed both daylight and slack tide to go safely through the pass and into the shelter of the atoll. In the strong winds, we couldn't slow *Stella Maris* down enough to delay our arrival, and we didn't fancy heaving-to for twelve hours close to an atoll in the Dangerous Archipelago. Instead, we decided to change course for Makemo some sixty miles further southwest, which had the added attraction of being closer to other atolls that we planned to visit.

By late afternoon, the wind had died, and we used the engine for the first time since setting off three days earlier. I sat on the port side and stared into the cobalt blue sea that was amazingly pristine in both colour and clarity and utterly smooth in the dead calm. The absence of breeze allowed the heat to envelop us, our only relief coming from the cooling seawater we hauled from the ocean by the bucketload. We were alone out there; we hadn't seen a single boat the whole trip.

The clouds returned with the night and brought rain and more dreaded lightning. We wrapped our backup handheld GPS in tin foil and placed it in the Faraday Cage that doubled as our oven. If we were struck by lightning and lost all our onboard instruments, we wanted to know our exact position in those treacherous waters. Thankfully the vicious forked electricity conducted itself elsewhere, and when we emerged into clear skies, it was as though we'd sailed into another, much friendlier world.

The joy didn't last long beyond daybreak. A final check

of our slack tide calculation revealed an error of two hours. At the speed we were sailing, we were going to arrive late at Makemo, when the tide would be on its way out. At maximum flow, the tide could reach speeds of up to nine knots, creating eddy currents and short, steep waves. We knew it would be impossible for us to enter the lagoon under such conditions, and we'd be forced to wait several hours until the next slack tide. Instead of the pleasantly calm final approach we'd been looking forward to, we were forced to turn on the engine and motor-sail at seven knots to make up for lost time. Meanwhile, we called other boats on the SSB radio to verify our new calculation and get advice from friends who'd already been to Makemo.

True to form, *Stella Maris* sailed valiantly and got us to the atoll entrance at midday, right on schedule. The French had marked the pass with both range and channel markers, and although it was overcast, the low tide made the reef and coral heads clearly visible. Our final calculations and determination to get there earlier were rewarded with dead calm water in the pass. Having worried about negotiating the entrance for days, it couldn't have gone more smoothly.

With Gjalt at the helm, I went to the bow to look out for shallow coral heads as we made our way to the anchorage beside the village of Pouheva, close to the pass. After four days and 500 miles, we were happy to have the anchor down, but we were a little bit disappointed by the atoll's appearance in the murky weather.

We had expected a picture-perfect paradise, and Makemo was falling short. One of the biggest atolls in the archipelago at thirty-five miles long and ten miles wide, we saw mostly water stretching into the distance, instead of the palm tree-covered motus and golden beaches we'd imagined. The island we were anchored beside had a large commercial jetty, hardly the image one has in mind when daydreaming about a desert island. But we were surrounded by crystal-clear water that was stunningly azure, even under grey skies, so surely all the atoll needed to be transformed was a little sunshine.

On the passage, a lot of necessary sail changes during the night had interrupted our watch schedule, leaving both of us exhausted. Safely anchored, we immediately slept for several hours, which was just as well because a strong southeasterly wind developed during the night, putting us on a lee shore. With 10 miles of fetch being whipped up across the lagoon, it didn't make for a peaceful night.

The following morning, the wind remained strong, and white-capped waves rushed towards us, making *Stella Maris* buck unnervingly. We sent an e-mail request for a weather forecast. If the strong wind was going to continue, we'd have to sail away from Makemo. Not wanting to leave so soon after arriving, we were relieved to see the forecast promised calmer conditions and even more relieved when the wind, and consequently the waves, actually died down. We seized our chance to go ashore and rowed across water so clear we could see coral and colourful fish as vividly as if we were snorkelling.

Without regular rainfall, the town of Pouheva lacked the abundant flora and lovingly tended gardens of the Marquesas, and it looked dry and dusty in comparison. The people, however, were just as friendly, and everyone we met seemed affluent. In 1999, eight tons of black pearls were produced in the Tuamotus, and business still appeared to be booming in Makemo six years later. Children rode around on new bicycles, teenagers listened to Walkmans, and adults had mobile phones clipped to their belts. I doubted the soft toys I'd brought from the USA as gifts would be greeted with much enthusiasm here.

We wandered into the large church, its high ceiling and tall, arched windows giving its white interior a bright, airy atmosphere. Long chains of shells stretched from the ceiling to the walls, and oyster shell chandeliers hung above the tiled central aisle. There we met Felix, guardian to the children who attended Makemo's boarding school from neighbouring atolls. He stopped reading his Bible to talk to us and said the island was home to around 1,000 people, half of them children. His grandfather had been Scottish, he said, but it was hard to imagine a pale, red-haired ancestor for this dark-skinned Polynesian. What an adventurer his grandfather must have been to leave Scotland and travel to the middle of the Pacific Ocean, all those years ago.

Along the shore, we stopped to talk to a group of men who'd just speared a variety of colourful reef fish in the lagoon. They gave us a large blue and green parrot fish, along with a guarantee that there was no ciguatera in Makemo. Prepared for such spontaneous acts of generosity, I offered some limes in return, a welcome gift since fresh fruit was scarce in the atolls. We looked forward to finding out if parrot fish was as delicious as we'd heard.

Too soon, the weather deteriorated, and we ran back to the dinghy knowing it would be difficult to row out to *Stella Maris* if the waves built up. Thankfully, conditions eased towards sunset, and we had a much more peaceful night than the one before. The sun even appeared the following morning, bringing out the glorious majesty of the blue lagoon.

We went on a short exploration in the dinghy to get a feel for the environment and investigate the coral patches. To move *Stella Maris* within the atoll, we would need sustained sunshine to safely avoid the large coral heads scattered in the otherwise deep water. Charts with all these hazards marked on them didn't exist, so we had to rely on eyeball navigation. I was reminded of the shallow waters of Belize, which had demanded the same care and attention, but at forty to sixty feet deep, Makemo's lagoon made me a little less nervous.

The wind never abated for long periods, and three nights on a lee shore was as much as Gjalt could bear; it went against every good seamanship bone in his body. The best protection would be found behind the islands at the eastern end of the atoll, but the weather remained too poor to navigate across ten miles of the lagoon to reach them. Other cruisers had told us of a protected spot in the far west, so we decided to exit the lagoon early in the morning and sail in deep ocean to the pass at the western end of Makemo, where we could re-enter at the next slack tide.

We prepared *Stella Maris* to go to sea, but when we tried to bring up the anchor, we found it was resolutely stuck. Gjalt had to get into the water and free it by hand. Despite having put two fenders on the anchor chain to keep it off the bottom, it had wrapped around a small lump of coral. He dived down and unwound it while I winched it in. As soon as the anchor was up at the bow, I returned to the helm and Gjalt climbed back onboard. This all went smoothly, but it delayed our departure, and by the time we reached the pass, water was bubbling and swirling within it, already flowing out at three knots.

This was not the nerve-soothing millpond that had welcomed us when we arrived. To add to my stress, the overcast skies and high tide conspired to conceal the reefs lining the channel, the ones that had been so clearly visible when we entered three days earlier. As we headed out, I looked at the range markers behind us, intending to help Gjalt maintain an ideal course by giving steering directions that would keep them aligned. Having a brain as nimble as an elephant in stilettos when it comes to spatial reasoning, however, I couldn't tell Gjalt if he needed to steer left or right to get back on course once the markers became misaligned. As usual, he remained cool and didn't need my assistance anyway, but by the time we emerged into the safety of the deep ocean, I was shaking like a leaf.

It was a lovely day to sail along the outside of the atoll, but I just spent the trip worrying about entering the next pass and gorged half a jar of Nutella to comfort myself. We had good wind and covered the twenty-five miles well within the six-hour window that preceded slack low water.

The channel was wide and well marked, but the tide was still flowing out, and there were choppy waves across the entrance. As we motored into the pass we had two knots of current against us, and I was not thrilled to be surrounded by bubbling, swirling water again. Gjalt maintained his ice-cool calm; I, on the other hand, was once again a nervous wreck.

Yes, there were red and green markers, but there were dozens of them sign-posting various different channels, and my panicking brain had to work out which ones we should follow. As *Stella Maris* lurched up and down in the short, sharp waves of the pass, I braced myself for the inevitable *thud* of a collision with hard coral. The stress became too much to bottle up, and tears streamed down my cheeks as I stood on the bow looking for the safe route to the elusive sheltered anchorage. Luckily, Gjalt didn't even notice this sorry emotional collapse, but it did at least have the same good effect as a slap in the face. I pulled myself together and managed to guide us to the promised haven nestled between a patch of shallow reef and a sandy motu.

I was intensely relieved to have the anchor down in a truly beautiful spot, even if it was a bit too close to a hut in which several men appeared to be living together. I sat anxiously at the helm, watching Gjalt as he walked over deck to survey our new surroundings from every angle. I could tell from his silence and his edgy manner that he was not as happy to have the anchor down as I was. I could also see for myself that our only protection from the fetch was the large patch of reef, exposed now only because it was low tide. The rising water would submerge this barrier and leave us no better off than we had been at the eastern end of Makemo. We would be worse off, in fact, since we were anchored in a relatively small area of water between the reef and the motu. Being on a lee shore was bad enough, but being on one with very little reaction time was madness. We could not stay; we had to leave immediately, before the tide turned.

At least I knew the way out, and since it was now close to slack tide the water had become benign. I actually relaxed and waved to the men fishing in the pass, who must have wondered what strange people had come to their corner of paradise and chosen to leave so quickly.

In the lee of the atoll, we got the sea berth ready for an overnight trip, and Gjalt planned our route to Fakarava, the nearest atoll with an easy pass and good protection from southeasterly winds.

We had a bumpy ride for the first twenty miles as we sailed close-hauled to skirt the southern reefs of Katiu atoll, maintaining speeds above seven knots. I frequently checked our position both on the paper charts and the computer, feeling the silent threat from the Dangerous Archipelago as we sailed through it in the menacing dark of night. It also became clear to me that we were going to arrive at the north pass of Fakarava too late for slack tide at 6 o'clock the next morning. I studied the charts, calculated arrival times and slack tide times, and became convinced that we should divert to the smaller atoll of Kauehi. This had the added advantage of being just a day's sail away from Toau, which was itself only a short fourteen-mile hop to the north pass of Fakarava. When Gjalt got up for his watch, I persuaded him to change our plan, and Kauehi became our new destination.

Two hours into my off-watch, we'd sailed sufficiently west of Raraka atoll to head for its northern neighbour,

Kauehi. Gjalt woke me up to help pole out the genoa, because after we changed course, the wind would come from behind the beam. Utterly exhausted I asked him to give me just another twenty minutes of sleep, but instead of agreeing, he let out a loud, disgruntled sigh. "I don't see what difference twenty minutes will make," he complained.

Muttering furiously to myself, I got up and tried not to let my intense irritation turn into a fully-fledged foul mood. After all, I had told Gjalt he should get me up whenever he needed help with sail changes, because I didn't want him going on deck without me watching him. In my top ten 'Worst Nightmares at Sea', waking up to find myself all alone onboard was right up there in joint first place with falling over the side while Gjalt was fast asleep.

After he'd fiddled with the pole *forever* and we finally had everything set up correctly, the wind veered just enough to turn the pole from a necessity to a hindrance.

When Gjalt calmly announced that we would have to remove it, without so much as a hint of remorse in his voice, I simply exploded. "I asked you to give me just twenty more minutes in bed but you couldn't wait and now the pole isn't even necessary!" I shouted. "You got me up for nothing."

Gjalt started to say something, but my mind had taken me beyond talking. I had hoped to be spending the night at anchor, but instead I was surrounded by treacherous reefs and not even getting a measly three hours of sleep. I suddenly felt unbearably claustrophobic, as though I was trapped inside a black bin liner and would suffocate if I didn't fight my way out. Overwhelmed by a need to escape the cockpit, I rushed downstairs, yelling furiously, but I felt just as trapped in the main cabin. I vaguely remember feeling and acting like a cornered wild animal, dangerous to approach and impossible to calm without a tranquilising gun.

A perpetually composed person himself, Gjalt was shocked at my sudden hysteria and didn't know what to do. He was afraid I'd try to leap over the side, so at least his worst fear was relieved when I went down below, where he was sure he could keep me confined.

Gradually, as all my frustrations were vented through the uncontrolled wailing and flailing of a lunatic, I came back to my senses, drained of emotion and strangely calm. Once Gjalt was convinced that it was safe to leave me alone, he went back to bed, and my watch passed quietly, as uneventfully as any other. In the cool light of morning, we attributed my temporary insanity to my nerves having been frayed by transiting Makemo's passes three times within six hours, followed by sailing through the Dangerous Archipelago at night. Even with our GPS, I'd found it highly stressful to chart a course between all those ship-wrecking atolls.

We arrived at the pass on the south side of Kauehi before daybreak and tacked back out to sea, timing our return to coincide with slack tide two hours later. The strong wind kicked up rough waves across the entrance, making it look particularly uninviting in the half-light of early morning. Above the atoll, an enormous bank of dark, threatening clouds lingered possessively. To reach the anchorage on the northeast side of the lagoon, we'd have to find a clear route through eight miles of coral-riddled waters, not the easiest thing to do in such conditions. And although the chart showed that the anchorage would offer good protection in southeast winds, it would be exposed to over eight miles of fetch if the winds turned to the south-southeast.

Having no intention of swapping one lee shore for another, we decided to sail westwards to Toau, another forty-mile hop through the low-lying atoll minefield. We were bouncing around the Tuamotu Archipelago like a pinball, and I began to fear we would never find safe shelter within it.

With strong winds pushing us along at more than seven knots, we had an excellent sail. We reached Toau well ahead of the next slack tide and stood off to observe the pass. Although it was wide, it didn't look any more inviting than the one at Kauehi; the waves were wild and stretched across the pass like a row of sharp teeth, just waiting to snap at any boat that dared to enter. There were range markers inside the lagoon; so far inside I had to use binoculars to see them. As we made our approach, I kept my eyes glued to the lenses and called out to Gjalt when the markers were aligned. Then, suddenly, he aborted the entry.

The waves were very short and too steep to negotiate. They curled over at the crests like surf against a shore.

The outgoing current was creating eddies and overfalls; our cruising guide noted that these sometimes stretched up to two miles from Toau's pass. We stood off for another half an hour to let the current diminish and the seas flatten out.

While we watched and waited, I noticed a lone figure perched on the island beside the pass, the arrival of a new boat providing the day's entertainment. I wished we were already safely anchored inside the atoll and were also in a position to enjoy the spectacle of sailors navigating the gateway to heaven.

We headed in a second time, and I diligently trained the binoculars on the range markers again. Thankfully, this kept me oblivious of the steep waves that were rising up on our leeward side as we crossed over the twenty-five-foot-deep entrance. My heart was thumping enough as it was.

Once we were through, I took up my usual position on the bow to look for coral patches, but the overcast skies made me doubt my ability to spot them. I replaced Gjalt at the helm, and he climbed up to the spreaders for a better view of the lagoon, just as his hero Bernard Moitessier had done. From the cockpit, I only saw some of the coral heads Gjalt alerted me to when we were right up close to them, so it really paid to have him perched in the mast.

At last, we had made it into a new atoll, and this one did live up to our dreams; it was breathtakingly beautiful. We headed straight for the southeast corner, which would afford us the best protection from the strong southeasterly winds. Gjalt was confident he could steer a clear path through deep water, so we pushed on until we were tucked up beside a sheltering island with sandy beaches, palm trees, and – most importantly of all – flat, calm water.

There were no other boats in the atoll; we'd finally arrived in our own private paradise, and that felt awesome. Maybe it was all the more special for having been so difficult to reach. Being on a lee shore in Makemo had been stressful for Gjalt, and transiting the passes and sailing around the Tuamotus at night had all but unravelled my nerves. In Toau, we were protected from the elements in every direction, and we could relax at last. We slept very well that night.

As if to prove that we had arrived in the right place, we woke up to a gorgeously sunny day. The water around us was a hypnotic tapestry of subtly changing turquoise, and beyond it beaches, islands and reefs waited to be explored. As far as we could tell, there was only one person to share it all with: the figure who had watched us come through the pass the day before. When we went ashore, we sought him out. We wanted to introduce ourselves and ask if he minded us being anchored in what was effectively his front yard.

We found him at his small house, a corrugated iron roof sitting atop walls of woven palm fronds, set a short distance back from the beach. The front garden was raked clean, and all his tools and belongings were neatly stored below the roof of the veranda. Copra had been laid out to dry at the side of the house, a large piece of blue tarpaulin protecting it from possible rain. Dressed in jelly sandals of the type that were all the rage in the eighties (and which The Dude himself sported), surf shorts, a fantastically dirty t-shirt, and a similarly soiled one wrapped around his head, Jean greeted us warmly. His weathered face creased up when he giggled, something he did often, and from within his bushy beard, a wonderful gappy smile emerged. I had been a bit apprehensive about how we'd be received by a man used to his own company, but I needn't have been.

I offered him some of our wind-fallen limes and the oranges we'd been given in Controleur Bay, and he accepted them cheerfully. Many yachts coming from the Marquesas brought fruit to the Tuamotus, where the soil was too poor to cultivate fruit trees. Jean immediately hacked open two coconuts for us to drink from and gave us some interesting shells and a shark tooth each (after Gjalt had asked if sharks were a problem in the lagoon). Jean told us he was the only inhabitant on that side of the atoll and that he had come there from Fakarava to harvest copra. When we asked if it was possible to catch lobsters on the reef, he invited us to go hunting with him the next night. The seeds of friendship had been sown.

We continued along the beach, the amazingly clear water exposing a wealth of marine life in its shallows: schools of bright blue parrot fish; large, open shells revealing the brilliant electric blue and green clams within; and even small blacktip reef sharks, their large dorsal fins piercing the surface alarmingly. We cut through the coconut groves to reach the outer reef and revelled in the sight of the ocean crashing onto it, whilst *Stella Maris* was so snugly anchored on the other side.

The next day, we dinghyed across an expanse of shallow water to reach a neighbouring island and walked around it, collecting shells that had washed up on its shore. Afterwards, as we snorkelled in the wondrously clear water around it, a blacktip reef shark appeared close by. I grabbed Gjalt and hid behind him like a coward. Soon, there was another, then another. "Are we safe?" I asked after we'd stuck our heads up, expecting him to reassure me as he always did.

"I don't know," he replied.

That was all I needed to hear to send me shooting back to dry land. I got used to the sharks before long, but at that point, I'd yet to be convinced that I wasn't on their menu.

At sunset, we met Jean at his house for the lobster-hunting trip. His kerosene lamp needed a new wick, so Gjalt returned to *Stella Maris* to get one and also dug out our own lantern. Gjalt had only lit this once before, and having to arm himself with the instructions did little to impress Jean.

To me, the casual observer, there seemed to be a crucial sequence of pressuring up the thing with the pump, lighting it, then pressuring it again. Atoll Man strode across to take over the operation, while Office Man tilted the instructions towards the failing light. "*Allez, allez,*" Jean kept muttering, while Gjalt murmured, "Hang on, hang on". When Gjalt referred to the instructions for the third time, Jean could bear it no longer. Taking matters into his own hands, he struck match after match, furiously pumping away. I feared the worst from Office Man at this unwanted interference, but he happily continued to ruminate over the instructions while Atoll Man pursued the practical approach. Eventually the lantern burst into action, and an intense ball of bright white light radiated out from it. Satisfied, Jean went over to his lantern, and only then did we see that the mechanism was exactly the same. He lit the thing every day; it was little wonder he'd been so exasperated by Office Man and his instructions.

Jean donned a home-made backpack that was essentially an old plastic drum with straps, a hunting glove (only one, Michael Jackson style) and produced an enormous, deadly knife that made me momentarily question his intentions. Gjalt had also brought a glove, as instructed, but he was told to leave the lobster pot we'd found on the beach behind (Jean clearly didn't have high hopes of success for Office Man). Jean took a shine to our brand new lantern and left Gjalt to carry his older, more lacklustre affair. I, a mere woman, was given a torch.

At last we were ready, and Jean marched off, with Gjalt and me trotting faithfully behind him like innocent ducklings. He moved through the coconut grove at a cracking pace. Gjalt stumbled over so many palm fronds in an effort to keep up that I expected to see him and his lantern to go flying through the air, setting the atoll ablaze on impact.

Once we reached the beach, Jean told me I was allowed to go no further. Lobster-hunting was apparently an unsuitable job for a woman. I didn't feel the least bit affronted by this. I was more than happy to keep my ankles safely on dry land, because the hunter-gatherers weren't the only creatures searching the shallows of the reef flats at night. Small sharks were on the prowl, too, and from their viewpoint, a human ankle was nothing more than tasty snack.

Jean marched along the edge of the reef as if he was in an Olympic race, and he soon ordered Gjalt to move further inland. I think he feared that Office Man would fall into the ocean and be swept away. After a while, Gjalt's vintage lamp gave up the ghost, and he joined me on the beach, where I lay sprawled on my back, enjoying the magnificent night sky in its full, unmasked splendour. Gjalt had only spotted one lobster, and it had scurried away before the gloved menace could grab it. Jean, meanwhile, carried on tirelessly, the glow of his lamp fading to a pinprick in the distance. Eventually he must have noticed that the novices had given up. After a good two hours on the flats, he returned to us with half a dozen lobsters clawing hopelessly inside his plastic drum and three small groupers that he'd whacked on the head with his knife.

Jean marched us back through the coconut plantation to his house, his pace unchanged despite his extensive foray along the reef. He gave us all the lobsters, and we promised to return with them the next night for dinner. We'd been given our first lesson in atoll survival; clearly we both had a lot to learn.

Feeling the need to prove his hunting skills to Jean, Gjalt decided the time had come to go spearfishing. We dinghyed to the closest beach and plunged into the turquoise aquarium. It turned out that I had a knack for spotting groupers hiding in the nooks and crannies of the coral heads. I pointed one out to Gjalt, but I felt like a traitor as Office Man went after his first real kill (shooting the spiny spider crab in Belize at point-blank range didn't count). One minute I was enjoying the underwater world, feeling privileged to be part of it, and the next I betrayed it.

Fearing the frenzied interest of sharks, I sought refuge in the dinghy and was quite amazed when the hunter returned successful. Having shot the creature in the body, he was anxious to end its misery. He started to pierce its brain with the spear, but the fish managed to squirm out of his hands and somehow, with a gash in its body and a half-bored hole in its head, quickly swam away.

Not to be deterred, Office Man rearmed and returned to the water to track down his prey. He could not face Atoll Man empty handed. With a wounded fish in the water leaking blood, I decided to stay in the dinghy. Sure enough, I saw a blacktip reef shark cruising around a coral head near the one Gjalt was searching. With his face in the water, he couldn't hear me warning him of his imminent death, but luckily for him, the shark just cruised on by. After a while, Gjalt returned with a grouper, and we were both relieved to discover that, miraculously, it was the same one that had briefly got away.

In the evening, we prepared a lobster curry and then went onshore to keep our dinner date with Jean. Brimming with pride, Office Man triumphantly presented his grouper to Atoll Man who, without any to-do, stoked up a fire and grilled the fish then and there on a barbecue fashioned from a Castrol GTX can.

It was a lovely evening, good food washed down with a litre of the white wine we'd bought in Panama. We communicated in fits and starts, long silent interludes peppered with sudden bursts of conversation, and although my French teacher would have winced in agony, we did okay.

After a morning of boat maintenance, including a trip up the mast for Gjalt to repair the line holding the gennaker block, we went to Toau's wide reef flats to look for

GJALT CONTEMPLATES A DIP ON THE OTHER SIDE OF TOAU'S OUTER REEF WITH
HIS ANTI-SHARK BAMBOO POLE

cowry shells. Gjalt decided it would be fun to venture into the ocean and snorkel on the outer reef wall, which was said to be home to spectacular coral and a wealth of marine life. Over the years, I'd slowly come to realise that I didn't actually have to do everything he suggested, so I stayed on *terra firma*, enjoying my search for shells, and left him to it. I'd frequently been told not to interfere with his God-given right to do the kind of things men feel the need to do, so I didn't try to stop him and made a concerted effort not to worry.

He had found a nine-foot bamboo pole on the beach and thought it the perfect weapon to deter a shark with hundreds of razor-sharp teeth. Thus armed, he plunged into the ominous surf, powering hard against it to reach deeper water and avoid being pummelled against the hard reef. Some time later, I glanced up from my pleasant shell-collecting efforts and saw him slowly treading water in a circle, the pole thrust out in front of him. I assumed he was trying to stop himself from being hurled back onshore by the mighty ocean. I watched him swim and scramble his way onto the red reef flat and was relieved when he was out of the water and still alive.

It turned out that he hadn't been trying to protect himself from an unplanned hard landing at all, but from a silvertip shark. This potentially dangerous predator had taken an interest in the blond Dutchman, who'd suddenly appeared uninvited in his territory, and had begun to circle, sizing up the intruder. At first Gjalt was fascinated by this encounter; the water was so clear he felt as though he was hanging in mid-air and the shark was flying around him. It was big, with a bulky, diamond-shaped body, distinctive white-edged fins, and sharp teeth visible in its grinning mouth. But when it swam between Gjalt and the reef, fascination turned to trepidation, and he thrust the bamboo pole towards the shark to 'warn' it not to mess with him, a scare tactic that works with black-tips. But being around nine feet long itself, and with a girth rather more substantial than that of the bamboo pole or the human being holding it, Jaws was not the least bit impressed by this threat. It continued to circle, convincing Gjalt to opt for a fast exit.

After a few minutes on dry land, though, his trepidation gave way to fascination again, and all sanity evaporated into

CORINNA WEYRETER

thin air. Instead of celebrating the fact that he'd escaped being hideously chewed to death, he decided to return to the water and repeat the exhilaration of being considered for lunch. Realising that the bamboo pole had been antagonistic, this time he armed himself only with the underwater camera. Meanwhile, I pondered what would become of me should I suddenly see an unholy commotion in the water: limbs desperately flailing, an occasional glimpse of Gjalt's horrified face amidst a spreading patch of blood-red ocean. Too scared to skipper *Stella Maris* alone out of Toau, I would have to spend the rest of my life harvesting copra with Atoll Man. Thankfully Gjalt emerged from the water alive; the shark hadn't bothered to wait for him to return. Death and its consequences were kept at bay for another day.

We must have done something right the first time we hunted lobsters with Jean, because he invited us to go with him again. When we arrived at his house just before sunset, an atoll delicacy awaited us: a kind of sea urchin meant to be slurped raw, like an oyster. It looked highly dubious but, incredibly, it tasted delicious, especially with some fresh lime squeezed over it. How nice that I brought limes from the Marquesas, I thought, but then I realised that he was not using the ones I'd given him. Those had been rather tired-looking affairs, while these were magnificently green Lilliputian cannonballs of juicy citrus. They were undeniably fresh. "You have a lime tree?" I asked.

"Yes," Jean said, breaking into his gappy grin, his brown eyes creasing up at the joke.

Atoll Man had his own lime tree! I had stood before him on that first day glowing with benevolence for handing a stranger some wind-fallen efforts, and all along he was growing his own. I contemplated asking him if he had an orange tree, too, but decided against it. After all, it's the thought that counts, isn't it?

Jean had asked if we could spare some fish hooks, and Gjalt beamed proudly as he now put his entire collection on display for Jean's perusal. "Take whatever you want," he offered grandly.

"Don't you have any smaller hooks?" Jean asked, uninterested in those spread out on the table.

There were many Gjalt considered small, but none that Jean did, who indicated a length the size of his small fingernail. Crushed by Atoll Man's rejection of every single one of his hooks, Gjalt scooped them all up and quietly packed them away.

After Atoll Man and Office Man had squatted on their haunches for an eternity to fix Jean's ailing lantern, we finally set off through the coconut grove for the reef flats. This time I decided that twenty-first-century woman could not be so pathetic as to obediently wait on the beach while the men went hunting. Into the shallows I traipsed, shining the torch in search of the nocturnal lobsters, staying alert for ankle-biting blacktips. It didn't take long for the futility of my actions to become obvious, though, and disinclined to keep pace with Olympic reef flat sprinter Atoll Man, I returned to the beach and my preferred night time activity of star-gazing.

Soon afterwards, Gjalt joined me, empty-handed once again, while Jean walked so far that he even wore himself out this time. When he finally gave up, he was utterly exhausted. He'd caught a gaggle of lobsters and managed to stun six small groupers with swift whacks of his knife.

We returned to the reef in daylight and spent several relaxing hours searching for cowry shells. At low tide, the flats were peppered with shallow rock pools, and there was nothing more satisfying than finding a pristine cowry gleaming in the clear water. We continued to be amazed by the ability of these humble snails to decorate their thick shells with such elaborate and beautiful designs. The money cowry (the old currency of the South Pacific) was a fairly simple white shell with a yellow ring surrounding a blue centre, but the helvola had bright purple tips, a light brown rim, and tiny white dots scattered over the dark brown shell. Unweathered, the cowries were highly polished, as shiny as if they'd been varnished, as magnificent as if they'd been created by artists, which I suppose they had. Our eyes, more used to the harsh metal and cement of the urban landscape, were reopened to the everyday wonders of nature.

That evening we kept our regular dinner date with Jean, bringing with us the prepared lobsters and grilled fish from the previous night's hunt. He had promised us that the

DEAD CALM: STELLA MARIS ANCHORED IN TOAU'S LAGOON, TUAMOTU ARCHIPELAGO

smaller groupers would taste better than the large one Gjalt had speared in the lagoon, and he was right. We complemented this sumptuous dinner with another litre of wine from our trusty Panama collection. We did consider if it was irresponsible to give alcohol to Jean, because we'd heard that Polynesians were prone to alcoholism. We obviously didn't want to encourage his downfall, but we reasoned that he was a grown man who didn't require any patronising nannying from us and that, in any case, he was unlikely to become a drunkard after only one or two glasses of red wine.

Our politically correct thoughts were trampled on after dinner when Jean decided to get the party fired up with his home-brewed coconut toddy. He brought out a huge drum of the stuff and filled our glasses using a bowl as a scoop. The toddy had a decidedly odd taste, verging on the unpleasant, but this was compensated for by an undeniably potent kick. As Jean had insisted we eat most of the dinner, the alcohol affected him first, and before long he was very, very merry, giggling in his disarming way, the laughter spreading to us like an infection. There was a steady stream of announcements along the lines of '*nous sommes les trois amis*', followed by laughter and hearty back-slapping between Atoll Man and Office Man. Meanwhile Jean began referring to me as '*Maman*', which made me feel old and matronly, yet strangely flattered at the same time.

I'd seen Jean burying two coconuts on the beach opposite our boat earlier in the day, and now he told us that these were for us. In five years, we could return to Toau, he said, and see the two tall palm trees that had been planted when we first visited. In the wonderful alcoholic haze of the evening, we thought there was a good chance we might just do that.

Our heads spinning with coconut toddy, we went back to *Stella Maris*, tied the dinghy to her stern, and just lay down in it, gazing at the stars. For over an hour, we deliberated if our presence would ultimately wreak havoc with the emotions of our good friend Atoll Man, who was so used to being the sole inhabitant of his island on Toau. *How will he cope when we leave?* we wondered. Coconut toddy can do weird things to the mind.

Minor hangovers aside, all was fine the next day. We

went ashore to check on Jean; he was hard at work split-
ting husks from coconuts with a metal spike embedded
in a block of wood. He didn't interrupt his labours for us,
and we happily acknowledged that our thoughts of the
previous night had been alcohol-induced, self-flattering
nonsense.

I started to film Jean at work, only to have the camcorder
die on me. I hoped it was just a flat battery, but back on
*Stella Maris*, nothing brought the gadget back to life. It
was our backup camera, and with it out of action, we were
down to our small digital Canon. This should have stopped
me from putting the camera into its waterproof housing
and taking it along when I went snorkelling, but it didn't.
The underwater world was simply too stunning not to
photograph.

After a long walk along the island, we passed Jean's
house, where we were treated to a mouth-watering meal of
sea snails and urchins. Atoll Man had clearly taken it upon
himself to provide for us. He'd already spent hours on the
reef gathering lobsters and groupers, and the next morning,
he was on the hunt again before sunrise. We lazy cruisers
were still fast asleep at seven, when a distant voice woke
us up. It was Jean, calling from the beach, and it was quite
obvious to me whose attention he was after. I stayed in bed
while Gjalt got up and dinghyed to the island, where Jean
was waiting with more freshly caught fish and lobsters. (The
early morning food deliveries continued the next day, with
the shouted alarm brought forward to half past five; definitely a wake-up call for Office Man.)

It was utterly windless, and a heavy heat smothered the
atoll. The lagoon was still, its surface like liquid glass,
and we could clearly see fish swimming forty feet below
*Stella Maris*. Conditions were perfect for exploring, and
an unhurried dinghy expedition took us to the pass some
three miles away. We got there at slack high tide, and it
was as smooth as a millpond, a benign Jekyll to the fierce
Hyde that had greeted us when we arrived one week earlier.

It was so calm that I felt comfortable dinghying into the
pass and waiting there while Gjalt snorkelled. He saw a
few small reef sharks, but little coral. The water was still
and clear enough for me to see all the way to the seabed
from the safety of the dinghy. Once we had drifted level

with the outer reef wall, we headed back into the lagoon. We knew if the tide picked up too much, we wouldn't be able to motor against it with our five-horsepower outboard engine, and we'd be carried out to sea unnoticed, our lack of shade and water condemning us to a slow and agonising death.

We anchored in the calm shallows at the edge of the pass, but when Gjalt went over the side to snorkel, he was nearly swept away. It took an energetic burst of front crawl for him to reach the dinghy, and with him safely back onboard, we quickly motored into the shelter of the lagoon. We went ashore and watched the pass, which transformed into a bubbling cauldron of eddies before our eyes. Atoll currents were not to be messed with.

Downloading the day's e-mails brought a nasty surprise from the last person who belonged in a South Seas atoll – the U.S. taxman. Somehow Gjalt had failed to file his 2003 tax return, and the IRS posse was hot on his tail. The e-mail was like an unwelcome hand that had reached · across the Pacific, grabbed us by the scruff of the neck, and attempted to drag us out of Toau's beautiful blue lagoon back to America. We dealt with it as best we could by sending e-mails to people we thought could help, and then went onshore to wriggle free from that unpleasant neck hold.

Close to Jean's place was an abandoned house that had two oil drums brimming with rainwater in front of it. These had been filled via gutters running along the edge of the corrugated iron roof, and I had my eye on that water for washing our dirty clothes. When Jean said I could use it, I left Gjalt to his boat chores and took the bulging laundry bag onshore.

I couldn't imagine a more idyllic place to do the washing, surrounded by palm trees, their fronds rustling in the wind. I loved the solitude – such a rarity in my life now – with only a few hermit crabs crawling across the sand for company. Two hours and one drum of water later, fresh laundry hung on the line I'd strung between two palm trees, drying in the tropical sunshine and Pacific breeze. It was bliss, pure and simple.

The evening presented another hunting trip, but this time it was the coconut crabs that had to watch out. We'd heard that these crustaceans were endangered and tried to convince Jean they were too rare to be killed, but he just replied that they weren't rare on Toau. They weigh up to four kilos and can reach the ripe old age of sixty, and it just seemed wrong to devour one, endangered or not. With our French too poor to convince him that the creatures shouldn't be eaten, we found ourselves outmanoeuvred. Perhaps we should have been more insistent, but it would have been rude to refuse the invitation after all the kindness and generosity Jean had shown us. Reluctantly we met him at his house after sunset and followed him along the dark beach to a spot he thought would bring success and we secretly hoped would bring failure.

Jean cut down two coconuts and hacked them open with his lethal knife. Nestled in the centre of the nuts was a kind of soft candy floss we'd never eaten before, and it melted in our mouths like sweet foam. Jean started a small fire on the beach, and whilst the coconut meat cooked on it, he hacked a short path through some tangled shrubs. Then he tied the warm coconut to the trunk of a palm tree as bait.

He put three large palm fronds on the sand for us to lie on and then gathered another set of coconuts, hacking them open so we could drink the water which, this time, was sweet and fizzy. Atoll Man knew everything there was to know about life on a desert island. We lay down on our palm frond mats, stared at the stars, and waited for the crabs to be lured by the roasted coconut meat. This was hunting for the lazy, far more preferable than trudging across a reef flat at night - as long as we didn't actually catch anything, of course.

For three hours, we lay there communicating in our clumsy French. Jean told us of a giant pig that had escaped from an enclosure on the island some years earlier and was now on the rampage. It was apparently such a nuisance that he wanted to kill it, but the creature remained elusive. It had become the Abominable Pig Foot of Toau.

Also roaming the island, apparently, was another giant: "*Un grand chat blanc.*" Jean had come home to find the feline nosing around the high bar-like table in his front room. Disturbed in mid-curiosity, the large white cat jumped onto the floor, smashing Jean's radio in the process. We'd seen paw prints in the sand that had indeed looked larger than those of an average domestic cat, so we were inclined to believe the creature was no myth.

He checked the bait every now and then, and to our great relief, the only crustacean it attracted was a small, inedible hermit crab. We were glad that the coconut crabs of Toau would live to see another day.

JEAN AND GJALT DISPLAY THEIR CATCH :
TOAU, TUAMOTU ARCHIPELAGO

Sunday brought an invitation to lunch, and Jean again surprised us with his culinary skills. He'd imprinted the shape of a tropical leaf into a bed of cooked, desiccated coconut and artfully placed sea snails on top. A side dish of fried bread patties completed the exotic spread, and it was truly delicious.

In the spirit of sharing that had formed so naturally between us, we gave him kerosene for his lantern, olive oil, sugar, and some more limes (I hadn't found his tree, but apparently the harvest was over). The only difference between our Western and his Polynesian culture appeared to be our need to say 'thank you' so many times that he couldn't doubt our gratitude, while he didn't utter a single 'merci'. Perhaps he realised that with such a balanced friendship on such an isolated island, the appreciation was obvious.

When conditions were favourable for navigating the lagoon, we seized the opportunity to explore a completely uninhabited part of it. After all, we'd had lessons from a master of atoll survival, so there was no reason not to put all we'd learnt to the test. The time had come for Office Man to fly the coop.

With Gjalt perched on the spreaders and me at the helm, we set off for an island four miles to the southwest. Our polarised sunglasses revealed shallow coral patches invisible to the naked eye, and from Gjalt's high vantage point, a clear path was easy to see. An hour later, we dropped anchor in our own private kingdom and went ashore, leaving our dinghy at a small covered boat dock.

There were two islands separated by a channel, which we later had to swim across when the tide came in. The reef flats, so broad and perfect for shelling by Jean's island, were narrow and far from the island here, and the deep rock pools held too much water, even at low tide. But the coral in the lagoon was more abundant and healthier, so we were compensated by the snorkelling. Drifting amongst the colourful fish in this real-life aquarium was as close to meditation as we were likely to get. Everything else simply vanished from our minds.

We set ourselves up beside a padlocked house, its walls woven from palm fronds, to experience life on land for a change. Living on a boat, our world had changed into one dominated by water; we were surrounded by it all the time. Land had become something in the view, like a painting hanging on a wall. We observed it from a distance, savoured all it had to offer during brief forays ashore, and then retreated once more to our waterborne home. After nearly six months at sea, I craved the presence of trees and plants; I wanted to hear the songs of land birds again. We set up camp beneath the high, shady canopy of the coconut palms, stringing a hammock between two trees, facing a deckchair towards the lagoon. We enjoyed lazy hours reading and beachcombing, but inevitably Office Man felt the need to put his survival skills to the test.

The coral was home to a wealth of fish, including sharks. The latter deterred me from joining the spearfishing trip, and I remained safely on land. Eventually Office Man emerged from the water, with every extremity still attached. He brought with him a grouper and a trigger fish, but both had taken two shots to finish off. "I'm the Mr. Bean of spearfishing," he announced glumly. His inability to kill with a single, clean strike made him feel terrible; the novice hunter had discovered that he did not enjoy hunting.

Our LPG tank ran empty, and Gjalt replaced it with the one we'd had filled in Panama, only to discover that it too was almost empty. We wouldn't have starved without cooking gas, but life would certainly be a lot less pleasant without coffee or hot meals. Secretly, though, Office Man loved the emergency, because it gave him the opportunity to truly become Robinson Crusoe. He disappeared behind a palm tree, spun around three times, and emerged in a ripped shirt and tattered shorts, sporting a long, straggly beard. He immediately set to work building a woodburning stove, his bouncy demeanour betraying his true state of mind.

With the stove successfully constructed, all that was needed was a fish to cook on it. Back in the water, with my fear of sharks overcome, I reverted to my treacherous role of pointing out groupers to the man with the speargun. This time, he succeeded in killing the target quickly, with a single shot to the head. It made us realise that it wasn't the hunting we minded so much as the suffering our ineptitude might inflict. After all, if we were prepared to eat tinned tuna, we ought to be prepared to kill fish ourselves. As with everything in life, doing this well simply took practice. Gjalt cooked the fish and the accompanying pasta on his home-made stove, proudly proving that we could survive without LPG.

After a few days, we decided to return to Jean's island. By early afternoon, the sun was high enough in the sky to be behind us as we made our way back, ideal for safe navigation – or so we thought. It was dead calm, and the water was so still its surface acted like a mirror; all I could see from the helm were the reflections of scattered clouds. The conditions were also a challenge for Gjalt, who was perched up in the spreaders, but from there he was able to make out all the hazards and guide us safely across the lagoon.

Jean had asked if we could take him to Fakarava with us, but we found his house shuttered and all his copra neatly stacked in plastic drums on the veranda, shaded from the sun by the roof. He'd been expecting friends of his to arrive by motor boat to collect their own copra, and we concluded that he had gone with them. We felt quite sad at his absence, not least because we hadn't properly said goodbye. Our relationship with Jean had formed so naturally and developed into a real friendship despite our appalling French; maybe it had been all the more special because of it. He'd taught us about life on an atoll, gladly showing us how he survived without electricity, running water, or shops. It had been a fascinating encounter with a truly self-sufficient man. We printed off some photos of Toau, including one of Atoll Man and Office Man proudly displaying their lobster haul, and left them in his house. We knew he'd return to collect his copra before leaving Toau at the end of the harvest season, and were sure he'd be happy to have the photos.

We spent our last day walking around the island and reef flats, absorbing the magic one last time. We'd lived in paradise for two weeks, and it wasn't easy to leave.

The next morning we got up at 6 o'clock to prepare *Stella Maris* for departure. The skies were overcast but it was calm, and we decided it was a good day to go. By seven the sun was out, and with Gjalt aloft in the spreaders we headed to the pass, needing to be there for high tide at eight fifteen. A ketch had anchored in the atoll a few days earlier, and just before we reached it the crew weighed anchor, pushing ahead as if racing us to the pass. We were happy to let them lead the way. Only when we got closer did we see that it was the Swan Gjalt had been attracted to in Panama when searching for replacement line-handlers at the eleventh hour. Erik, the Norwegian captain, had gamely stepped into the breach.

When the yacht arrived opposite the pass, it made a sharp turn for the exit and, without any hesitation, shot towards it at high speed, like a jet accelerating along a runway. Despite the benign weather, large standing waves stretched from the centre of the gap in the reef to the leeward shore. Erik's yacht charged towards them, the outgoing current increasing its already considerable speed. When it reached the steep waves, it was as if the yacht had collided with an impenetrable barrier. The bow plunged downwards, and the stern rose sharply into the air, a spectacularly wild movement that was repeated several times by the unforgiving power of momentum. As the boat rocked, it turned until it was broadside to the waves, at which point it was knocked down, the mast almost touching the water. It was incredible to see how such short, steep waves were capable of throwing a boat around like a toy in a bathtub, and this wasn't a small yacht, but a sixty-foot motor-sailor. It was a horrendous sight, not least because we were about to go next.

"Oh my God," I muttered over and over again as the awful scene unfolded, and when Gjalt lined up to go through the exit I asked him if we should wait.

"It'll be fine," he assured me, in his usual cool manner. "We'll stay to the windward side of the pass. Look at the range markers and tell me when they're aligned."

I sat facing the stern and stared at the markers through the binoculars chanting, "Aligned, aligned," like a mantra, grateful not to see what we were heading into. Despite everything we'd just witnessed, though, I did believe we would be all right, because we'd safely entered the atoll in much rougher conditions.

Our cruising guide advised going through the centre of atoll passes, but that day the standing waves were clearly less fierce towards the windward side. Toau's pass was wide and deep enough to steer closer to the reef edge, and because the range markers were so far inside the lagoon, they remained aligned for some distance away from the centre. Our exit was not without some drama, though, as a large wave did crash onboard, thoroughly drenching me. Unfortunately, I deflected some of the spray down the companionway and onto the navigation table, where the computer was sitting. Electronic equipment hates salt water – even a few drops of it. Our already fragile laptop was about to go into a coma.

As we motored out into the safety of the deep ocean, we passed Erik's yacht and saw that the crew were hoisting sails. I thought it was incredibly keen of them to sail out of the pass, having just been thrown around so violently, but it wasn't keen at all; it was essential. The worst-case scenario had happened to them – their engine had failed in the middle of the pass.

We stood by ready to help, as Erik battled the waves and building current to sail back into the lagoon. It was nerve-wracking to watch this tense situation unfold, and I was afraid that we would have to go into those standing waves ourselves to pull the yacht away from the unforgiving reef. With two genoas out, Erik managed to maintain his distance from the leeward shore, which looked scarily close from our vantage point. After several minutes of making scant progress, the crew hoisted the mizzen sail, giving enough additional power for the Swan to finally inch its way back into the safety of the lagoon.

At last Erik came on the radio; he had been far too busy to answer our calls before. He told us they were moving forward at an agonisingly slow one and a half knots, hindered by a three-knot current against them. He was grateful that we had stood by, and he sounded very relieved to be out of the pass. It would have been easier to sail with the current into the open ocean, but Erik wanted to fix his engine in a flat anchorage rather than in the Pacific swell. He wasn't likely to be able to enter another atoll without it. Ice cool Norwegian blood had kept Erik calm, but the morning's events must surely have pushed even his Nordic heart rate above sixty.

Gjalt suggested that the violent rocking had probably stirred up the dregs in the Swan's fuel tank, which had subsequently entered the fuel line, clogged the filter, and prevented diesel from reaching the engine. If this were the case, simply replacing the filter would have fixed the problem, but we never met Erik again to find out. We do know that he made it safely out of Toau, though, and that he didn't have to learn about atoll survival from our friend Jean.

Wiping the saltwater droplets from the computer and stowing it away left me decidedly seasick. As we had an upwind sail to Fakarava, fourteen miles to the southeast, all I wanted to do was lie down and make the nausea disappear. With the wind blowing steadily, it was a fast trip, and while I remained out of action battling seasickness in the main cabin, Gjalt was in his element. When we reached the north pass of Fakarava, I roused myself and tried, but failed to coax the computer back to life, while Gjalt cleaned and bagged a freshly caught tuna on the aft deck. The pass was comfortingly wide, and we entered the second largest atoll in the Tuamotus with a lot less drama than we left Toau.

We followed the channel markers to the anchorage beside the village of Rotoava, and as soon as the anchor was down, an ebullient retired couple from Texas, Iris and Terry, came over to welcome us. We'd last seen their yacht four months earlier in Colón, waiting to go through the Panama Canal. They were positively bursting with enthusiasm about Fakarava and told us everything we could possibly have needed to know about it, rapid-firing the information at us because, Iris explained, "We've just bought ice-cream and it needs to go in the freezer."

On their boat for drinks that evening, these irrepressible, plain-speaking Texans felt no need to offer us false hope about our ailing computer.

"You've had it," Iris said, her face remaining cheerful. "We got water on a laptop once. We took it apart, dried it out, sprayed it with contact cleaner, and while it did come back to life, the screen gradually faded, getting darker and darker until it finally died."

*Surely a few saltwater drops can't kill a computer*, I thought to myself and resolutely refused to believe her words of doom.

We went onshore with our garbage, which we'd stored onboard since leaving Nuku Hiva, along with our empty LPG tank. This we towed on a small dock dolly, like a sick person pulling his life-supporting drip. We asked at various establishments if it could be filled, but as we had anticipated, it could not. We continued cooking on the gas-fired barbecue that Gjalt had moved into the cockpit from its windy home on the stern. A few days later, we learned from Iris and Terry that their LPG tank, also filled in Panama, showed a pressure much lower than normal as well. Having had no desire to build wood stoves onshore, they'd continued to use their tank; so far it had lasted a fortnight. We realised that the gas inside must be butane, which shows a lower pressure on the gauge when the tank is full compared to propane. We could have happily cooked in the galley as normal, but I think, secretly, Office Man enjoyed living in a state of cooking emergency. Pressed back into action, the tank provided us with gas for the next three months.

Despite being the second largest atoll in the archipelago, Fakarava was home to just 700 inhabitants, and they clearly led unrushed lives. They were as welcoming as the people of Makemo, and we found the village of Rotoava to be much prettier than Pouheva, its gardens more lush and better tended.

To complement earnings from the pearl industry, Fakarava had opened itself up to modest tourism, and Rotoava abounded with small shops. After our two-week retreat into the purity of nature, we enjoyed browsing through merchandise that would normally have been unremarkable, and our mouths positively watered at the sight of fresh fruit and vegetables.

At the dive shop, we were offered a free snorkelling trip to the north pass by Philippe, the generous French owner. When we set off in the large, rigid inflatable boat that afternoon, it soon became apparent that the driver – like most of his ilk around the world – had obviously been trained at the James Bond School of Boat Handling. We couldn't have raced the five miles to the pass with more urgency if Dr. No had been in pursuit, and I clung on for dear life as we bounced and jarred our way across the lagoon.

While the scuba divers descended to drift their way through the pass, Gjalt and I were dropped near the outer reef a safe distance from the current. We were told to keep well clear of the pass so we wouldn't be flushed out into the ocean, never to be seen again. Taking these instructions seriously, I was shocked to see Gjalt immediately swim in the direction of the pass and then dive down. The boat had moved quite far away from us by that time, and I felt myself beginning to panic as I suddenly felt invisible, a mere speck adrift in the open ocean. When Gjalt resurfaced, I accused him of wanton irresponsibility, but he convinced me that he hadn't swum towards the pass at all and had no intention of doing so. Reassured, I calmed down and began to enjoy myself, although considering that Gjalt had encountered a rather too inquisitive silvertip shark on Toau's outer reef,

I'm not sure why. I wouldn't have been happy to snorkel outside the lagoon if a dive operator hadn't taken me there; illogically, that made it seem safe, even though the boat was a good distance away.

The underwater scenery of the outer reef was incredible. The ocean was crystal clear, and an expansive bank of healthy corals stretched off in both directions. Huge blue and green Napoleon wrasses seemed unperturbed by the many blacktip reef sharks patrolling the area, but this wasn't the case for two tiny yellow damselfish that were being tailgated by one mischievous shark. It was like watching a scene from *Finding Nemo* as the trio swam past, the small fish rapidly flapping their fins while the predator kept its nose glued to their tails. They disappeared out of sight, only to return a short while later, swimming back in the opposite direction. I could almost see the grin on the shark's face and the fear in its distressed victims' eyes. Fortunately I'd been in the water with reef sharks so often by then that I wasn't fazed by the sight of a dozen of these fearsome-looking fish swimming closely behind us. Had one of them chosen to tailgate me as closely as those poor yellow fish, though, I definitely would have panicked.

When we returned from the dive, we removed the keyboard from our laptop in the hope that letting it dry out overnight would lead to a miraculous recovery of our invaluable communication machine. Having gained courage from the stimulating effects of strong coffee, I screwed the keyboard back in place and, with shaking hands, pressed the power button.

Suddenly lights flashed and motors whirred as, against the odds, the computer came to life. I immediately set about sending an e-mail to let our families know we were all right, but it was only halfway into cyberspace when the laptop suffered a relapse. Nothing I tried could induce the lights to glow in that festive way again. It was with immense trepidation that I agreed to let Gjalt the handyman take the whole thing apart, a procedure so scary I couldn't possibly watch. He removed every single screw, detached every possible component, and spread it all around the boat to dry.

Left with no choice, we braced ourselves for the pain of parting with a small fortune in Rotoava's Internet café and went onshore. Not only did we want to send a reassuring e-mail home, but we also needed to print off Gjalt's U.S. tax return. The café had no printer, though, so the long arm of the Inland Revenue Service kept us in its grip and continued to torment us from afar. To console ourselves, we went on a shopping spree and splashed out on tomatoes, bell peppers, a jar of Nutella (chocolate Valium for my nerves), and a two-litre bottle of Coca-Cola; we were in urgent need of a rum-and-Coke, or maybe even a few of them.

Back on *Stella Maris*, our expensive computer looked so distressingly vulnerable that Gjalt immediately reassembled it. Amazingly, there was still a screw for every hole, and even more amazingly, the laptop came back to life. This time, it functioned long enough to send and receive e-mails and burn all our precious photos onto a CD. We were ecstatic at this success, but we knew the chances of our computing troubles being over were slim.

The south pass of Fakarava was said to be home to hundreds of sharks, a must for all serious divers. Early one morning, we set off on the twenty-eight-mile trip through the lagoon, with one of us stationed on the bow at all times. In the north of the atoll, the pearl buoys scattered in the water were of more concern than the corals; we didn't want to get a line wrapped around the prop. Once clear of the buoys, the trip went smoothly, and by early afternoon, we were anchored behind a sandy island close to the Tumakohua Pass.

The following morning, our dynamic Brazilian friends, Caju and Mariana, arrived in Fakarava. Like everyone else at the southern end of the atoll, they had come to dive with the sharks. The frenetic activity of eager divers racing to and from the pass, coupled with the noise of compressors refilling tanks, was far removed from the tranquil idyll of Toau. But we hadn't gone there for peace and quiet, so the next day we joined the thrill-seekers ourselves.

I was very nervous and secretly hoped that an early morning squall would scupper our diving plans. My last dive had been in the Galápagos, three months earlier, and this would only be my fifth since qualifying. We were going to drift through the pass, letting the inflowing tide flush us past hundreds of sharks. I wasn't looking forward to it, but

I wasn't going to bottle out either.

By half past seven, five of us were bouncing towards the pass in Caju's dinghy; ours was anchored around the corner from the pass, where we would be released from the current's grip. On the way, Guy, a nonchalant young Frenchman, coolly announced that his friend had died on a drift dive, swept out to sea and forever lost because nobody could see her. It wasn't exactly the pep talk I was hoping for, especially since the brightest thing attached to me was my rather short, pale yellow snorkel.

I descended easily to the bottom of the pass some ninety feet down, so easily that I landed on it like a dead weight. Aware that this was not the idea, I added some air to my BCD. Seeing my predicament, Caju, an ex-diving instructor, encouraged me to add more air, which I did. Unfortunately, this meant I had added too much, and instead of levitating a few feet above the seabed, I began to rise so quickly I was in danger of shooting all the way to the surface. Gjalt, my dive buddy, had gone off to photograph the sharks, and Caju had also mysteriously vanished, but thankfully Guy of the Inspirational Anecdote witnessed my ascent. He stretched up his hand to my rapidly retreating person, and I swam desperately towards him to grab it. He pulled me back down, saving me from the bends.

Somehow, I was able to get my buoyancy under control, and only then did I notice that a huge platoon of sharks was hanging in the current that streamed through the pass. Impressive as this was, the predators failed to distract me from the preoccupations of diving, and the interludes when I wasn't checking my depth, my air, or some other piece of equipment, were rather short. In order to stop and admire the underwater spectacle, it was necessary to hold on to something. I sought out dead coral but didn't always succeed, and it became sadly clear that the environment was paying a price for all the diving activity.

When we met the French Polynesian owner of the local dive shop on the island later that day, he confirmed our suspicions. Sunny might have lived up to his name when he was a boy, but as he told us about the damage tourists were inflicting on the coral in the lagoon and on the outer reefs 'Gloomy' unfortunately seemed altogether more appropriate.

In Toau, the flats we'd walked on were vast expanses

of dead reef rock, essentially a giant pavement, but those on Fakarava were home to a patchwork of fragile, living corals that could be all too easily crushed by human feet. Destruction can swiftly follow an influx of people who are determined to enjoy their expensive holidays, blissfully ignorant of the lasting damage they might be leaving behind.

Gjalt enjoyed the shark drive in the pass but he had expected something more spectacular. Intent on finding it, he joined Caju on the atoll's outer reef wall and, without his jittery novice buddy to worry about, was free to enjoy himself. The visibility was incredible, as was the abundance and variety of healthy coral. As he went deeper, he peered at the seafloor, puzzled to see it moving. Only when he got closer could he make out the individual groupers in an unbroken carpet of thousands, which stretched away in both directions. Above it, dozens of reef sharks circled. It was a David Attenborough moment; he'd got his spectacular dive.

We packed our dinghy away, planned the route to Tahiti, and prepared *Stella Maris* for sea. At sundown, we sipped margaritas and reflected upon our time in the Tuamotus. We'd had our nerves tested in Makemo by bad weather, were taught about atoll life by Jean in his paradise of Toau, and had dived with the sharks of Fakarava. We would be leaving it all behind when we went through the Tumakohua Pass the following morning and headed for the Society Islands.

# 11.

## Rejoining Society

*There have been seven bleaching events in French Poly-*
*nesia over the last two decades, with most of them in the*
*Society Islands. The apparently increasing frequency of*
*bleaching events (every three years on average) poses*
*a major threat to the corals of this region, with the real*
*risk that the more susceptible species may become rare*
*in the coral community.*

   *– Status of Coral Reefs of the World: 2002,*
    Australian Institute of Marine Science

I had observed the behaviour of the Tumakohua Pass at various stages of the tide's cycle ever since we'd arrived, intent on getting to know the devil's movements so we could sneak out when he was in a sympathetic mood. We were up early on the day of departure, and by slack tide at 8 o'clock conditions in the pass looked good to go. The anchor, however, was less inclined to leave, and Gjalt had to dive down to work it free. I winched in the chain and dashed back to the helm once the anchor was up, the same departure procedure as in Makemo.

We had two knots of current against us, but it was an easy exit, which I weathered unexpectedly calmly from my post on the bow. Once we were safely in open ocean, we set a course for Tahiti, some 225 miles away.

The wind was strong, and *Stella Maris* raced along at more than eight knots, feeling frisky after a month confined by the reefs of the Tuamotus. Gjalt dealt with a rain squall while I slept down below, succumbing to the drowsiness that usually overcame me on the first day of a passage. I got up when Gjalt caught a three-foot wahoo and needed help to bring it onboard. He soon had it gaffed, killed, bled, and filleted; practice had made the whole process less traumatic than it used to be for all involved.

I took the first watch from six to nine, a nearly full moon softening the harsh effect the wind's power had on the night. I didn't listen to my Walkman because we were sailing fast, and I wanted to be fully aware of the elements around me. By my second watch, conditions had eased, and I needed my music to keep me awake until it ended at 3 o'clock. We both slept well when we were off-watch and so we weren't grumpy with each other the following day, which was a rarity after a first night at sea.

We continued our high speed throughout the night. By morning, we knew that if we maintained seven knots during the day, we'd reach Tahiti Iti, the southern bulb of the hourglass island of Tahiti, before dark. *Stella Maris* kept up the pace until lunchtime, but then the wind dropped, and we had to hoist the gennaker to catch every puff. The anchorage in Tautira Bay on the northeastern side of Tahiti Iti has an easy entrance through the fringing reef and we were determined to reach it before dark. If we didn't make it we'd be forced to wait at sea until dawn, a far less attractive option than a full night of sleep at anchor. So, two hours before sunset, we enlisted the help of the engine to cover the remaining miles.

The sun seemed to hang in the sky just long enough for us to sail safely through the half-mile-wide pass and hook behind the protective reef. We never thought this trip would be a mere overnighter. We enjoyed sundowners in the cockpit while we took in our new surroundings.

The island had the same densely covered tropical slopes we'd seen in the Marquesas, but it was distinguished from those younger, eastern neighbours by a long beach of jet-black volcanic sand and a fringing reef. The Tuamotu Archipelago was the oldest of the three French Polynesian groups, its volcanic islands having eroded over time, leaving just the encircling reefs to attest to their existence.

The absence of other yachts in the bay gave us a feeling of adventure that we hadn't expected to feel in Tahiti, the largest of the Society Islands. With a population 160,000 strong, it was going to be very different from the atolls we'd just left behind, and not just geographically. Tautira Bay was the gentle introduction we needed.

We slept like logs; the fringing reef pacified the Pacific and kept the anchorage as calm as a millpond. After coffee the next morning, we set sail for Port Phaeton, a snug hurricane hole in the neck of the hourglass island, where we could safely leave *Stella Maris* while we went by road to Papeete in the far north. We had to go to the capital city to check in, sort out our lingering U.S. tax issues, and shop for a new computer.

The six-hour trip took us north along the scenic west coast of Tahiti Iti. There were so many pine trees covering the hillsides that with a little effort, we could imagine ourselves sailing on an Alpine lake. Whenever our eyes strayed down to the coastline that was so liberally lined with palm trees, the illusion was instantly shattered. I experienced the scenery in a regrettably fragmented fashion, because every fifteen minutes, I felt compelled to put our position on the chart. (We didn't want to have our fragile computer switched on for six hours while the GPS plotted our progress on it.) I was driven by a superstitious fear that being relaxed about the fringing reef would invoke some kind of malevolent supernatural force that would ensure we ran aground. My irrationality irked Gjalt tremendously, but nothing he said could sway me.

The Tapuaeraha Pass was wide and straightforward, but this time I lost my cool as soon as we were behind the fringing reef. There were red and green posts all over the place, marking a spaghetti junction of channels I couldn't make any sense of as we approached. They snaked north and south, some hugging the island shore and others skirting invisible coral patches. Yellow and black cardinals warned of isolated hazards, but I could only decipher which side was safe to pass when we got close. I asked Gjalt to let me take the wheel while he went on the bow, but I was bluntly told I had no reason to panic and should stay put and calm down.

Two miles north, an unexpected complication arose when we reached the next pass. The red and green markers switched sides without warning, so all of a sudden we had to keep green to starboard and not to port. Gjalt realised this just in time to alter course and prevent us from running onto a shallow. This nerve-wracking weaving lasted for a further mile as we made our way to Port Phaeton. I felt as though we'd earned a beautiful destination, but we seemed to have arrived in an ugly industrial harbour. It was, however, a very well-protected anchorage, which convinced us that we could safely leave *Stella Maris* anchored there while we went to Papeete, some sixty kilometres away by road.

Onshore, the twenty-minute walk to the supermarket was along a road much too busy for our senses. We hadn't been in such a hectic environment since Panama, nearly four months earlier. An endless stream of cars raced past us, a maniac behind every wheel. Overtaking was apparently compulsory, even if the car in front was already recklessly breaking the speed limit. The drivers seemed intent on killing themselves and unconcerned about taking innocent pedestrians down with them; sailors, who were used to travelling under eight miles an hour were easy targets.

We sought shelter in the supermarket, relieved to have made it there unscathed. Our spirits quickly lifted at the sight of shelves stacked to the rafters with all kinds of luxuries, including our old friend, Coca-Cola. Despite the long walk back, we couldn't resist the offer of four bottles for the price of three. Even at fourteen dollars, it seemed like a bargain. Our Coca-Cola abstinence had ended; rum just wasn't the same without it.

Outside the supermarket, several Tahitians were drinking beer. One of them was a frail, dishevelled old lady. She was very drunk, but still lucid enough to offer us sound advice: "*Attention à les voitures!*" she warned.

We hadn't come across such a sad scene in the Tuamotus or the Marquesas Islands. More people, more material goods, and more money seemed to result in less happiness.

Back onboard, we prepared the paperwork required for checking in. Although the computer did start, the ingress of seawater had somehow transformed it into an encryption device. Whenever I pressed a letter on the keyboard, a different one appeared on the screen. Progress was slow, as I tried guessing which letter might produce the one I wanted, but eventually the crew lists were typed. It was clear that our ailing laptop needed professional help.

We were at the bus stop bright and early the next morning, but Gjalt had a money-saving plan. Having been an avid hitchhiker in his youth, he had no problem waving his thumb in the air, and before the bus showed up, we were climbing into a small white van. Gjalt took the passenger seat beside the driver, and I perched on a toolbox in the back. A relaxed Frenchman in his forties, Frédéric had lived in Tahiti for twenty-four years and now built local fishing boats in a small town near Papeete. He dropped us off at his office, leaving us a much shorter bus ride to the capital. He even offered to give us a lift home if we met him back there before 4 o'clock. The day had got off to a good start.

Things continued to run smoothly at the Port Authority. They were used to clearing yachts into French Polynesia and were almost as relaxed about the required bureaucracy as The Dude would have been.

Invigorated by our good fortune and quick progress, we set our sights on the Fedex office, where packages containing anodes for our prop, Gjalt's tax return, and a new computer hard drive were waiting. We marched purposefully along the built-up Avenue Prince Hinoi, with me having to do odd little sprints every now and then to catch up with Gjalt, who was like a man possessed. Even with map in hand, we overshot the mark (at the pace we were going, this was inevitable), so we marched back, still refusing to slow down.

With Gjalt's usually precise homing-in skills failing to locate the target, we charged into a fishmonger to ask for guidance. We were sent back up the street and, sure we were finally getting warmer, sought fine-tuning directions in a pet shop.

"Fedex?" we gasped.

"Fedex? They moved to the other side of Papeete a year ago."

"But their Internet Site says they're in this street."

"Yes, I know; you're not the only ones who come here looking for them."

Luckily this heavy Fedex cloud was soon lightened by an unexpected silver lining: a computer shop with the desired Dell sign in its window a few doors from the pet shop. Inside was a French technician, who agreed to examine our laptop, although he did wince at the mention of salt water. He was convinced that a new keyboard would be the only solution to our encryption problem. And new computers (*ordinateurs* to the French, always determined not to use English words) were not as horrendously expensive as we'd feared, so we could buy a backup and still afford to eat. Of course, we were quite sure that if we did fork out for a new one our current laptop would last for years, but if we didn't, it would die the minute we sailed away from Tahiti. Such was life, according to Sod.

Thanks to the pet shop man, we finally tracked down Fedex at their new location, a long, hot walk across the frenetic town. We put our lives in the hands of the crazed drivers as we crossed the final obstacle, a kind of Tahitian Périphérique. Sweaty and exhausted, we stumbled up the stairs to the office, only to find that Fedex had refused to accept two of our packages because they'd been sent via DHL and UPS. Well, we might have sympathised with their standpoint if we hadn't spent a hot day stomping along miles of polluted streets to track them down, but since we had, we were not impressed.

Having spent a fortune in an Internet café to access and print off our tax returns in preparation for exactly this kind of failure, we were at least able to mail the documents and finally rid ourselves of the unpleasant IRS invasion into our lives. I hadn't yet heard from the taxman myself, but I sensed his footsteps thundering towards me and made a pre-emptive strike while I could. We'd soon be far away from Internet cafés and Fedex offices again, and I didn't want to be grabbed by the neck a second time. It turned out to be the right thing to do.

Certain we wouldn't make it to Frédéric's office in time to drive back to Port Phaeton with him, we went instead to the airport, where UPS had set up shop. When the man muttered that we couldn't have our package until we'd been to Customs, which happened to be closed, Gjalt lunged over the counter and ripped his head off – okay, that's just what he felt like doing. What he actually did was calmly persuade him it was only paperwork (which was even true), and we left feeling victorious, despite the fact that our expensive visit to the Internet café had made the tax return we held in our hands completely redundant.

Sensing we were on a roll, we duelled once more with the Périphérique, survived, extracted our new hard drive from the clutches of DHL, and thus accomplished all of our missions. Gjalt thought we deserved to reward ourselves with a Big Mac meal (the subject of many a fantasy on our eighteen-day crossing to the Marquesas), but I wanted to get back to *Stella Maris* and save that pleasure for another day. As purser, I kept a tight rein on the budget, and we'd had an expensive day, sending a substantial cheque to the U.S. taxman and agreeing to buy a backup laptop. It didn't seem the right time to indulge in frivolities. We took the bus back to Port Phaeton and enjoyed the picturesque ride that took us away from the hectic, man-made jungle of Papeete.

After the unimpressive disintegration of my nerves as I'd tried to decipher the channel markers leading to Port Phaeton, Gjalt sat me down and delivered his captain speech, the upshot of which was that if there was any worrying to be done, he would do it. This liberation from responsibility made me unflappable when we negotiated the passes of the fringing reef to move a few miles east the next day.

Port d'Ataiti was on Tahiti Nui, the larger bulb of the hourglass island of Tahiti, and with its tree-covered slopes and pretty reef-fringed bay, it was a refreshing contrast to Port Phaeton. The absence of other boats was wonderfully calming after the manic activity in Papeete; we felt the stress melting away. It was clear that we would have to ease ourselves back into society very gently after all the months of blissful solitude.

We set off in the dinghy to explore our new surroundings and pulled up at what we thought was a public jetty. A middle-aged Frenchwoman promptly emerged from a mansion that turned out to be private and set us straight. Apologising to her in French for our ignorance thawed her frosty heart, and she became quite helpful, directing us to nearby natural springs and waterfalls. She didn't go so far as to invite us in for a glass of wine though.

The springs were pretty but cold, and as we headed off in search of the waterfall, we came across an expertly landscaped botanical garden. Ignoring the well-maintained paths that led past impressive trees and exotic plants, Gjalt proceeded to scramble up a muddy hill. I left him to it, only to scramble up a hill of my own soon afterwards, unable to resist the rare opportunity to view the world from a height far above sea level. The best ways to see the true beauty of reefs are underwater and from the sky. From where we stood, we could appreciate the grandeur of nature: the coral barrier able to stand firm against the power of the Pacific, the luminous mix of blues spanning the placid lagoon, and the luxuriant flora covering the slopes of Tahiti Iti in a soft green cloak.

Back at ground level, a herd of blubbery Americans in shorts and white trainers had been released from their tour bus for a brief excursion around the botanical gardens. We fled quickly, now that the beauty of the natural world had faded behind a sea of pallid flesh and booming human voices.

Early in the morning, we left for Papeete. The sun was too low to highlight the shallows, but the channel to the pass was well marked. It was about thirty miles to the capital, and we had to motor for many of them, but when we had enough wind to sail, it was wonderful. We trolled the lure and got three strikes: first was a tuna that got away; second was a barracuda we let go because of the risk of ciguatera poisoning; and third was a tuna that ended up in the fridge.

The pass south of Papeete was incredibly narrow, but it was a calm day, and conditions for entering were ideal. The more passes we went through, the less nervous I became, and at least the transits didn't need to be timed with slack tide, as they had in the Tuamotus. The water didn't bubble or swirl, and there were no powerful currents. The price we had to pay for such benevolence was the presence of human beings in far greater numbers.

We found a space amongst dozens of other yachts in an anchorage with a stunning view of the island of Moorea, its jagged peaks jutting up from the ocean ten miles to the west. In the opposite direction, expensive houses clung to the Tahiti slopes – a scene so European we might have been anchored on a Swiss lake. It wasn't all perfect though: speedboats and jet skis tore along the channel that ran past the anchorage, tourist toys that got Gjalt's blood boiling. He buried his head in his Robert Ludlum thriller and tried to pretend it wasn't happening. For me, the view of Moorea, the aquamarine water stretching to the reef and the pretty hillside enclave, made up for the Club-Med atmosphere.

After the Dell technician had written off our salty keyboard, we had nothing to lose by resorting to drastic measures. We dunked the thing in fresh water to flush away the salt and then let it dry, a technique that had apparently proved successful for other cruisers. Alas, it finished off our keyboard once and for all. Back at Dell, the excellent technician sprayed every crevice of our salt-infused computer with contact cleaner and attached a brand new keyboard, which eradicated its encryption tendencies. Naturally, the French had moved a few keys around just to assert their Gallic identity, so I was forced to unlearn years of tapping away on an English keyboard to avoid doing the encrypting myself. But the joy of having a fully operational computer far outweighed the temporary reduction in my typing speed. I didn't think Gjalt would suffer much, because it's hard to work up a speed worth mentioning with two fingers, but the inexplicable French decision to require the shift key be pressed to type a full stop or a number did draw expletives from him quite regularly.

We wouldn't get another chance to buy a new computer before we got to Australia, and we didn't dare sail away without a backup. So, we bought a laptop that was on sale and hoped the hard drive wouldn't play up, like its predecessor's had.

The resolution of our computer problems was cause for celebration. In the evening, we dinghyed over to the McDonald's opposite the marina, and I waited for Gjalt while he ordered the Family Meal Deal. For a mere twenty dollars, we became the excited recipients of two Big Mac meals, two cheeseburger meals, and nine chicken nuggets. Back on *Stella Maris*, we wolfed down every last morsel, and although it was good, it just wasn't as great as we'd imagined it would be during all those long and hungry night watches. Perhaps life at sea was beginning to cure us of the desire for the junk food we'd frequently indulged in back in Texas.

In town the next morning, we heard about a fifty-five-foot catamaran that had been wrecked two days earlier on the outer reef of Manuae, an atoll west of Bora Bora. After spending a night on the reef, the family was rescued and flown to Papeete. While the father was treated in hospital, the four young children stayed with another cruising family, people we knew. We met the eldest boy, Ben, who was just sixteen and remarkably calm for someone who'd just lived through a cruiser's worst nightmare.

Late in the afternoon, a day after leaving Bora Bora, the father concluded they were about seven miles from Manuae. He could see the tall palm trees through the binoculars. As the family was sitting down to dinner, the pin connecting the boom to the mainsail broke. They tried to fix it for over an hour but eventually chose to lower the sail, lash the boom, and continue the repair in daylight. At about seven in the evening, just after it got dark, they heard scraping under the boat. They thought they'd hit something in the water, but this was quickly dispelled by another sound; Ben compared it to bones crunching. Distracted by the problem with the boom, they'd failed to pay attention to their position and the catamaran had run onto the submerged reef on the southern side of Manuae.

Caught in the surf, the pounding waves relentlessly pushed the yacht onto the reef. Water poured in from the starboard hull. The family grabbed emergency supplies, put out a Mayday on the radio, set off their EPIRB, and hurried on deck. Ben and his father went to the bow to inflate the life raft. By now, the catamaran was breaking up, and suddenly the seventy-nine-foot mast came crashing down. Ben was hit on the head by the falling rigging, but his father was more seriously injured when a spreader sliced through his shin and practically severed his foot. He was pinned down by the heavy mast and couldn't be moved until one of the hulls broke apart, nearly an hour later. The family stemmed the blood flow with tourniquets above and below the knee, not knowing which position was best, and eventually managed to get off the boat and spend the night on the reef.

The EPIRB signal was picked up by a satellite, and the boat name subsequently relayed to the U.S. Coast Guard. It took two more hours before a GPS position was received. At dawn, a French Navy jet flew to the location, but the crew didn't understand from the family's hand signals that someone needed immediate medical care. The pilot fired flares to attract the attention of Manuae's few inhabitants, and when the locals reached the scene in their motor boat, the jet left. At around midday, a helicopter arrived and evacuated the family to Bora Bora, from where they took a plane to Papeete.

Young Ben was stoical about his family's harrowing

event. "The important thing is that we're all alive," he said.

His father's leg had to be amputated below the knee in Papeete. Back home in the USA, a second operation amputated it above the knee. It was a high price to pay for not paying enough attention to their boat's position. The accident happened on the family's second day at sea, after a five-month break in the USA. They were sailing on a tight schedule, making their way to meet friends who were flying in to Fiji to holiday with them. And they'd been distracted from navigation while they tried to repair the boom. Modern-day cruisers may have advanced technology, but it's still good seamanship that keeps them safe at sea.

Later, we heard that people we knew had sailed their catamaran onto a coral head in the lagoon of an atoll. One of the hulls had been holed and a prop badly damaged. It was another reminder of the need to be vigilant in these beautiful, but hazardous waters.

One morning, the wind suddenly started gusting through the crowded anchorage. Gjalt instinctively went on deck and saw that a neighbouring boat was dragging. While he dinghyed over to it, I radioed other yachts in the anchorage to find someone to help. I didn't want to leave *Stella Maris* in case she dragged too; we'd learnt from our Isla Mujeres experience to protect our own boat before others. Soon, another cruiser joined Gjalt aboard the drifting boat, and they managed to put out a second anchor, which stopped the yacht before it hit the reef.

The middle-aged American owners were on a tour of the island, and we felt sure that once they returned and found their boat in a different position, with a second anchor deployed, they'd be ready to thank the people responsible. From the cockpit, we saw them dinghy back to their yacht, where they duly stayed until the next morning. Only then did Mrs. Drifting Boat come over to say thank you, going some way to make amends for her late appearance by giving us a bottle of white wine. Her husband, however, was nowhere to be seen.

The couple weighed anchor a short time later, and it seemed to take all the man's might to muster a curt "Thanks" as they passed us on their way out. The other cruiser who'd helped to re-anchor their boat received the same gratitude: a solo visit and a bottle of wine. Perhaps the couple was embarrassed that their boat had dragged while they weren't onboard, something they probably felt shouldn't have happened to them after seven years of cruising. This was the only reason we could come up with to explain their reticence to thank those who had saved their boat. Had the tables been turned, we would have immediately invited them for dinner and celebrated till the sun came up. Anyone who protected *Stella Maris* would be our friends for life.

We braved the busy streets of Papeete a few more times to buy provisions, browse through chandleries and dive shops, and finally to check out. We'd had enough of the noise, heat, cars, and pollution of so-called civilisation and were ready to sail away from it all. The bewitching island of Moorea beckoned from across the water.

Fresh from the fuel dock, with *Stella Maris*' tanks full of diesel and water, we left Tahiti through the narrow pass. The absence of wind removed every last ripple from the ocean and turned the water a wondrous deep indigo it was tempting to dive into. Cook's Bay was only fifteen miles away, so we didn't mind having to use the engine to get there.

As we sailed along the fringing reef guarding the bay, we saw that the anchorage was crowded with sailing boats, and – even worse – a cruise ship was there too. There were no such vessels in any place we could call paradise, so we carried on a further two miles to Opunohu Bay, where there were just a handful of yachts and no cruise liners.

It was an easy entrance through a wide gap in the reef, and the turquoise water directly behind this coral barrier invited us to nose into the anchorage as far as we could in order to find solitude. When the hook was down, we took in the fantastic view of Moorea's dramatic volcanic peaks, the kind of South Seas vista people dream of. The reef was just a short swim away, and in the afternoon sunshine, the abundance of coral heads in the clear water proved irresistible. Even I could do the anchor check in thirteen feet of water, and having seen it firmly dug into the sandy bottom, we snorkelled over to the reef.

There we discovered a spectacular garden of coral more enticing than anything we'd seen so far, and it just stretched on and on. It was healthy, the variety was incredible, and it was exactly the right depth below the water to allow hours of meditative exploration.

It felt wonderful to have escaped from the clutches of Papeete, and it was the perfect place to recover from the mayhem we'd been drawn into there – well, almost perfect. Gjalt had already spotted a few jet skis and taken imaginary shots at them. We'd seen 'unexploded ordnance' marked on the chart at a location not so far away, and Gjalt wanted to retrieve it and blow the motorised monsters out of the water.

When friends Chris and Lisa, a sunny, easy-going British couple with two young sons, sailed their catamaran to a small anchorage a mile to the east, we tied our dinghy to the stern and climbed aboard for the short trip outside the fringing reef. Not wasting the chance to catch some fresh fish, they trolled a brightly coloured squid lure and quickly hooked a huge wahoo, from which we happily accepted two thick steaks.

The pass leading to the new anchorage was narrow and shallow, but neither Chris nor Lisa seemed particularly perturbed by the challenge. In their shoes, I'd have been a nervous wreck. They even remained calm when their depth alarm went off as they edged further towards a pretty island; the corals underneath us looked close enough to touch. They tied their catamaran to a huge concrete mooring and had their adventurousness rewarded by being the only yacht there.

We dinghyed back to Opunohu Bay along the small boat channel and stopped at a spot famous for the stingrays that congregated there. Knowing that the rays gathered because they were fed by tourists had put us off coming earlier, but now that we happened to be passing we were drawn in by the spectacle. The stingrays were climbing up the sides of visiting motorboats, somehow managing to propel their entire bodies out of the water. Keeping one eye on the blacktip reef sharks patrolling in the small boat channel, we snorkelled towards the rays and were immediately approached as possible providers of food. They slithered up against us, often several at a time, a silky sensation that was strangely and unexpectedly pleasant. Their diamond-shaped bodies glided over us, their wide, flat fins flapping gently as they rose up and out of the water.

I enjoyed stroking their soft, smooth skin but remained wary of their tails with the painful sting lurking at the tips. We don't like animals being turned into performers for the entertainment of human beings, but at least these creatures were free to swim away whenever they chose.

It was July 7th, 2005, and while we were immersed in an exotic and peaceful world, suicide bombers killed fifty-two people in London. I e-mailed home as soon as we heard the news to make sure everyone was all right. Chances were slim that my sister would have been injured, but she worked in central London, and I wanted to be sure. Our life on the ocean was so heavenly and refreshingly free of all the troubles forever flaring up in the world we'd left behind; there was little incentive to give it up.

We loved our time in Moorea and spent so many hours snorkelling that the skin on our hands began to slough off. It would have been nice to stay there longer, but our visas were due to expire in two weeks, and so much still lay ahead of us that after a week, we moved on.

With good wind for an overnight sail to Huahine in the Leeward group of the Society Islands, we set off in the late afternoon, despite it being grey and drizzly. We'd intended to tow our dinghy, but soon after exiting the pass, it got tangled in the line of the towing generator, so we hove-to, pulled it onboard, and secured it to the aft deck.

By now, the wind was blowing strongly and while *Stella Maris* raced along at an enthusiastic seven and a half knots, I got tired and seasick, so I swapped watches with Gjalt, and I did feel better by the time I relieved him at 9 o'clock. When a small freighter came within a few miles of us, I woke Gjalt up to confirm that we needed to alter our course. I always woke him up if I wanted a second opinion in the confusing darkness of night. Unfortunately, this interruption to his sleep made him so grumpy that I hesitated to wake him when a second freighter came close to intersecting our path. By the time I did, the ship passed us just 200 metres away, a distance I felt was too close for comfort. There was no one on deck, and we both had a feeling that the crew hadn't even seen us.

The short trips of just one or two nights were the most testing, because neither of us slept well when we were off-watch. Once again, we renewed our promise to get up whenever necessary and not complain about it. Being woken up by each other was a lot better than being woken up by a collision with a freighter steaming along at twenty knots.

The winds were so strong that to avoid making landfall in the dark, we sailed with the main alone. We rounded the north coast of Huahine at daybreak and entered the wide Avamoa Pass an hour later.

A marked channel between the island and its fringing reef led us nine miles south to a pretty bay. We anchored in aquamarine water that stretched all the way to the outer reef a mile away; onshore, a sweeping sandy beach was backed by green hillsides. And yet we didn't find the bay as appealing as previous anchorages. It was beginning to dawn on us that we'd become spoilt, in the same way as the Frenchman who'd shrugged his shoulders when I remarked how beautiful Hiva Oa was. Then Gjalt detected tourists, an unwelcome part of the scenery in the Society Islands, and their presence only added to the feeling of discontent.

I suppose the snorkelling was bound to be disappointing after Moorea, but there was very little coral in the bay, and the expansive aquamarine shallows were overrun by hundreds of sharply spiked black sea urchins. There was also a strong current due to all the water washing across the lagoon, which made swimming hard work.

We dinghyed around the southern tip of Huahine and crossed a channel leading from a narrow gap in the reef to reach a small island. The ocean was breaking heavily across the gap, and there were even breakers inside the lagoon; it was not a good day for locals to take their fishing boats out to sea. We walked around the island, enjoying being on land again, especially since it was free of tourists and home to just two families.

We dedicated a day to boat chores, with me lavishly using three jerry cans of water to do a load of washing on deck. Sixty litres was two weeks' supply of drinking water, but we could easily spare it, as we'd filled our tanks in Tahiti. I was enjoying the simple satisfaction of transforming our dirty clothes into clean ones when the crew of an American yacht, apparently blind to the vast emptiness of the enormous bay, anchored so close to us that they could have helped me wring out our things. As if this wasn't

intrusive enough, they then proceeded to argue, unabash-
edly hurling expletives at each other until my tranquillity
was well and truly shattered.

We left Huahine the next morning, together with our
Australian friends, Jo and Jason, on board their yacht
*Reverie*. An enterprising couple in their thirties, they'd
bought their fifty-foot Juneau in the Caribbean and
planned to sell it for a profit in Australia before returning
to the Caribbean, buying a new boat and doing the whole
trip again. Jo was more bubbly than champagne, Jason
had a wry sense of humour, and both were irrepressibly
fun company.

We motored north to the pass and raced each other to
the island of Raiatea, a twenty-mile hop to the west. Gjalt
and I would normally have been lazy on such a short trip,
but having competition made such slackness unacceptable. The genoa was poled out, and sails were trimmed
constantly, our eagerness boosted by the sight of Jo and
Jason busily coaxing speed out of *Reverie*. It was an excellent day for sailing, and *Stella Maris* raced across to Raiatea
at seven and a half knots, reaching the pass just ahead of
her friendly rival.

Finding little of obvious appeal on the northern coast of
Raiatea, we continued north to the sister island of Tahaa,
which was protected by the same fringing reef. We investigated Apu Baie and found it too deep and unattractive, so
we moved a few miles further to Hurepiti Baie, which was
unfortunately no better. Nothing seemed to satisfy us, and
we pushed on northwards, determined to find a pretty spot
before the sun went down. At last we succeeded, anchoring
beside a palm tree-covered motu (albeit tarnished by some
over-water tourist bungalows), with Bora Bora rising might-
ily in the distance.

Once again, the snorkelling failed to match that of
Moorea. Most of the coral was dead, the marine life was
sparse, and the sea urchins carpeted the bottom with
sharp black spikes. We moved to a string of motus on
the eastern side of the island, but the anchorage was too
exposed to the wind, which made the water quite choppy.
The time had come to take a closer look at Bora Bora.

We left Tahaa early in the morning, and Gjalt refused to
take the helm, forcing me to sail out of the pass. It was

the first time I'd done anything more than fret about it. I kept *Stella Maris* steady between the markers, dead centre of the pass and well away from the waves that were breaking threateningly on the fringing reef. Seeing the white foam in the corner of my eye and hearing the crashing breakers made my heart beat faster and focused my mind. I sailed us clear of danger and felt pretty good about it.

We had a wonderful sail to Bora Bora, some twenty miles to the northwest. Perfect trade winds pushed *Stella Maris* gracefully towards the most famous island paradise of the South Seas, its legendary volcanic peaks rising enchantingly from the ocean. We skirted south of its protective ring of fringing reef to reach the Teavanui Pass on the western side. Gjalt had dreamt of making this landfall for years, but now he gave me the honour of taking us through the pass and into the famous lagoon. It was quite a feeling.

We made our way to the south and dropped anchor near a dozen other sailing boats and yet another set of overwater tourist bungalows. In the bright sunshine, the pure sand bottom coloured the clear water a vivid azure. From the cockpit, we could enjoy one of the best views in the world: the magnificent green peaks of Bora Bora towering to a height of over 700 metres. It was a magical scene, and not even the buzzing jet skis could tarnish our mood at that moment.

The following day, we went ashore to see if the island looked as good up close as it did from a distance. As we walked along the road, moments of tranquillity had to be snatched between bursts of speeding cars. How can people possibly be in a hurry on a tropical island in the South Pacific? There were also far too many tourist haunts for our tastes: bars, restaurants, hotels, and souvenir shops, all vying to attract the holidaying hordes. It was too hard for us to accept this intrusion of the wider world after having experienced the wonder of places it cannot reach.

The coral close to the anchorage was visited by multitudes of tourist boats every day. We ventured there at lunchtime, when the operators took their break, but the coral was mostly dead, and there were hardly any fish.

In January 2002, the entire south barrier reef, eighteen kilometres long and eighty metres wide, was killed by a red tide. Following a period of heavy rain the previous December, the island's sewage system had failed to cope with the amount of wastewater being produced, so the hotels dumped their waste directly into the lagoon. A north wind subsequently lowered the sea level inside the lagoon, and the water temperature rose to 36°C. This encouraged the growth of phytoplankton, creating the red tide, which in turn allowed the zooplankton population to explode. All the oxygen in the water was consumed, and visibility was reduced to zero. Light could barely reach the bottom, and any organism needing oxygen died. As a result, millions of dead fish washed up on the beach.

The red tide was gradually broken up by waves, and a week later the water was completely clear – so clear, in fact, that newly arriving tourists had no idea that anything had happened. But while the corals looked almost normal, live tissue was detaching from the skeletons. Eighty per cent of coral died on some reefs in the area. Bleaching events caused by raised temperatures used to occur once a year in Bora Bora, but now they happen three times a year, making it harder for corals to recover. In May 2003, sixty per cent of corals bleached.

I discovered a healthy coral patch within swimming distance of our boat, one not visited by the tour operators. I spent a long time watching a pipefish, a slender relative of the seahorse that I'd never seen before. Whirring its delicate fins, this small, intriguing creature moved around the coral, seemingly unperturbed by the huge monster looming close by. It was wonderful to be able to observe it without being disturbed by anyone else.

As I swam slowly back to *Stella Maris*, I came across a group of tourists whose foray into the underwater world seemed better suited to an aquarium in Disneyland. They were standing on the seabed, their faces visible through the clear glass of the gigantic rectangular dive helmets they were wearing. Long hoses snaked from the top of their heads up to the surface, feeding oxygen to them from the boat above. They walked along the bottom like scantily clad astronauts in a bad sixties sci-fi, luring nearby fish with food. At one point, four of the 'divers' held hands and started to jump up and down together, twisting in a ring as they hopped. This strange performance was filmed by their guide, a souvenir video bound to be inflicted upon unsuspecting friends back home.

In spite of all those years dreaming of Bora Bora, we

both got itchy feet after just three days. A full moon the next day would make the night watches a lot more enjoyable, something worth taking advantage of.

Our last day was filled with a series of highs and lows. After a trip to the main village to spend the last of our Polynesian Francs, I felt cooped up on *Stella Maris*, so I swam over to some coral heads we'd dinghyed past on the way back. Healthy and varied, they were home to some colourful fish, but it was an encounter with a stingray that really lifted my spirits.

I drifted along with him while he hoovered back and forth across the sand, sucking up shellfish and whatever else he felt inclined to eat, with a trumpet fish hitching a ride on his back. It was just the three of us, none minding the other, and it was wonderful. I was deeply immersed in this experience when in the distance, emerging out of the deeper blue, two creatures came flying towards me.

They were spotted eagle rays, flapping their wings in synchronised slow motion like graceful birds. It was one of the most sublime sights I had ever seen, and I watched, entranced, as they swum past me, side by side.

Then, all of a sudden, the sound of an engine broke the spell. I lifted my head out of the water and saw a motor boat filled with tourists hovering nearby. It must have had a glass bottom, because it was following the rays. I was relieved that the tourists didn't all plunge into the water to snorkel, but the experience was spoilt nonetheless, because I had to make sure I wasn't run over by the boat. It eventually left me alone, but I ended up ruining the experience myself by diving down for a closer look at the eagle rays, which scared them away.

I swam back to *Stella Maris*, euphoric. I wanted Gjalt to return to the water with me, but before we could leave, a Dutch sailor arrived to see him, so I went back in alone. This time I took the camera with me, despite having a premonition about the integrity of the waterproof housing.

In the water, I was reunited with my stingray friend, and later one of the eagle rays appeared, but it flew past me just as a large catamaran was making its way through the anchorage. Yet again, instead of enjoying the sight of the eagle ray, I had to keep my eyes on a boat so as not to be run down.

Once the catamaran had passed, I looked at the ray one

last time, surfacing just as a speedboat raced past me in a blur, little more than six feet away. It was no surprise to find that it was a dive boat. Everywhere we went, those vessels tore through anchorages, flouting the etiquette of not creating a wake. The boat had been going so fast that the driver hadn't seen me until he was almost on top of me. He did at least, turn the boat around and ask if I was all right, but then his French companion proceeded to reprimand me for not towing a dive flag. She accused me of being further than fifty metres from my boat (which I only realised wasn't true after the shock had worn off), and idiot as I was, I practically apologised to them!

The trauma of the near-hit upset me enough, but when I got back to *Stella Maris*, I discovered that the waterproof housing had leaked. Even though only a few drops had found their way inside, it was enough for the camera to die a slow, spasmodic death. So I went from a great high to a devastating low that was compounded by the fact that our backup camera, the camcorder, had died a few weeks earlier in Toau. A disposable camera was all we had left, and we were unlikely to come across a camera shop before we reached Australia.

Sunny Jo and Jason made me feel better when we visited them to say farewell, and then the sight of giant manta rays, their wingspans six feet or more, feeding by the underwater lights of the Bora Bora Hotel, cured me completely. These enigmatic creatures swept through the water in elegant circles as they fed on plankton, their large mouths wide open, their smooth white undersides gleaming in the glow of the lamps. It was the best possible tonic to end an emotional day.

The next morning, I steered *Stella Maris* out of the lagoon I'd brought her into four days earlier, and we sailed away on the deep blue ocean. It was a beautiful day to leave Bora Bora, with ideal wind for sailing. We planned to visit Beveridge Reef, a submerged atoll some 930 miles away, before continuing on to Tonga. Not many cruisers stopped there, and it was rumoured to have pristine coral and vibrant sea life. Conditions would have to be perfect to enter the lagoon, though, as the pass wasn't marked, and without any islands it would be hard to identify. If it didn't look doable or the weather wasn't good, we'd just sail on to Tonga.

When I got up after our first night at sea, the palm trees on the atoll of Maupihaa, part of the Society Island Group, were visible to starboard on the horizon. The sight reminded me of the Tuamotus, and I felt drawn towards it. We hadn't planned to stop at Maupihaa, because the entrance into the lagoon was described in our cruising guide as 'one of the trickiest in French Polynesia'. Having already aged several years going through atoll passes, I'd decided this was excitement I could do without.

But now the gods were conspiring to lure me there. I studied the cruising guide's checklist for safe entry into the lagoon: *Calm seas? Yes; Easterly winds? Yes; Slack tide? Yes.* (The tide tables showed it was two hours away, exactly the time it would take us to get there.) Then there were considerations unique to our situation. A weather system to the west threatened storm force winds just when we expected to arrive at Beveridge Reef, and there was no way we could enter that submerged atoll in such conditions. I realised that Maupihaa might be the last Pacific atoll we'd be able to explore.

I also thought there was a good chance of having it to ourselves. In 1997, Cyclone Martin destroyed every house on the main island and killed eight members of an extended family. Afterwards, all the surviving inhabitants left. And with a difficult pass to deter cruisers, I didn't expect crowds; that was an appealing thought after the busy high islands of the Society Group.

Gjalt was perplexed by my running commentary of the information I gleaned as I studied the cruising guide and tide tables. He was fully geared up for a long passage, and we'd only been at sea one day. Making landfall in a few hours simply did not feature in his thoughts. He couldn't understand why I was investigating Maupihaa in such detail. Me, of all people; the person with a near-morbid fear of atoll passes seemed to be seriously contemplating a transit through one of the trickiest in French Polynesia. I admit it was bizarre, but part of me wanted one final taste of the paradise we'd found in Toau. Another part thought that going through the pass might cure me of my phobia. It wasn't hard to convince Gjalt that all reasoning pointed towards visiting Maupihaa, so on the spur of the moment we changed course for the pass ten miles to the north, and *Stella Maris* raced to get there in her usual enthusiastic style.

Courage being inversely proportional to the distance from the battle, mine began to fade as we got closer to the pass. Then something eerie and upsetting set my head spinning with omens and supernatural warnings.

That morning, I'd woken up from a nightmare about catching a bird on a trolled fishing lure - a bird with the body of a man. Now, as I was scanning the pass with binoculars to look for markers to help guide us into the lagoon, Gjalt noticed something pulling on our fishing line. A seabird was squawking above it, and we assumed it was after the fish we'd caught. But as Gjalt reeled in the line, we saw that we had hooked a bird. There was nothing we could do to save it, and we pulled it onboard, feeling the terrible weight of responsibility for its pointless death. It was so beautiful, with extremely soft, dusky brown feathers and a long, hooked beak. We'd never caught a bird before since they normally knew to steer clear of fishing lures. We assumed it was a juvenile, and on such a remote atoll, trolled lures were surely a little-known hazard.

That my nightmare seemed to have suddenly become a premonition was just too creepy for me, and I was sure it foretold certain doom. The problem was deciphering the message. *Should we not enter the pass? Would our boat be wrecked on the reef if we did? Or should we enter to avoid being wrecked by the storm waiting for us to the west?* None of this irrationality affected Gjalt in any way, and while I laid the bird down on the aft deck, he steered *Stella Maris* towards the pass.

It was arrestingly narrow, a mere sixty feet wide, but at least it was short. The deep water was clearly visible in the bright midday sunshine, as were the hard reef edges due to the low tide. There were no swirling eddies or whirlpools, no short, steep waves. The pass looked completely benign, welcoming even. We couldn't have timed our arrival better. I went to the bow to watch for coral heads and help Gjalt to steer through the deepest part of the channel. On either side, the hard reef edges stopped abruptly and plunged steeply into the water; they were perilously close. At the end of the pass, a white buoy warned of a large coral head and, keeping it to starboard, we entered safely into the sheltered waters of the lagoon.

Gjalt climbed up to his usual position in the spreaders and alerted me to shallow dangers as I steered us across to the long island at the eastern edge of the atoll. The presence of pearl buoys in the lagoon told us that Maupihaa was inhabited after all, and five yachts had got there ahead of us as well. With four of them anchored opposite the few houses in the south, we stayed north.

The atoll was small, just three and a half miles wide and four and a half miles long, with wonderful shelter from the trade winds. We had found paradise lost. We might not have had it completely to ourselves, but it wasn't exactly teeming with people either. There were no speedboats to chop me into mincemeat and no tourist bungalows blighting the landscape. We planned to stay for two or three days and then continue on to Beveridge Reef.

We dinghyed ashore and buried the seabird in the shade of a palm tree. We couldn't find the species in our comprehensive sea life book, which convinced us that the poor thing was indeed a juvenile.

We walked north to the reef flats and looked for shells. I didn't find any, but a blacktip reef shark found me. It was only small, just two feet or so, but it was much more aggressive than any of the sharks we'd encountered so far. Even when I frantically splashed a stick in the water, it continued to circle my ankles, salivating at the prospect of a late afternoon snack. I'd read somewhere that in this type of sticky situation, you should lie down in the water and show Jaws the true magnitude of the meal it was sizing up. The hungry shark would then quickly realise that the tasty-looking ankles were, in fact, merely the puny foundations to a monstrous skyscraper of humanity, and scarper. At that particular moment, though, the advice seemed only certain to win me a Darwin Award 'for ensuring the long-term survival of the human race by removing myself from the gene pool in a sublimely idiotic fashion'.

Gjalt had marched on ahead, so when my stick-thrashing antics failed, I screamed for help and he dutifully rushed back to save me. "Is that it?" he said, peering dismissively at the shark and then at me. He soon discovered for himself how persistent the thing was, though, but with four ankles in the water, it did realise that it was outnumbered and at last swam away.

The next day, we dinghyed to an island south of the pass to see if we could find any trace of wreckage from the

*Seeadler*, a German three-masted schooner that was used to raid allied supply ships during World War I. Having captured and sunk eleven ships in the Atlantic during the first three months of 1917, Count Felix von Luckner, the *Seeadler's* superbly named captain, took the 245-foot schooner around Cape Horn and into the Pacific in search of more. In this vast ocean, his mission became much harder, but by July, he'd captured three American vessels and taken twenty-eight men and one woman captive. After two weeks of vainly searching the shipping lanes for traffic, the ship's doctor reported signs of beriberi onboard. As the *Seeadler's* fouled bottom was in desperate need of scraping, von Luckner agreed to head for an uninhabited atoll. Maupihaa was chosen because of a reported abundance of fish and coconuts.

Too large to navigate the narrow pass into the lagoon, the *Seeadler* anchored outside the entrance, relying on the wind and current to keep her clear of the reef. Just two days later, however, the schooner was wrecked on the coral. Exactly how it happened still remains a mystery.

Von Luckner, a man renowned for telling stories as dramatic as his name, claimed a tidal wave created by an earthquake that followed the eruption of an underwater volcano had swept the ship onto the reef. It certainly out-dazzled the more plausible versions of events, which suggested the grounding was due to a sudden wind shift or the force of the current after the wind had died. If von Luckner did invent the story, his reasons were lost with his ship, but only an act of God could have absolved him of responsibility, and he came up with three!

Taking a crew of five, von Luckner set sail in a thirty-two-foot open lifeboat rigged as a sloop to search for a new ship with which to continue his raids. Incredibly, after sailing more than 2,000 miles, having stopped at two islands in the Cook Group, and aborted landfall at a third to avoid capture, the men reached Fiji. There, von Luckner was bluffed into surrender and became a prisoner of war, but this wasn't a man who gave up easily. A daring escape took him all the way to the Kermadec Islands, northeast of New Zealand, before he was recaptured.

Meanwhile, the fifty-eight German crew members he left on Maupihaa managed to commandeer a French trading ship that stopped at the atoll. Leaving their American prisoners behind, they sailed to Easter Island, where the vessel ran aground on uncharted rocks. The crew were interned by the Chilean authorities until the end of the war.

In a final feat of heroic seamanship, the captain of one of the American ships captured by the *Seeadler* took three men and sailed almost 850 miles in a small lifeboat to reach American Samoa. A French relief ship was then sent to Maupihaa, and the forty-four marooned merchant seamen were rescued from the atoll and taken to Tahiti.

Not surprisingly, we found no sign of the *Seeadler*. Any remnants were probably long gone even before the 1997 cyclone, which would surely have swept the most persistent wreckage away. It did, after all, blow down every house and seventy-five per cent of the coconut palms. As these trees grow to full size in five years, the only evidence of their destruction were the many sunken trunks close to the shore, strewn amongst a lot of coral rubble.

The small islands near the pass were home to thousands upon thousands of nesting seabirds, and we saw many adorable, young frigates and boobies, their fluffy white feathers giving them a rather comical appearance. The fairy terns looked stunning as they soared above us in the cloudless blue sky, their jet-black eyes standing out against bodies of the purest white. We found a single egg balanced on a bare branch, an amazing trick peculiar to terns that offered easy pickings for locals. Well aware of this, the birds became highly agitated whenever we strayed too close to a nest.

On one occasion, a bird that looked identical to the one we'd caught outside the pass flew out of the bushes and swooped low over my head, an act of aerial aggression that I felt sure was motivated by revenge. I fled from it like an actor in *The Birds*. "I think the wildlife here is out to get me," I said to Gjalt, after a subsequent attack by a moray eel on the reef flats.

He just looked at me as if I'd lost my mind.

Later in the day, two welcoming inhabitants of the atoll, Henna and Lionel, stopped their motor boat alongside *Stella Maris* and generously gave us two reef fish and half a dozen small eggs. We suspected the eggs were from the tern colony we'd visited, which made us feel awkward about accepting them, but we didn't want to refuse a gift from our hosts. Besides, we'd bought eggs in the States from chickens that surely had worse lives than the wild Maupihaa terns, so we could hardly claim the moral high ground. The eggs had strikingly orange yokes and slightly translucent whites, but they tasted good, albeit a little fishy.

Henna and Lionel had open, kind faces, and we managed to chat a little to them in French. They told us that people had returned to Maupihaa in 1999, and a population of fourteen now made a living there, growing pearls and producing copra.

By our third day in the atoll, the weather en route to Tonga had deteriorated. If we'd sailed past Maupihaa, we would have faced gale force winds, strong thunderstorms, and, according to the forecasts, no wind at all after the system had dissipated. We heard yachts on the radio reporting ripped sails and damaged equipment. We were grateful that we'd been lured into this special atoll, a final chance enjoy the kind of paradise we'd found in Toau.

On an expedition to the eastern edge of the atoll, we had to push our way through a tangled, overgrown forest of palm trees and stubborn bushes to reach the outer reef. For an atoll that supposedly saw little rain, it had a veritable jungle of thriving flora. With extensive lacerations on our exposed limbs, we emerged onto a narrow, sandy beach that bordered an equally narrow reef. The landscape was very different from Toau, where a wide belt of jagged rock had separated the trees from the beach and expansive reef flats had stretched a long way to the ocean.

The tide was high, and the rock pools were fully submerged, which limited our shelling to the beach. Even so, we had the pleasure of finding many empty cowries, some in good condition. Unfortunately, human garbage was far more plentiful, with plastic bottles, crates, and the odd flip-flop strewn along the shore. Even this far out, the so-called civilised world was leaving its mark.

The bad weather to the west kept us in the atoll for days. We had expected steady trade winds to blow across our Pacific route, but a series of fronts, followed by calms prevented us from setting off on the 800-mile passage to Beveridge Reef.

The first week brought little wind to Maupihaa, keeping the lagoon flat calm and giving us peaceful days and nights. We made several exploration trips ashore, combing the reef for shells and walking along a shady palm tree-lined path that stretched the length of the long eastern island. We passed some padlocked cabins and abandoned shacks along the way to the new community of fourteen people at the southern end of the island. There we met Frankie and his family, who had moved from the island of Maupiti, some twenty-seven miles west of Bora Bora, to manage the pearl farm.

Soon other yachts arrived in the atoll to wait for better weather. One of these was *Illusions*, with our sociable Californian friends Katie and Jeff onboard. They had also hooked a seabird just outside the pass, but luckily theirs lived and was able to fly away.

A burly man with a personality to match, Jeff had a wonderfully sarcastic sense of humour and a boisterous desire to have a good time. Katie was in her late twenties, a few years younger than Jeff but definitely more mature. She was sweet-natured and possibly the most laid-back person we'd ever met; even Jeff's antics couldn't faze her. We told them about the survival skills we'd learnt from Atoll Man, and they were as keen as we were to put our lobster-hunting expertise into practice.

Armed with our kerosene lamp and some torches, we ventured onto the reef just after sunset. My quest wasn't helped by the fact that my torch had a weak beam, but I don't think a stronger one would have increased my enthusiasm. I soon got bored, just as I had in Toau, and even though I carefully watched where I placed my feet, I felt the occasional crunch underfoot. Not wanting to damage the coral, I returned to the beach and lay on the sand, gazing up at the stars.

The stellar band of the Milky Way stretched across the cloudless black sky like a sparkling diamond bracelet. Venus shone as brightly as ever, and seeing the lustrous Southern Cross made me appreciate that we really had sailed our way into the Southern Hemisphere. We rarely stopped to reflect on how far we had come and what a special time in our lives it really was. I watched a satellite moving swiftly in its orbit and witnessed the dying moments of two shooting stars. I was impressed by the unwavering patience of the lobster hunters, but above all, I was glad that their perseverance allowed me to enjoy some welcome solitude beneath a bewitching Pacific night sky.

The lobsters remained safe that night, but a dozen turban shells weren't so lucky. Gjalt had plucked them from the rocks, determined to introduce Katie and Jeff to at least one atoll delicacy that Jean had treated us to. We boiled the snails and served them to our friends, who declared they tasted just like lobster. They were certainly easier to collect.

We prepared *Stella Maris* for departure several days in a row, but on each occasion, the weather reports forecast new lows and cold fronts that would deliver gale force westerly winds along our route to Beveridge Reef. We were getting impatient to move on, but there was no sense heading out into strong headwinds, and it wasn't exactly a trial to be in Maupihaa, where we were mostly blessed with wonderful weather.

When the possibility of strong southwesterly winds arose, we relocated to the south of the island. Had we stayed in the north, those winds would have put us on a lee shore with four miles of fetch. We had been surprised by such winds one night already, and *Stella Maris* had ridden some substantial waves at anchor. We'd stayed up through several ominously dark hours with the anchor alarm on, worrying about dragging and having to re-anchor when there were so many coral heads around us.

The change of scenery helped to scratch our itchy feet. Onshore we met Henna again, as well as Monique, a petite woman who had moved to Maupiti from France, after marrying a French Polynesian soldier when she was young. Like the others, she came to the atoll in 1999, after Cyclone Martin polluted Maupiti's lagoon and made it unsuitable for pearl farming.

The women told us the best place to spearfish, so we set off to try and catch our dinner. For Gjalt, this endeavour involved wedging himself in one of the gullies that cut into the edge of the outer reef. The strategy yielded two groupers, but it cost him a flipper. By the time he noticed that it had been swept away, it was already sinking into the abyss, another piece of detritus to join the estimated 100 million tons of man-made rubbish adrift in the Pacific.

On the dinghy ride back to *Stella Maris*, we stopped to talk to some men on a French Polynesian fishing boat that had just arrived in the lagoon. They looked as wild as the Honduran fishermen we'd met in the Vivarillo Cays. A young man with a fierce look in his eyes explained in very good English that they had been fishing for two weeks. They'd put out longlines baited with sardines and caught marlin, tuna, dorado, and wahoo. They undoubtedly also caught marine life that was of no commercial interest to them, known as 'bycatch', which they'd have simply thrown back into the ocean. Each year, over four million sharks, billfish, marine turtles, seabirds, and marine mammals are estimated to be injured or killed, on longlines in the Pacific.

When we were about to leave, the young man offered us a coconut crab, another creature threatened by man's pitiless insatiability. We turned down the gift, but he persisted with such aggressive insistence that refusal seemed unwise. The poor crustacean was being kept alive on the aft deck for future consumption, suspended from a metal bar on a piece of nylon fishing wire.

Knowing that coconut crabs were an endangered species, we were not about to eat our gift. We took it back to *Stella Maris* and kept it in a bucket on deck, its nylon line tied to the handle. We named it Coco and decided to release it on the island the following day. Its horny carapace was a vividly coloured mix of blue and orange, as were its ferocious-looking pincers. Since it was a fairly large adult crab, it was probably a decade or two old. Being captured had cost it an eye and part of a feeler, but otherwise it was very much alive and kicking, rightly upset by the loss of its liberty – so much so that at two in the morning, Gjalt woke up to find it on its way through the aft cabin hatch and about to drop into the bed. If I'd woken up to find it anywhere near me, I would have freaked out. Aside from the fact that it was quite capable of severing my fingers with its strong claws, in the dark shadows of night it would have looked like a giant spider, not something an arachnophobe would handle well. I suppose it just wanted to find somewhere more comfortable to sleep than the bucket, but the poor thing ended up hanging from the boom instead.

The next morning, we took Coco ashore and released it back into the wild. It certainly seemed very happy about that, and we felt pretty good about it too. Gjalt hacked open a coconut for it to eat, but it was only interested in getting as far into the undergrowth, and as far away from humans, as it could.

At last, after nearly two weeks kept in the atoll by the weather gods, the series of lows that created storms to the west finally plummeted south. A succession of yachts headed for the pass early in the morning. We timed our arrival to coincide with slack tide, and the short trip through the narrow channel went smoothly, which was a great relief, as always.

From inside the lagoon, the ocean had looked flat, but once outside, we immediately felt the Pacific's power, its long period swell unnoticeable behind the protective reef. But it was nothing more than the deep, placid breathing of the ocean, a gentle reintroduction to life at sea. The wind was very light, ideal for the gennaker, and soon *Stella Maris* was moving along at five knots, finally on her way after an unplanned and unforgettable stop of sixteen days.

YACHTS ANCHORED IN OPUNOHU BAY, MOOREA, SOCIETY ISLANDS

# 12.

## Forced to Steer a Different Course

*Fifty-two percent of the world's fisheries are fully exploited and 24 percent are overexploited, depleted, or recovering from depletion.*

*As many as 90 percent of all the ocean's large fish have been fished out.*

*Several important commercial fish populations have declined to the point where their survival is threatened.*

*Unless the current situation improves, stocks of all species currently fished for food are predicted to collapse by 2048.*

– WWF, February 2008

The wind grew stronger as the day wore on, and during the night, frequent squalls forced us to replace the gennaker with the genoa and mainsail. The wind strength was much greater than forecast, and we made tremendous progress that first day. The squalls were accompanied by forbidding dark clouds and sudden downpours, but luckily for me, Gjalt saw more of it on his watch than I did on mine.

I slept incredibly deeply on my second off-watch, and I woke up at 7 o'clock in the morning, feeling as though all my limbs had disconnected from my body. I had to get up just to reassure myself that I was still in one piece. I wasn't sure if this decidedly odd feeling meant the main cabin berth was comfortable or uncomfortable, but in any case, it was a sensation I never experienced when I slept in the aft cabin at anchor.

Later that second day, the wind died down, so the gennaker went back up again, and we kept sailing at a pleasant five knots. We caught our first fish since Tahiti, a three-foot wahoo, and devoured sashimi for lunch and fried fillets for dinner. Our towing generator had started to vibrate so violently that we could no longer use it, and as the solar panels weren't producing enough power to run the fridge, we had to eat the entire fish in one day. By sundown, we had both overdosed on protein.

My first watch of the night was heavenly, the gennaker capturing every breath of wind and allowing *Stella Maris* to glide peacefully over the calm seas. After two weeks in Maupihaa, the full moon we'd enjoyed when we left Bora Bora had become a brilliant smiling crescent, and Venus seemed to fall from it like a diamond tear. The sky was so clear that light from the Milky Way and some of the brightest stars was reflected on the surface of the ocean. I saw so many shooting stars that I ran out of wishes. It was one of the most peaceful watches I'd ever had, but it wasn't to last. The wind gradually died, and when Gjalt came on watch, we were forced to resort to engine power.

In the morning, some wind reached us from the south, and even though it was light, we were able to sail close-hauled, making speeds between five and six knots over the flat seas. Eventually the wind died away, and the engine took over again. It was a gorgeous, cloudless day, and only the swell of the Pacific rocked *Stella Maris* gently from side to side. It was breathtakingly tranquil out there, as far away from man-made troubles as anyone could possibly get.

I became engrossed in *A Voyage for Madmen*, a book about the 1968 Golden Globe race that saw nine competitors set out to become the first man to sail single-handed and non-stop around the world. Now that I was slowly becoming a sailor myself, I could better appreciate their exploits, although sailing was a different game back then, and the adventures of those men was in a completely different league to ours. For a start, they had been alone; in the case of eventual winner, Robin Knox-Johnston, this meant 313 days of solitude. Without GPS, they had to navigate using a sextant, and for the three entrants who made it that far, there was also the might of the Southern Ocean to face. I enjoyed being at sea, but not in conditions that scared the living daylights out of me. And whilst our ocean passages did save our minds from the feverish assault of modern-day media, it was the islands that restored an appreciation of nature that years spent in cities had taken away.

During my night watch, the wind picked up, and we started sailing again. It was always such bliss to turn off the engine and be left with only the sounds of the wind and the waves. When distant lights suddenly pierced this tranquillity, the shock sent me reaching for the binoculars. I saw a red, then a green, and finally a white light, but they were rising so quickly above the dark horizon that a plane seemed a more likely source than a ship. For several unsettling moments, I struggled to think what it could be, until at last it became obvious. It was a star, twinkling in a night sky so devoid of artificial lights that it was brightly visible low on the horizon. The best watches held such wondrous surprises.

By the fourth day, the trade winds finally found us, and with them came the ocean's more familiar liveliness. By sunset, the wind had picked up with a vengeance and blew strongly throughout the night. The ocean became quite wild, and my lethargic senses were shocked back into 'real' sailing. *Stella Maris* was rolled vigorously from side to side, making life onboard exhausting. With two reefs in the genoa and a reefed main, *Stella Maris* settled down to a steady run between seven and eight knots. Her speed had picked up just minutes after we'd calculated that we wouldn't make it to Beveridge Reef during daylight the day after next, if we couldn't maintain a speed of six knots. There was nothing like such a challenge to get her racing.

While Gjalt was on watch that night, he noticed some small vibrations resonating through the boat. His hand, as always resting on a hard surface to detect such things, felt a persistent, almost rhythmic knocking. Having latched onto it, waiting for the next vibration became an unpleasant obsession that ruined his enjoyment of the sailing. He had to find the source.

Thinking it might be the autopilot, he removed the bedding and mattress from the aft cabin to examine the arm on the rudder quadrant. There was nothing wrong with the autopilot, but he could see that some minor wear in the nylon rudder bush was causing the heavy steel rudder to jolt every time the ocean swell rocked *Stella Maris*. He wasn't sure how much damage it might lead to, but in his worst imaginings, he saw a hole bashed into the stern by an irreparably loose rudder.

We discussed our options and decided prudence had to override everything else. We would sail straight to Tonga, still some 500 miles away, and see if we could replace the worn bush there. In hindsight, we probably overreacted, but when the image of a sinking boat enters your mind in the middle of an ocean, it's hard to push out again.

In any case, I had been mentally steering myself away from Beveridge Reef. As I mentioned earlier, courage is inversely proportional to the distance from the battle, and every day we got closer to the submerged atoll, mine grew a little weaker. We only had a GPS position for the pass, and without any surface landmarks, we'd need to use the radar to help locate it. The recent turbulent weather had done nothing to encourage me to enter an atoll for which we had no chart. Gjalt was disappointed at having to sail past such a unique and remote place, but his priority was to get *Stella Maris* and us safely to land.

At sunset the following day, we sighted another yacht on the horizon. Out in the vast Pacific, we marvelled that the paths of two small sailing boats had intersected. It was *Tin Can*, a yacht we'd seen for the first time all the way back in the Marquesas. The crew had left Palmerston atoll and were on their way to Beveridge Reef. It made us ponder our decision to sail straight to Tonga, but we didn't change our minds.

The captain of *Tin Can* was a boat builder and gave us some good advice about the rudder. Out in the middle of a great liquid nowhere, another sailor had helped us, and that felt incredibly comforting. They headed southwest while we continued west and a strange sadness came over me as I lost their navigation lights to the horizon.

By now, we were so far south that we had to dig out our foul-weather gear to prevent hypothermia on night watch. It seemed like another good reason not to head any further south to Beveridge Reef.

The moon joined me on watch and rose like a bright smile high into the night sky. Then a visitor arrived in the cockpit, fatally out of its element. I heard frantic flapping, and seconds later, the unmistakable stench of flying fish hit my nose. The unfortunate creature was floundering in a suffocating world of hard, unforgiving surfaces it hadn't even known existed before that moment. And as if that wasn't traumatic enough, a giant fleshy hand then scooped it up and hurled it back into the ocean. I guess it was the flying fish equivalent of being abducted by aliens; none of his friends were going to believe *that* fishy tale.

The flying fish wasn't the only one to suffer that night. I stupidly put my thumb between the door and frame of the forward head, and it took no time at all for the Pacific swell to make painful sandwich meat of it. I screamed louder and more blood-curdlingly than a victim in a horror film and was left with a throbbing thumb and a nail that rapidly turned a bluish black. I managed not to cry, but did suffer an attack of the vapours when I tried to type an e-mail. I felt so faint that I had to lie down immediately to stop the world from clouding over.

"I won't need to amputate above the elbow," Gjalt said, examining the thumb.

The next day, the wind eased, taking the anger out of the ocean and the menace from the skies. The calmer conditions encouraged us to fish again, but the result was a case of the one that got away. And we heard from our friends on *Reverie* that both they and *Tin Can* had made it safely into Beveridge Reef. Without any islands, they experienced the strange sensation of being anchored in the middle of the Pacific.

The wind petered out during the night, and I woke up early on the seventh morning of our passage to find us alongside Niue. It was quite a sight. The long, flat, two-tiered island seemed to hover above the surface of the ocean, like an enormous flying saucer about to land. I gazed at it through the binoculars and wondered if we were right to sail past a country few people had even heard of. It was just the kind of destination we loved: sufficiently remote to deter tourists and very few inhabitants. It was marked on our chart as Savage Island, a strangely appealing name dating from Captain Cook's 1774 encounter with unwelcoming locals, who refused him permission to land.

Our rudder concerns would have won a battle against our exploration desires, but then the weather gods intervened and sucked the final puffs of breeze from the air. We downloaded the forecast, which duly declared that it was set to stay windless for the next four days. So we had a choice: motor the remaining 200 miles, or stop at a unique island that we might never get another chance to see. The decision was easy. We turned north to Alofi Bay, the island's only anchorage, and after receiving a warm welcome on the radio from the authorities, we cheerfully tied up to a mooring buoy.

SAILING TOWARDS THE SUNSET IN THE PACIFIC OCEAN

# 13.

# Swimming with Whales

*The industrial fishing methods used by the foreign fleets are highly effective at stripping fish from our ocean. For example, a modern super-seiner can take up to 11,000 tons of fish per season. In comparison, a fleet of small aluminium boats and outrigger canoes in Niue caught an estimated 100 tons of the main tuna species for the whole of 2003 – a super-seiner would catch this much fish in just two days.*

- Greenpeace Australia Pacific, *Stolen Fish, Stolen Future*, 2007

After a week at sea, with no contrast to the blues of the ocean and sky, the sight of the trees clinging to the jagged black cliffs of Niue hit us between the eyes like a hefty green punch. The smells of plants and burning wood fires shocked our noses out of their apathy. Our senses had been heightened by their retreat from land and were almost overwhelmed by these new experiences.

Alofi Bay was a gentle scoop out of the middle of the island's west coast. With no significant headland to protect it from the ocean, the swell rolled in almost unhindered, making it a very rolly anchorage, even in fair conditions. When we arrived, the absence of wind significantly reduced the swell, and *Stella Maris* sat remarkably steady behind her mooring. Niue plummeted into the ocean, so even though we were close to shore, there was 100 feet of water below us. And yet it was so crystal clear that we could see corals on the seabed. Gjalt spotted whales beyond the bay, and we watched them as the sun went down, landfall drinks in hand.

Early the next day, I cleaned *Stella Maris* thoroughly in preparation for a sanitation inspection that never happened. Gjalt picked up the police and Customs officers in our dinghy and brought them back to the boat. This made the paperwork easy, but the officials were enormous Polynesians, and I eyed their big boots nervously as they thundered aboard. With their feet safely planted on the cockpit floor, my next concern was for our table, which the robust Customs officer decided to destruction test by leaning on it with all his might. For several minutes, I considered how best to tell a man capable of giving Mike Tyson a run for his money that his weight might be a tad too much for our table. Finally, when I was sure it was about to break, I asked him – as tactfully as I could – to show mercy. He took it well, but I still tried to get back into his good books by asking him how to say 'hello' in Niuean. Later, I tried it out on the quarantine officer. "*Fakaalofa atu,*" I said, proudly.

"Are you swearing at me?" he barked. He scowled just long enough for me to open my mouth to apologise and then burst out laughing.

Once all the forms were filled in, signed, and stamped, we were free to go ashore. As the bay was exposed to the ocean, our dinghy couldn't be left in the water, so we hoisted it on land with the wharf's large crane. This was our first taste of how different this island was from others we'd visited. It even had a Tourist Information Office, and there we discovered how much there was to do on Niue. If the wind hadn't died at exactly the right moment, we'd have missed it all.

About 10 miles long and with a central plateau just 200 feet high, Niue is one of the largest emerged coral islands in the world and is peppered with limestone chasms and caves. A terraced limestone reef rings most of the island, protecting its sheer cliffs from the ocean, and living coral abounds in the unpolluted waters. Without any rivers or streams, rain flows out to sea free of sediment, leaving visibility around the coast incredibly clear.

Since it was a self-governing nation in free association with New Zealand, with historical links to Great Britain, everyone spoke English as well as Niuean. The atmosphere was relaxed, and the people were so friendly and welcoming that we felt at home right away.

Katie and Jeff from *Illusions* arrived that day, and we met up in one of the cafés in town. We'd said goodbye to them in Maupihaa, and it felt strangely emotional to be reunited a week later, having each sailed across 930 miles of open ocean to reach the next speck of land in the Pacific.

Walking along the main road out of town, we appreciated the complete absence of traffic. A pleasant jungle of tropical plants grew on either side of it, but to my horror, spiders the size of small mammals hung in enormous cobwebs between the trees. I had to summon up the courage to walk beneath each of these sticky traps, as it didn't look beyond the spiders to drop down on a silk thread, inject an innocent passer-by with poison, and yank them back up to the web to be cocooned and consumed at leisure. Why does nature always find some way of tarnishing paradise?

Back in town, we went in search of the supermarket, where we intended to purchase such essentials as Coca-Cola, crisps, onions, and baked beans, the latter having been the subject of many a fantasy on the passage. Most things were much cheaper than they'd been in French Polynesia, so we could finally afford to live a little. We asked two men for directions, and it turned out that Sri Lankans Rio and Hershel were from the supply ship *Pacific Express*, which was off-loading cargo in the harbour. I asked them a few questions, trying to impress them with a smattering of rig parlance, which must have worked, because we were invited to dinner onboard the ship that evening.

We arrived at six thirty as instructed, and Rio, the first mate, and his compatriot, Leki, one of the engineers, were waiting for us up on the enormous ship's dizzyingly high deck. We tied our tiny dinghy to the ladder dangling over the side, a highly mobile rope and wood affair that didn't encourage any lingering stops to admire the view as we clambered up it. We were taken to the galley, where we met Hershel again and Captain Aseri, a confident 31-year-old Fijian, who made quite an impression, not least because of his imposing 130-kilo physique.

We spent the evening being wined and dined in style. A heap of delicious dorado sashimi was followed by an assortment of main courses: chicken curry, tuna curry, chicken drumsticks, and chips. The chef was from Sri Lanka and certainly knew what he was doing. I think the crew thought we were starving, because they hardly ate anything while we gorged ourselves, rather shamelessly I must admit. It was only because I felt obliged to finally demonstrate a modicum of politeness that I turned down a third bowl of raspberry ripple ice cream (something else my taste buds had salivated for at sea).

While we ate, Captain Aseri entertained us with stories about Fiji and his family. One of his ancestors had been nine feet tall, he said, his eyes telling us he was serious. His brother had killed him with a spear made from coral, which was still lying on his chest when the grave was excavated. He talked about the Indians who'd been taken to Fiji to work in the sugar plantations and insisted they would never be able to own land there because that would be 'like poking a Fijian in the eyeball'.

There were only nine men onboard this 280-foot ship, the kind of monster we kept a very good lookout for at sea. It round-tripped between Auckland, Raratonga, Aitutaki, and Niue every three weeks, bringing subsidised supplies courtesy of New Zealand, part of an annual aid package of five million dollars.

After dinner, Hershel and Leki gave us a tour of the highly maintained engine room and the crew's cabins before handing over to Captain Aseri and Rio, who showed us around the bridge. With the ship's watertight doors, the smell of grease, and the overwhelming size and power of all the machinery, I could have been back on an oil rig. I felt quite at home.

At the end of the evening, Captain Aseri handed us an extra-strong garbage bag full of tinned food. They obviously thought we were in desperate need of it after our greedy display at dinner. It was like getting a large sack of presents from Father Christmas, and we accepted it gratefully. We invited them all on a tour around our more humble vessel, but in the end, only Captain Aseri accepted our invitation. Given the capacity of our small dinghy, that was just as well, because it barely stayed afloat for the short trip across the harbour with three of us in it. We were sure the crew realised that any more passengers would have sunk the boat.

The tour of *Stella Maris* was a tad shorter than that of the *Pacific Express*, but I think Captain Aseri was as interested in our boat as we'd been in his. He couldn't imagine sailing across the Pacific in such a small yacht (and I couldn't imagine being the captain of a ship the size of the *Pacific Express*, which he actually considered quite modest). Gjalt explained our rudder problem, and Captain Aseri told us he had lost rudders from two ships he'd captained, including the *Pacific Express*. In her case, the bolts had sheared, and the rudder had just dropped off; he used his bow thrusters to steer until a tug arrived to assist. He'd had the same first mate on both occasions, so the pair had become known as the 'rudder-f**kers'. A new rudder for the *Pacific Express* had cost 165,000 dollars; we were banking on a significantly lower sum to repair ours.

Throughout our second day onshore, we had blue skies and sunshine, perfect weather to rent a motorbike and explore the island. First we had to get a Niue driving license, which entailed parting with 10 New Zealand dollars and filling out a few more forms at the police station. With that done, Gjalt was legally permitted to whiz us around the island's entire 225-kilometre road network on a nifty 125cc Suzuki bike.

We headed north along the west coast, stopping first at Avaiki which, like every other place we would visit on Niue, we had all to ourselves. Pools of intensely blue, clear water were liberally scattered across the reef flats, giving the coastline a magical, slightly surreal quality. As it was low tide, exposed pathways of dead reef rock snaked around these oases of life, allowing us to admire them up close without causing any damage. Each was home to colourful schools of small fish and healthy coral.

The ocean was so calm that we ventured over the outer edge of the reef to see what treasures clung to the side of the island. Although there were quite a few fish, the coral was not as dramatic as I'd expected, but I soon got all the drama I needed when I came face to face with one of Niue's famous inhabitants: a black and white striped sea snake that writhed past me up to the surface, took a breath, and then writhed back down again. There was always some kind of aquatic creature lurking in the water to jangle my nerves, and this one had venom poisonous enough to kill ten horses. Now, I had read that the snake's tiny fangs were too far back in its mouth to even bite me, let alone inject me with venom, but being within striking distance of the creature and not safely on the boat did make this fact seem altogether less convincing. Therefore, I decided to put some distance between me and his fangs and made a beeline for the reef.

Further up the west coast, we stopped at Limu, where a scenic path led to the coast and a pool in the reef large enough to swim in. The sun turned the water an inviting shade of aquamarine, and we hung up our clothes on natural, ancient coral hooks and slipped into the pool.

Fresh water and seawater mixed together, distorting our underwater vision like hot air rising from a desert road. The sensation was weird, as if we were swimming in gooey ectoplasm. There were many fish in the pool, colourful patches that rippled around us, the blurred outlines of their bodies melting into the water. When we swam through the pool's famed coral arch, it was like entering the spectacular drowned city of a fairytale. The separate layers of fresh water and seawater created wispy clouds that drifted at different depths in a liquid blue sky. The bright sunshine burst to the bottom, seeking out every rock, coral, and fish, the shadows highlighting the magical scenery caught in the light. It was truly enchanting.

Afterwards we hit the road again, and as we whizzed around the island, we discovered more graves than people. They were scattered everywhere, some next to houses, others at the side of the road. The dead were buried on family land and not in a communal cemetery. The graves added to the impression that the island had been abandoned, as we passed untold numbers of deserted houses in largely deserted villages. Niue was like a ghost island full of ghost towns.

Some of the houses had been damaged by Category Five Cyclone Heta, which tore into Niue in January 2004. The waves had been so high that they climbed the cliffs and stretched up to 200 metres inland. Luckily, only two people lost their lives, but the coral, vegetation, and many houses were destroyed. During the one and a half years since the cyclone struck, the coral and vegetation revived, but many of the islanders had moved to New Zealand. They left behind their ruined houses, which helped give the island its end-of-the-world atmosphere. But the roads were maintained, gardens were well tended, and there wasn't a scrap of litter to be seen. Not for the first time on our trip, we thought we'd found somewhere we could live, but having been turned into gypsies by the oil industry, it was hard to see us ever settling anywhere.

In the evening, we indulged in hamburgers on the terrace of a sea view café called the Crazy Uga (Crazy Coconut Crab) and unexpectedly rubbed shoulders with Niue's high society. A smartly dressed local man wearing an elaborate necklace swaggered in, clearly under the influence. He was looking for a policeman to drive him home when, as luck would have it, the chief of police himself arrived with his wife. Like us, they hadn't been able to resist the lure of Burger Night.

"You told me I should call in at the police station whenever I needed a lift, but there was no one there," the man complained.

"Well, I'd be happy to drive you home myself, Prime Minister," replied the utterly sober chief of police and duly escorted the premier to his car.

Freshly flown in from New Zealand just two months earlier, the chief of police had brought with him notions of 'policies and strategies', words that brought back the horror of modern corporate life to us. Of course, eradicating drink-driving was a good thing, but when we saw police stopping traffic in town to check people's licenses, it did seem overly zealous for a remote island with only 1,700 inhabitants. This was the official population of Niue, but the real number seemed closer to 170 to us. We hardly passed any cars when we rode around the island, and even at the few houses that did show signs of habitation, we rarely spotted a living, breathing human being. Other estimates of the population at the time were between 1,000 and 1,200, but even those seemed too high. Niueans have been steadily migrating to New Zealand for decades, and the remaining population had become small enough to threaten the nation's very viability. With global warming expected to result in more frequent and more intense cyclones, the last inhabitants may eventually be forced to leave.

Our third day in Niue got off to the best possible start with the arrival of two humpback whales in the bay, a mother and her calf. We instantly abandoned our coffee and jumped into the dinghy, and while Gjalt took us close to the whales, I pulled on my wetsuit. He and an Australian cruiser were the first in the water, but I decided to wait and see if joining them was a sensible thing to do. When it was clear that they weren't going to be eaten or flippered into the air, I couldn't wait in the dinghy like a coward any longer.

I slipped into the water and immediately saw a pale grey whale swimming away from me, its fluke going up and down, effortlessly propelling it forward. It stopped beside an enormous black rock, the existence of which confused me as I hadn't worried about it when we'd arrived in the bay, and I'm nothing if not wary of treacherous rocks. As I drifted a little closer, I suddenly realised that it was not an enormous boulder at all, but an enormous creature. The pale grey whale I thought was the mother was merely the baby; the gigantic black mass looming ahead of me was the mother. The instant this penny dropped, I stopped dead in my tracks; in fact, I started to back-pedal, frantically sculling my hands to retreat. Junior was plenty big enough to impress me, but the sight of his mother just blew me away. She was absolutely, phenomenally huge; I hadn't even seen an animal that big before, let alone attempted to share its personal space.

I observed the whales for a while, and seeing that they weren't upset by the presence of the snorkellers, I dared to swim closer. I was amazed at how the mother just hung in the water, suspended almost vertically with her eyes closed, dozing. Little Junior nuzzled up to her like any baby to its mother, and she caressed him with her flipper when he swam underneath her. Her flipper was at least as long as Gjalt was tall (he didn't hesitate to get close enough for this comparison to be possible). With one flick, she could have catapulted him clean out of the water.

Junior was an inquisitive little chap, and every now and then, he'd leave his mother's side to take a closer look at the strange creatures floating around him. First he swam towards Gjalt, who wasn't the least bit afraid, and then he set his sights on me, who was. Well, most baby animals are rather small, but this baby was big, at least fifteen feet long with an equally formidable girth, and I was well aware that his protective mum – four times his length and a hefty forty tons – was keeping her eye on me. I'd been in trouble with a mother from the animal kingdom once before, and I didn't want to be in trouble with one again, especially this one.

It happened on holiday in Zimbabwe, when I couldn't resist the urge to stroke some adorable baby warthogs that had wandered up to our tent. Their mum, taking offence at this intimacy, made her feelings about it quite clear. Years later, I still have to suffer through Gjalt's frequent recollections of how I was chased by a small warthog through a campsite full of amused people. In truth, the beast was monstrous, with horrifying tusks capable of inflicting fatal wounds. And for the record, I did not *run*; I merely took a few sedate steps backwards.

Anyway, the experience left me in no doubt that mothers don't appreciate people interfering with their offspring, and I was profoundly mindful of this as Junior approached me. I was holding onto our dinghy, and when it became obvious that he had every intention of nosing up to me, I quickly scooted behind it. From my hiding place, I could see all the strange lumps and bumps on his head, and it was a long time before his eye appeared, much further back than I expected, close to his flipper. It was the most wonderful and moving experience to see him actually looking at me as he swam past, not more than three feet away. Even so, his proximity made me retreat further behind the dinghy, and suddenly he flicked his fluke and dived down. In the corner of my eye, I saw his mother swooping beneath me to reach him, but thankfully she didn't blame me for the encounter. Reunited, the two of them nuzzled each other contentedly.

We swam with them for at least an hour, and when Junior came up to me again and looked me over for a second time with his inquisitive eye, I was more relaxed. Gjalt swam much closer to the mother than I would ever dare, and it was an amazing sight to see how tiny he was next to her. His body was shorter than the length of her head, and I estimated her size at fifty to sixty feet by seeing how many Gjalts would stretch from nose to fluke. When he dived down to see the whales underwater, they rolled together in a graceful ballet, displaying their white, grooved bellies before swimming away. Every movement was effortless, and they patiently allowed us to spend time with them, letting us share their world. This magical experience wasn't just a highlight of our trip, but of our lives.

The only dampener came when a claim was made by an unnamed person onshore that someone had tried to ride the whale. Well, no one in their right mind would do that (humpbacks may be gentle giants, but they *are* giants), and no one in the water with us was anything but respectful to the whales, so we were all upset by the accusation. The alleged perpetrator had supposedly been in the water just after sunrise, over an hour before we got there, but the more people we spoke to, the more ludicrous the stories became. One local woman had heard that the infamous whale rider had, presumably at the height of his escapade, leapt from the mother across to Junior. Even James Bond would have had difficulty pulling off such a stunt.

We began to wonder if local politics were involved, if someone was simply stirring up trouble for their own ends. All kinds of pernicious concoctions can be brewed in small communities. In the best case, we could say that at least the locals cared about the whales, which are sacred to the Niuean people. If only we humans could make up for the merciless slaughter of the past, when we hunted these magnificent creatures to the brink of extinction; the privilege of swimming with them in their natural environment made mankind's crimes against them all the more upsetting.

We rode our zippy Suzuki to Vaikona on the east coast of the island and followed a rambling path to reach a cave deep within the forest. Long tree roots crawled over giant lumps of ancient volcanic rock, and enormous cobwebs spun by monstrous, hairy spiders (there were far too many of these on Niue for comfort) quivered between branches. We climbed over fallen trees, scrambled up hills and slipped down again, and somewhere along the trail, we met a local guide and two tourists on their way back from the cave. The tourists were men, but they acted like mildly hysterical schoolgirls as they described the treacherous descent into the cave, one they assured us we wouldn't survive if we attempted it alone. "You have to crawl along an edge with a sheer drop," one of them said. "If you slip, you'll be killed."

"Then you have to climb down a vertical rock face on a rope," his friend continued. "If you fall and break a leg, you'll never be able to get back up."

Kitted out in sturdy mountain boots, they stared disapprovingly at our feet, naked beneath the straps of our sandals. Unbeknownst to them, though, these were no ordinary sandals but Tevas, which were worth their weight in gold. They had thick rubber soles with the tread of off-road car tyres and had already taken us across jagged volcanic landscapes, up steep, slippery hills, and across miles of sharp reef rock. But the tourists looked at them now as if the Grim Reaper himself had put them on our feet. Thankfully, their Niuean guide seemed less concerned and even lent us his underwater torch, which he said we'd need in the cave. We reasoned that he wouldn't have given it to us if he didn't think he'd get it back, but maybe he just thought he could pick it up from beside our skeletons the next time he went.

We carried on through the forest, and after taking a wrong turn to the coast, which was all steep cliffs, red reef flats, and pounding waves, we eventually found the cave. I waited by the entrance while Gjalt went inside to scout out the route. After nearly an hour of searching, he still hadn't found the rope we needed to climb down. By this time, I was all for aborting the mission, but Gjalt persuaded me to follow him in for one last look.

At last he spotted the rope and edged deeper into the cave. I crawled after him, moving carefully along the ridge of the smooth, sloping rock so as not to plummet into the pitch-black gorge below. I put my faith in my Tevas, and they didn't let me down.

We reached the rope and peered over the edge to see it dangling fifteen to twenty feet down a vertical drop. The appeal of going further into the cave was stronger than my fear of falling, because it was so enticing. Far from being a dark and forbidding cavern, daylight streamed in through a hole in the ceiling, lighting up this secret underground world. Tropical plants had taken hold on the surrounding walls, and luxuriant green leaves trailed over the barren rock. Beyond a group of huge boulders was a clear blue pool. We could have been inside a giant terrarium.

Gjalt climbed down first, testing the strength of the thick nylon rope and finding the easiest way to the bottom. Then I eased myself over the edge, placing my feet on the first ledge and gripping the rope so tightly that my knuckles turned white. I took my time to find the best places for my Tevas to glue me to the rock, mindful that if they slipped, I would end up hanging from the rope. I interjected a little melodrama to the descent, complaining about lack of foot-holds, sheer drops, and imminent death, but it wasn't really that hard, and before long, I was standing beside Gjalt. The wimpy tourists had overplayed the technical difficulties a bit, but if we had fallen, it would have been quite a chal-lenge to climb out dangling a broken leg and pretty much impossible with a broken arm.

Safely on solid rock, we clambered over the enormous boulders to reach the pool. It was like liquid aquamarine, its clarity made brilliant by the afternoon sun beaming through the hole above.

Gjalt plunged into the icy-cool water, while I eased myself in gently. I took a single stroke and came face to face with a small black fish. We hung there staring at each other, an aquatic Mexican stand-off. He was admittedly somewhat braver than me, given that I was roughly a hundred times bigger than him. Suddenly I was the whale, but this little fellow made no cowardly attempt to hide from me.

Gjalt and I swam to the end of the pool and reached the point where the underwater torch came in handy. We dived down and swam through an arch that led to an adjoining cave. Without a hole to let in light, this one was pitch dark. We climbed out onto some rocks, but soon claustrophobia and cold encouraged me to return to the giant terrarium. Finding our way out of the cave was easier than finding our way in, and not for the first time in my life, I had to admit that Gjalt had been right to persevere. We'd been on an adventure into the exotic heart of Niue, and it would have been a real shame to miss it.

That evening, we went back to the Crazy Uga, where we met its owner, Willie, a home-grown Niue entrepreneur. He'd made a success of his café by locating it atop a cliff with a fantastic view of the ocean and catering to people's fundamental desires (i.e. burgers and beer). He was hoping to show other Niueans that they didn't need to rely on New Zealand aid. "You should visit Joseph," he said after we'd been chatting for a while. "He grows the best vegetables on the island and loves showing people around his garden."

Joseph, as it turned out, lived right next to the golf course – in Niue's prison.

So the next day we turned down a track off the main road and parked our Suzuki near a building that looked more like a large shed than a prison. There was no barbed wire – not even a fence – but then, if the prisoners did try to escape, there was really nowhere for them to go. The closest land was Tonga, 230 miles away. The locals called Niue 'The Rock', but apart from being surrounded by water, this prison and Alcatraz had nothing obvious in common. Clint

Eastwood wouldn't have needed to go to all the trouble of fashioning a papier-mâché replica of himself to sneak out of this jail, but he would have faced one hell of a swim.

We approached a man sitting on a doorstep, intent on repairing a lawnmower. He was barefoot and bare-chested, his shorts were somewhat tattered, and his dishevelled hair reached down to his shoulders. Perhaps it was the lawn-mower that made us ask him if he was Joseph, or perhaps we just didn't expect anyone else to be there.

"I'm the warden," the man replied blithely. Ordinarily, this faux pas would have made for a very bad start, but he didn't seem to take offence. "Joseph's over there," he said, pointing to the shed.

It was open to the elements at either end, and inside a man sat at a table, writing letters. We walked over and introduced ourselves, mentioning Willie to explain our uninvited presence. Joseph greeted us with a polite hand-shake, a smile, and eyes that seemed too warm for violence. He was sixty-two but proud of looking a lot younger; there wasn't a single grey hair on his head, despite his loss of liberty. He invited us to follow him to an open plot of land behind the prison, where he had nurtured an impressive garden. As he showed us around, he began to relax and enjoy having company. He explained that since the island's soil was so poor, he made his own compost, and he was writing a book to help Niue's housewives grow better vege-tables. His garden was a treasure trove of lettuces, toma-toes, cucumbers, cabbages, spring onions, garlic chives, and a variety of other herbs. He selected vegetables that were ripe for the picking and filled a plastic bag with them for us to take along. They looked wonderful and tasted even better, the best we'd had on our trip.

Afterwards we sat down at the table beside Joseph's cell and listened to his story. He had been a chef in the merchant marine for thirty years and travelled the world, even living in Liverpool and Motherwell for a while. Follow-ing his career, he returned to Niue and became the warden of the very prison in which he was now incarcerated. A New Zealander living on the island had been convicted of rape, but instead of being sent to New Zealand to serve his nine-year sentence, he'd been jailed on Niue. Sitting inside the prison, we could see that it amounted to little more than a stable in which the stalls had been converted to cells;

hardly maximum security.

The convict was a bully and made a sport out of stirring up trouble, antagonising Joseph at every opportunity. Finally, one and a half years after being thrown together, they got into a violent fight that ended when Joseph shot the prisoner dead. He argued that he had fired in self-defence, but he was found guilty of manslaughter because he'd shot the prisoner in the back. He was sentenced to eleven years in his own prison and with seven years still to serve, continued working on his appeal.

Joseph spoke eloquently and with confidence, sure of himself and his opinions. He told us that he was happy, although he understandably longed for his freedom. It was clear that he was making the best of the situation and wasn't sitting around feeling sorry for himself. He was able to visit his family's plantation every now and then, and some mornings he sneaked to the golf course, but his fishing trips had been stopped after an islander reported him. It sounded just like an open prison for white-collar criminals, right down to the golf course.

He showed us his cell, which had shelves crammed with books and magazines, a music system, a TV complete with video, and a small statue of Buddha. I wished we'd brought something to give him and felt a little sad as we rode away. It seems strange to admit, but meeting Joseph was another highlight of our visit to Niue.

A fterwards, we drove to Togo on the southeast coast to find another of the island's hidden wonders. The hike through the overgrown forest was all Indiana Jones, a winding path beneath a dark canopy that promised to lead us to long-lost treasure. We emerged at the coast, a dramatic black moonscape of towering, jagged coral pinnacles that stretched the length of the barren shoreline. A path had been cut through the jumble of rocks, and, free of the enclosing forest, we walked in the afternoon sunshine towards the ocean. The path came to an abrupt end at the top of a sheer vertical wall that formed the end of a chasm some sixty feet deep. Inside this harsh, black fissure, scattered palm trees rose up to the sky from a bed of fine golden sand. It seemed improbable, but there was a slice of Arabian desert in that crack in Niue's coastline.

A strangely oversized wooden ladder invited us to climb

down, and its widely spaced rungs made us feel too small, as if we were entering a giant's lair. We walked around on the soft sand that was hemmed in by sheer rock walls, the still air muffling all sound, creating a magical atmosphere. As the chasm stretched towards the ocean, it grew narrower, and a huge pile of massive, jumbled boulders seemed to protect a secret that lay beyond the open sandy space. We clambered onto them, each of us finding our own route over the top, wanting to discover what that secret was. We dropped down onto a soft carpet of moss that lined the base of a dark, damp gorge. Before us lay a vivid green pool, guarded by palm trees. It was as if we'd stepped into a painting by Salvador Dali, mysterious and surreal.

Niue must have been one of the last places on Earth untainted by tourism; in 2005, less than 1,300 people went there on holiday. It was an island where we could swim with whales, motorbike safely on empty roads, and discover exotic freshwater pools hidden in caves and chasms; all without having to share it with another soul. Providence must have made the wind die when we sailed alongside this enchanting island. In every sense, Niue really was far out.

GJALT SAILING AWAY FROM NIUE

GJALT WORKS ON DECK IN LIGHT WINDS: THE GENNAKER IS TO
LEEWARD AND THE GENOA IS POLED TO WINDWARD

# 14.

# *Strikes and Gutters*

*Since 1977, El Niño events have become more frequent,*
*which may be attributed to climate change. Each El*
*Niño event has resulted in water shortages and drought*
*in the Pacific Islands. For Tuvalu, Tonga, Samoa, Cook*
*Islands and French Polynesia, there is an increased*
*risk of tropical cyclones associated with El Niño events.*

– www.SeaWeb.org, March 2005

We left Niue after five days. The swell in the bay had increased considerably since we arrived, and *Stella Maris* had begun to roll badly, making life onboard less comfortable in the anchorage than it would be at sea. More importantly, a cold front was heading to the island, bringing west winds with it. These would blow unhindered into exposed Alofi Bay, kicking up waves and putting all moored boats on an extremely dangerous lee shore. Some cruisers chose to stay, but conditions were so bad that one yacht's concrete mooring actually shifted on the seabed and a local fishing boat ended up on the reef after its mooring line broke. That was not the kind of excitement we enjoyed.

We set sail in bright sunshine and got off to a fast start on our passage to Tonga. Being at sea again made me feel tired, so I went down below to sleep, but I was soon woken up by strong gale force winds and heavy rain when we passed through a squall. Gjalt said I could stay in bed while he brought in the sails, and I wasn't about to argue. I saw a big smile on his face as he revelled in the challenge presented by the adverse conditions. *Stella Maris* was utterly cosy down below and easily took such weather in her stride, so I felt very comfortable and safe. I didn't appear topsides until we emerged from the squall, when strong northwesterly winds meant we had to sail close-hauled. We wrapped up against the sudden cold in our foul-weather gear and, with reefed sails, progressed between six and seven knots throughout the night.

The following morning, the wind turned westerly as forecast, and because we were heading due west, we had to motor into it for a day. We were glad we'd left early enough to be able to sail half the 250-mile passage. The weather steadily improved as the day wore on; the sun reappeared and the seas flattened out, so going against the wind was altogether bearable.

During our second night at sea, we crossed the International Date Line, and Sunday evaporated into the ether, taking a day of our lives with it. Suddenly we leapt ahead of our family and friends at home, after months of lagging further and further behind the more distance we covered. The imaginary line swerved quite significantly to the east of 180 degrees, preventing the people of Tonga and Fiji from existing at the same moment in different days of the week. We also crossed the Tonga Trench, a submarine valley that stretches roughly north to south for almost 750 miles and has an average depth of 19,500 feet, plunging to 35,702 feet at its deepest point. It was a very long way down.

On the third morning of the passage, Gjalt woke me up to say he thought he could see land. I climbed into the cockpit bleary-eyed, expecting to see a hazy smudge on the distant horizon, but instead I received a kind of visual electric shock when I saw the high, chalky cliffs of Vava'u right alongside us. The unfortunate after-effect of that jolt to my senses was an irrepressible urge to sing *The White Cliffs of Dover* with gusto. Luckily for Gjalt, I only knew the song's two famous lines, but it was still enough to scare away the humpback whales he'd seen before I opened my mouth.

Sailing into the Vava'u Group of islands, the most northern of the three groups that make up Tonga, was an absolute joy. It was completely different from everywhere else we'd been, with scores of coral limestone islands, all vibrantly green, nestled close to one another and separated by gloriously deep channels. There were hardly any reefs for me to worry about bumping into. It felt as if we'd sailed into a system of lakes somewhere far inland; the water was so flat calm that it seemed impossible that we were still in the middle of the Pacific.

We reached the anchorage beside the town of Neiafu, where we were required to tie up at the wharf to check in. The wharf didn't appeal to me at all. It was a high concrete construction with massive, hard rubber fenders that were more welcoming to rusty fishing boats than cruising yachts. The tide was out, and I didn't see how I was going to scramble up to the top, where I needed to attach our mooring lines to the bollards.

Once we'd prepared all the necessary lines and fenders, Gjalt made his approach. As he manoeuvred *Stella Maris* alongside the wharf, it loomed above me. I was going to have to stand on one of the rubber fenders and then quickly hop up. A close inspection of these fenders revealed that they had sloping sides. I was convinced that if I attempted to step onto one of them, I would slip down into the narrow space between *Stella Maris* and the wharf and be instantly crushed. Not surprisingly then, I bottled out of stepping onto the first fender, but, wilfully ignoring my protests, Gjalt persisted with the landing. Before I'd even thought about backing out again, I was stepping onto the next sloping fender and, just a microsecond later, stood safely on the wharf. I rushed to the bollard and secured *Stella Maris*, while Gjalt climbed up with the stern line. Mission accomplished.

Soon afterwards, a large yacht pulled up behind us. The short, tubby man on the bow threw me a line, but as he'd forgotten to attach it to the cleat on the boat, this proved rather pointless. Then, with hands on hips and the pompous air of someone used to bossing people around, the captain began issuing orders that he apparently expected me to obey. I considered letting his line fall in the water before I walked off, but as his incompetent bowman had hopped up beside me, I charitably handed it to him instead.

Customs and Quarantine officers came and went almost unnoticed, their procedures were so straightforward. They had willingly worked during their lunch hour for a twenty-dollar overtime fee, which wouldn't have been an utter waste of our money if the Immigration officer had been prepared to do the same.

While we waited for him, Gjalt went into town to change money, and only when he was standing in the bank queue did he realise he had entered Tonga illegally. Thankfully, he made it back to *Stella Maris* before he was caught out, but our neighbours, the obnoxious captain and his incompetent crew, weren't so lucky. They had gone into town for lunch and were nowhere to be seen when the Immigration officer turned up. He was *not* impressed.

An imposingly large man, both in height and bulk, his authority was not diminished by the fact that he was wearing a long black skirt, traditional attire for Tongan men called a *ta'ovala*. In fact, his presence was actually enhanced by it. Visibly seething with anger, he told us that he was going to refuse the others entry into Tonga for going ashore without his clearance. We sat there quietly, feeling mighty relieved that Gjalt had been back onboard when he arrived.

Fully cleared in, we left the wharf and picked up one of the mooring buoys in the anchorage. Onshore, the many bars and restaurants gave the small town of Neiafu a distinct holiday feel. For the first few days, we simply relaxed in its laid-back atmosphere. There was a large community of yachts, many from New Zealand and Australia; we were now so far across the Pacific that we'd made it to a sailing destination within reach of these countries. We ate out a lot, indulging in such healthy foods as hamburgers, pizza, and the delicious ice cream for which Tonga was renowned. After the scarce and prohibitively expensive restaurants of French Polynesia, we were beyond ready to eat someone else's cooking, and because they made it affordable, we did. All those months of abstinence were swept away by a sudden flood of free-flowing money. I was also able to indulge in the luxury of machine-washed laundry again. It was heavenly.

On Sundays, the town virtually shut down; shops were closed, and streets were deserted. Nineteenth-century Christian missionaries had succeeded in making Tongans deeply religious, and on this day of the week, they weren't allowed to do much more than pray. Religion had also taught them to dress modestly in public, and in deference to their conservatism, cruisers and tourists refrained from showing too much flesh when in town. In fact, it was actually illegal to venture out without a shirt which – considering that ninety-two per cent of Tongans over the age of thirty were reportedly clinically obese – was something to be grateful for. Such a statistic gave the country the dubious honour of 'fattest nation in the world', but as far as we could tell, the residents of Neiafu belonged to the remaining eight per cent. Most were certainly overweight, but compared to some of the enormous people we'd seen in Houston - America's 'fat city' - they seemed quite modest in size.

We found the Tongans less readily friendly than the people of Niue and French Polynesia. Perhaps this was because the higher number of tourists made visitors less of a novelty and more of an irritation. Our experience was opposite to that of Captain Cook, who called Tonga 'the Friendly Islands' (still so-named on our chart), after getting a warmer reception than he'd had at neighbouring Niue.

We inspected the facilities for hauling out *Stella Maris* and decided they weren't good enough for her. She would have to be pulled up on a slipway, and it looked too rickety for our liking; we weren't going to take any risks. Fiji had a choice of yards with travel lifts to hoist her out of the water, and it was only 450 miles away, a 3-day sail. We ordered the replacement rudder bush from England and left the bright lights of Neiafu to explore quieter anchorages while we waited for it to arrive.

A fter a short sail, we anchored opposite the golden beach of a small, sandy island that was the irresistible main attraction in a sheltered bay. The water was so clear we could see fish swimming amidst the coral. I couldn't resist joining them and shamelessly left Gjalt to fix a leaking drain nipple on the engine's lube oil cooler that a routine maintenance check had brought to light. While I happily snorkelled, Gjalt faced the horror of a corroded nipple that simply came off in his hands. Without that piece firmly in place, the boat would flood with water if we ran the engine. The severed nipple couldn't be reattached, so he had to jury-rig a repair. He found a piece of rubber amongst the useful bit and bobs he kept in the forward cabin for just such a crisis and held it securely over the hole with two hose clamps. He turned on the engine and held his breath as he watched for water: none came, not even a drop. He was absolutely euphoric; it had been inconceivable to carry on without the engine. The leak was fixed so completely that when we got to Australia, a mechanic told an exceedingly pleased Gjalt that it could be left as it was.

In the late afternoon, we dinghyed ashore to the island's small resort and splashed out on two expensive beers, mine admittedly less deserved than Gjalt's, although I enjoyed it just as much as he did. An American behind the bar introduced himself as Dave, and after some preamble, announced that he used to be in a band called The Cure. This was not a claim I'd expected to hear from a man serving beer on a small Tongan island. I was just about to ask him if he meant The *actual* Cure, when he went on to say he was now the lead singer of The Offspring, a band I knew from our time in the States. His refusal to remove his sunglasses added a certain authenticity to his professed rock-star status, and with his bleach-blond hair, I thought it possible that he really was the lead singer of The Offspring. Sadly, I felt a frisson of excitement at meeting someone famous, which I fear must have been obvious enough for him to feed off for the rest of the evening. Still, rock star or not, we weren't prepared to fund his lifestyle by buying a second round of overpriced drinks. We did decide to return for his more modestly priced dinner, though, an event that would be attended by the tourists staying in the resort and cruisers from the three other yachts in the anchorage.

Back on *Stella Maris*, my brain mulled over Dave's claims, searching through its archives for real data. Pop trivia from the 1980s was pulled from dark and dusty recesses, and when we returned for dinner, I was ready to impress Dave with my knowledge. "Wasn't Robert Smith the lead singer of The Cure?" I asked.

"Yeah. He was my boss," he answered, which struck me as an odd way to refer to the lead singer of his own band.

"Which instrument did you play?" I persisted, but Dave's reply was addressed to the fridge in which he had inserted his head in an overly determined rummage for a beer. I caught fragments of sentences as they bounced out of the cool enclosure and got the distinct impression that if he'd had anything to do with the band at all, it was back stage, not on it. Consequently, suspicions about the true brilliance of Dave's stardom began to grow.

"The Cure was a British band, wasn't it?" I asked.

"Yeah, I was living in Chelsea at the time. I was only fourteen and had to add a few years to my age to be able to tour with the band. My passport says I'm fifty now, but I'm only forty-four," he said, laughing.

*Hmm.* "So, where is Robert Smith these days?"

"Rehab."

This was the only part of his story I thought plausible, but a subsequent enquiry to my best friend and ex-The Cure fan in England revealed that Robert Smith was actually back on the road with The Cure at the time.

"I spent four months in a coma after being in a car crash," Dave announced a few minutes later. "Have you heard of Reiki?"

I told him I had not.

"It's a Japanese healing treatment I mastered when I had to learn to walk again. You know, I couldn't help noticing that your hips are a little bit out of balance," he said, fixing me with a deadly serious stare. "Not much, but enough to benefit from realignment. All I need is twenty minutes with you to put it right."

Considering Dave was not a doctor and I hadn't consulted him about my gait, his sudden diagnosis did take me aback. I'd never had any problem with my hips, and there was no way I was going to allow him anywhere near them for a realignment.

As the night wore on, Dave's stories moved steadily away from possible reality to certain fantasy, whilst the confidence with which they were told just kept growing. He was allegedly one of the original Jackasses, a group of men who display the maturity of pubescent teenagers by performing stunts almost certain to cause serious physical injury, preferably to the testicles. To back up this claim, Dave announced that he had base-jumped off the statue of Jesus in Rio de Janeiro, not once but four times – twice off each arm! He also found time to produce such minor TV shows as *The Sopranos* and *Sex and the City* and owned a music company called DreamWorks Records. In fact, he said he recorded music right there on the veranda of the resort.

"Are the acoustics good enough out here in the open?" I asked.

"Modern technology," he answered, quick as a flash.

His links with the music business extended beyond the mere dating of Gwen Stefani (who apparently kept calling him because she was jealous of his new girlfriend) to managing and producing her band, No Doubt. He claimed she was going to arrive at the resort the following week, and that Tom Cruise had been there a few weeks earlier. Dave also found time to manage the careers of Shania Twain, Eminem, and Metallica (for twenty years!). By midnight, he was showing us assorted music videos in which he claimed every single guy with blond hair was himself (which they clearly weren't). The only videos not in his collection, oddly enough, were those by The Cure and The Offspring. He had apparently also been asked by Madonna to arrange her multimillion-dollar concerts in China because – and this really was the crowning glory of the entire evening – he was fluent in Cantonese! By the time he made this grand revelation, it was nearly two in the morning, and events had taken us to such a surreal plane that we urgently needed to make our way back to the planet on which we'd anchored *Stella Maris*.

Dave was quite simply the undisputed world champion of bullshit, as cool as ice and just as slick, with a rapid-fire response to every question designed to throw him off balance. It proved impossible to trip him up. We might have achieved it had we asked for a few words in Cantonese, but he really was a very nice guy, and trying to expose him seemed rude. Besides, he'd brought out bottle after bottle of excellent red wine during dinner, all on the house, which certainly helped put us in the mood to just sit back and enjoy our host's prodigious narrative talents. By the end of the evening, I didn't believe we'd met a founding member of The Cure, or the lead singer of The Offspring, probably not the owner of the music division of DreamWorks either, and maybe not even a man who worked at the resort. Perhaps he was just a cruiser who'd washed up on the beach one day and convinced everyone he was supposed to be there. Now, *that* would have been impressive. But whoever Dave really was, I did know that he was quick-witted, generous, and very entertaining company.

The next morning, we snorkelled in an area called the Japanese Garden because of the abundance of plate corals that looked like Bonsai trees. I found our biggest and prettiest shell to date, a tiger cowry, but the snail inside it was still alive. We'd pondered the ethics of taking live shells for some time, and it was in Tonga that we decided to stop. Whilst I loved collecting shells, it slowly dawned on me that I experienced the most joy at the moment of discovery. Admiring a live shell for a few minutes and then putting it back was the right thing to do, but it had taken me a long time to realise that. Arriving in an area with a high number of visitors had made it obvious that humans can quickly have a lasting detrimental impact on the environment whenever they decide it has something that they want.

We returned to Neiafu to find DHL and let them know we were expecting packages; we didn't want our replacement towing generator and new rudder bush returned to sender. Rosabella was the delightfully chirpy, softly rounded DHL representative whose office was conveniently located inside Lonnie's Video Store. On the many occasions a visit to her did not yield our packages, we did at least leave with a film for the evening. Rosabella giggled when she talked to Gjalt and told him he looked like Sting (which he didn't take as a compliment). She giggled even more when he told her his surname was van der Zee, because she thought he'd said 'fantasy'. I'm pretty certain Sting and fantasy were one in the same to her.

A fter a few rainy days stranded in Neiafu, we headed for the nearby island of Vaka'eitu. We had a difference of opinion, of sorts, when Gjalt appointed me helmsman and took the chart with him to the bow to navigate us past a submerged coral patch. I was supposed to switch my brain off and obey his instructions without question, something I found impossible to do. I got the there-is-only-one-captain-onboard speech, which I rebuffed with my fervent this-is-not-the-Navy response, and we both agreed to a truce as we turned into the anchorage.

It was a very hot day, and as soon as the anchor had dug into the seabed, we jumped over the side to cool off. We swam to the beach, where we ended up going our separate ways, needing to let the air clear between us after the argument.

I headed inland and came across an enormous ficus tree, the type of hardy plant I was more used to seeing in pots in the corners of rooms. It must have had a circumference of at least 50 feet and been 100 years old. A great mass of branches spread out from its core, each supported by a vertical stem the size of a tree trunk. I felt drawn to it and sat down so I could properly appreciate its beauty.

After all the months of constantly sharing the same small space with another person, the solitude itself was wonderful, but I also looked at the plants, smelt the earth, and listened to the birdsong as if for the first time. I was unwilling to pull myself away and stayed there so long that Gjalt was convinced I'd come to harm.

When the weather threatened to put us on a lee shore, we returned to Neiafu for one of our regular visits to DHL. Winds were strong, and there was significant chop away from the protection of land, but we had a fast and thrilling sail back to town. Rosabella had our towing generator, as promised, but not everything was going our way. Our U.S. tax returns were waiting for us in the Internet café, and the size of the payment demands induced severe heart palpitations. The taxman was determined to muscle himself onboard *Stella Maris* and try to spoil our trip across the Pacific. We always managed to push him over the side, but it took too much time and effort, and the bastard just kept hauling himself back onboard.

The following day brought more bad news in the form of a strange e-mail from our British boat insurance company. We were informed that from now on we could only contact them through their Spanish office and this set off alarm bells in our minds. When preparing to leave Texas, it had been nigh on impossible to find a company that would insure a yacht with only two people onboard. When a reputable broker finally found one that did, we were so relieved, and it was so late in the day, that we didn't look into the company in any depth. Now the time had come for us to do just that.

With great trepidation, we went to the Internet café, and before we could say 'bogus insurance company' the Web threw up a slew of damning reports that made us doubt *Stella Maris* was covered at all. We couldn't have had less confidence in the owner of the outfit if he'd been an estate agent who sold second hand cars in his spare time. He had moved from one European country to another, leaving a trail of unpaid claims and failed companies behind him. We clearly had to find a new insurance company – just what we wanted to be busy with in the South Pacific. The Tongan weather had been a mixed bag of rainy, windy days interspersed with glorious sunshine, and this was a good metaphor for our stay in the country: strikes and gutters, as The Dude would say.

One pleasant distraction for Gjalt was the opportunity to be the sail trimmer on *Medea*, a fifty-three-foot J16 yacht, in a race against her sister ship, *Seraphina*, in the channel opposite Neiafu. Taking the challenge seriously, the captain held training runs, which *Seraphina's* crew (rumoured to have won a Los Angeles-to-Honolulu Transpac race) observed keenly through binoculars. By race time, the crews were raring to go, and the spectators were raring to support them spiritually, so to speak, from the comfort of The Mermaid bar. This was by far the best place to be, as the heavens opened up just as the race began, releasing a torrential downpour onto the competitors.

*Medea* made the best start, and Gjalt enjoyed the thrill of sailing on a big boat that was lively and responsive to the wind. He felt her accelerate with every gust, and having taken the early lead, *Medea* never gave it up. The yachts sailed three times around the race buoys, and before the spectators had a chance to grow restless, the amateurs had thrashed the alleged professionals, a sure bet for tension in the bar afterwards.

Later in the evening, I was innocently sitting at what had morphed into the winning yacht's table when I noticed an abrupt movement out of the corner of my eye. Turning to investigate, I saw that the incompetent *Medea* bowman had gripped his neighbour – a mild-mannered Canadian yachtie – by the neck and was forcing him to carry out an intimate examination of his own kneecaps.

"What are you doing?" I asked, more quietly outraged than alarmed; the Canadian seemed uncomfortable but not in any immediate danger. Still, it wasn't usual for yachties to interact with each other in this way.

The Canadian's wife tried to reason with her husband's assailant, and then a Norwegian mother of three young children appeared from nowhere to mediate, clearly used to this kind of thing. Eventually the vice-like grip was relaxed, and the Canadian was allowed up for air, at which point *Medea's* captain got involved. "What are you doing at this table, anyway?" he demanded from the victim. "Nobody invited you."

"This was *our* table," the Canadian responded meekly, clearly shaken by all the sudden hostility towards him. And it was true, the *Medea* crowd were the gatecrashers, not him. But in the strange way of these things, after a few more pointed exchanges, the two men shook hands. Even so, it had all been too much for me, and I left in search of less testy company.

I managed to find it on the other side of the bar, but my convivial conversation was cut short by Gjalt informing me that we were leaving. Having stayed in the hostile atmosphere of the competitors' table, he'd ended up in an argument of his own, although thankfully no heads were forced anywhere they didn't belong. The American owner of *Seraphina* had told Gjalt he needed to keep an eye on both his boat and ours, because they were moored so close they might touch.

"Why didn't you choose a different mooring then?" Gjalt demanded.

"I put a fender on my mooring when I left the anchorage a few days ago. You're the one who should have chosen a different mooring."

This was the yachting equivalent of placing a towel on a deckchair at five in the morning and only returning to sit on it after lunch.

"What kind of a captain are you?" Gjalt said after a succession of other insults, and then he stormed away from the table to find me.

We went back to *Stella Maris* to make sure she was all right, and thankfully she was; for the time being, anyway.

The morning after the morning after, though, we were woken up early by the unwelcome sound of *Seraphina* bumping into us. It was dead calm, and without the wind to keep boats aligned behind their moorings, they drifted haphazardly on the glassy water. The strategic placement of a few fenders prevented any damage, but when the owner appeared on deck, we exchanged words, most of them focusing on the key question of exactly who amongst us was the complete and utter dickhead. The first sunshine in days couldn't warm the frosty atmosphere that had engulfed our boats, so we left the crowded anchorage in search of solitude.

It was such a calm day that we decided to look for the famous Mariner's Cave. Situated in a channel that was too deep to anchor, I stayed on *Stella Maris* while Gjalt jumped overboard. The entrance to the cave was underwater, and the only clue to its location was a supposed patch of pinkish rock on the cliff directly above it. This proved exceedingly difficult to distinguish from the many splashes of colour on the rock face, and Gjalt dived under at various places to try and locate the entrance. Just as he was about to give up, I was certain I'd identified the elusive patch of pink that marked the spot. Gjalt dived down one last time, and – sure enough – he found the entrance to the cave. I was pleased to hear his verdict that it had been nice inside but not spectacular; I didn't fancy swimming underwater into a hidden cave, but I would have felt compelled to had he told me it was worth it.

We made our way to Port Maurelle, a sheltered bay formed by picturesque Kapa Island, its curved sandy beach luring us in. All alone, we felt able to breathe again, but our oxygen was stolen bit by bit when one boat after another arrived as the afternoon wore on. By sunset, six yachts had joined us in the anchorage, and we felt hemmed in yet again.

Our moods improved after a long night of sound sleep and got even better after we'd snorkelled and explored the island. I found an exquisite Arabian cowry, which I took pleasure in returning to its hiding place amongst the coral, but only after fully admiring the elaborately patterned shell. Onshore I enjoyed walking in the shade of the leafy trees and listening to birdsong once again. Slowly but surely, the irritations of our human encounters faded away.

At the tip of Kapa Island, a long vertical gash in the rock wide enough for our dinghy formed the entrance to Swallows Cave. There was no need for the underwater heroics required to explore Mariner's Cave, we could just slip through the gap like the birds the cavern had been named after. The deep blue water was so clear that we could see schools of fish shimmering in the sunshine and an enormous coral head spreading down the steep edge of the island. Above water, impressive multicoloured stalactites reached down from the high roof, but humans had not been able to refrain from leaving their own mark. The walls were still daubed in graffiti from the crews of whaling boats, and it was strangely interesting to see Norwegian names dating as far back as 1892. There was ugly modern graffiti as well, but we only felt angry towards those people for having defaced such a naturally beautiful place. Our conflicting responses to the different vintages of 'personal expression' begged the question: At what point does vandalism become fascinating history?

We tied the dinghy to a rock, then clambered over some boulders and negotiated a narrow ridge until we reached a huge, dry cave. Sunshine streamed through a tree-lined hole in the roof, filling the interior with light. At the turn of the twentieth century, feasts were held in the enormous cavern, and the food was lowered down through that very hole. Presumably the spongy, malodorous carpet of bird guano that would have covered the ground then as surely as it did now, was shovelled out before the VIPs were ushered inside for those grand occasions.

On the short trip back to *Stella Maris*, we trolled a lure behind the dinghy. We rarely managed to catch fish that way, but surprisingly, we hooked a good-sized albacore tuna, its tender white meat providing delicious sashimi to round off a fantastic day.

We returned to Neiafu to collect our rudder bush, but Rosabella told us it was due to arrive on the afternoon plane, and we'd have to collect it the next morning. She was dressed in black, with a ceremonial mat of finely woven pandanas around her waist, because she was in mourning for her aunt. We offered our condolences, and something in the way Rosabella explained that her aunt had never married gave us the impression that spinsters weren't all that highly regarded in the community.

To my immense disappointment, the late arrival of the rudder bush meant we had to spend yet another night anchored beside Neiafu. The town I'd found so alluring when we arrived nearly three weeks earlier had lost most of its appeal. Now I craved the unspoilt nature and solitude of the outer island anchorages.

The next day, we awoke to overcast and drizzly skies. I couldn't face another trip ashore, so Gjalt went alone. Having waited patiently for forty-five minutes outside Lonnie's Video Store, he was finally told that everyone had gone to the funeral of Rosabella's aunt. There would be no handover of packages that day, and the next day was Sunday, when everything apart from the churches would be closed. Unable to spend another minute in Neiafu, we weighed anchor and sailed east, aiming to get as far from the busy town as we could.

We followed a marked channel through a broad expanse of shallows and coral patches and then sailed on towards the Group's outermost anchorage beside Kenutu Island. Beneath overcast skies, it was hard to see two unmarked reefs that we needed to keep to port whilst skirting 'foul ground' to starboard. With Gjalt at the helm and me searching from the bow, we managed to steer clear of the hazards and into the deep channel leading to the most striking anchorage we had seen in Tonga. Kenutu was a link in a chain of tree-covered islands bounded by the Vava'u Group's fringing reef on one side and an open expanse of aquamarine water on the other. In all this splendour, only a single boat was anchored, and it was so far away it might as well have been on another planet. It was perfect.

Onshore we walked along the golden beach and found a path that wound through dense shrubbery up to the top of Kenutu Island. We were at the eastern edge of the Vava'u Group's sheltered waters and had a glorious, sweeping view of the vast Pacific. We watched waves crashing against the island and onto the outer reef that stretched south into the distance. Seeing the mighty ocean held back by the protective barrier of coral restored our spirits and made us feel adventurous again.

The next day the wind disappeared and the sun returned, perfect conditions to go exploring in the dinghy. The ocean was so calm we tried to catch a pelagic fish in a small boat pass that led out to sea, but we had no luck. We headed north to the island neighbouring Kenutu, looking for good places to snorkel, but wherever we stopped, visibility was poor and coral was scarce. Onshore, a trail on the island led a short way inland to a small sinkhole, but it was no rival to the wonders of Niue. By late afternoon, a motor boat arrived in the anchorage, followed by a sailing yacht; it suddenly became easier to contemplate returning to Neiafu in preparation for leaving Tonga.

The following day was windless, and the mirror-smooth surface of the water made it impossible to see the channel leading out of the anchorage. Fortunately, by the time we were ready to leave, a breeze had stirred and produced ripples that revealed the shallow reef. We steered safely away from Kenutu and sailed the fifteen miles back to Neiafu.

At Lonnie's Video Store, our rudder bushes were in the safe care of Rosabella. We also entrusted her with our belated U.S. tax returns and the weighty cheques we hoped would finally keep the wretched taxman at bay.

A farewell pizza in our favourite Italian restaurant brought an encounter with the owner of *Seraphina*. His wife had arrived since we'd thrown insults at each other a few days before, and she must have had a good influence on him, because he came over to our table to apologise. Such magnanimity produced a snowball effect, and soon we were apologising as intently as he was. The air was cleared, and the dirty water flowed away under the bridge.

Check-out day was jam-packed with things we had to do before we could leave. I collected three loads of washing from the laundry service, Gjalt called various brokers to come to a landing on a reliable insurance company, we had our LPG tank filled, collected water in jerry cans, and bought fresh groceries from the open-air market. We called in at Immigration, the port captain, and finally Customs, located in a big warehouse by the wharf.

We'd been warned that one particular officer should be avoided at all costs; he'd made Jo and Jason take *Reverie* to the wharf to be inspected, something other officers didn't demand. So we started loitering by the open door, walking away when it looked as though he would be the next available officer. After some time playing at these shenanigans, we decided our behaviour was ridiculous and we were sure we'd be able to manage the tricky character easily enough. We returned to the warehouse at just the moment he became free, and he called us forward.

We chatted to him using our tried and tested 'interaction with officials' routine, and although he was sour-faced, we did manage to engage him in conversation. Everything went smoothly, and we weren't asked to bring *Stella Maris* to the wharf, so we left feeling quite pleased with ourselves. It was only when we discovered that other cruisers hadn't paid a twenty-dollar fee that we realised we'd been duped. I'd had a bad feeling about the charge at the time, because no one had mentioned having paid to check out, but not wanting to bring *Stella Maris* to the wharf (one landing against that thing had been enough for me), I kept my mouth shut and coughed up. We'd thought we were smart enough to play him, but he'd played us instead. Apparently Tonga ranked fifth in the world for corruption at the time, but it was also extremely poor, with the average yearly income amounting to just 2,200 dollars.

It had been a very hot and exhausting day, and I went to bed with a throbbing headache, thinking more about the lost twenty dollars than the fact that we'd finally got everything sorted out: our tax returns, our boat insurance, the towing generator, and the rudder bushes. I don't know why my mind chose to wallow in the small puddle of badness instead of the great big sea of goodness, but it was very 'un-Dude'.

We got up at six the next morning to the eerie silence of windlessness. The Neiafu waters were flat and littered with ugly detritus, man-made garbage suspended on the surface, marooned in the doldrums. We downloaded a weather forecast that promised the winds would kick in that evening, so we decided to leave. After a month in Tonga, we were itching to move on. We now had only six weeks before the start of the cyclone season, and the devastation Hurricane Katrina had recently inflicted on New Orleans demonstrated why we wanted to be safely in Australia by then.

Gjalt was forced to have an early dip in the mucky water in order to dislodge our anchor from between two rocks. Luckily, it was only thirty-two feet down, and after three dives, he had wiggled it free.

As we left the protection of the Vava'u Group, we saw plumes of water spurting out of two blowholes, one bigger than the other. It made me think of playful Junior and his trusting mum. Swimming with whales was regulated and jealously guarded by the tour operators in Neiafu. Of course there must be rules when such interactions become part of the tourist industry, but the joy of cruising comes from the freedom to marvel at the world far from the madding crowd. We felt so privileged to have had our unique experience with the humpbacks in Niue. If it had been controlled and directed by someone we'd paid, it just wouldn't have been the same.

CORINNA: GETTING AROUND IN THE DINGHY

# 15.

# Hauling Out

*Fiji's marine systems are showing increasing signs of over-exploitation. Over-fishing, unsustainable and destructive harvesting of live coral and fish for aquaria, and pollution are all taking their toll. In addition, Fiji's reefs took a major hammering in the 2000 and 2002 bleaching events from higher than normal sea temperatures, leading to widespread coral dieback.*

– WWF South Pacific Programme, 2005

It was dead calm out on the ocean; very pretty and very hot. We had to motor, but as there was no swell, *Stella Maris* didn't roll from side to side, so it was painless.

Just as we passed the small volcanic island of Late, we finally had success with our fishing efforts. We simultaneously caught a three-foot wahoo and a four-foot dorado on our trolled lures; we must have sailed through a school of fish they had been hunting. Their beauty – especially that of the dorado, with its metallic green and gold markings – aroused familiar feelings of guilt, but their tender white meat was a fully appreciated alternative to tinned tuna and the dreaded corned beef. We'd bought new tins of the meat in Tonga, but the contents didn't resemble any corned beef we'd seen before. Suspended in a creamy white gelatinous fat were gristly, pallid lumps that appeared to come from cow body parts one wouldn't normally consider eating. Thankfully, we'd just caught enough fish to last the three-day passage to Fiji, so we wouldn't be chewing on unappetising cow offal any time soon.

My first night watch was tranquil, with a calm ocean and a nearly full moon. By 9 o'clock, the promised wind had arrived, and after fourteen hours of motoring, it was a relief to turn off the engine and restore peace onboard. The wind breathed life back into the Pacific, and *Stella Maris* was rocked gently as she coursed through the waves under a black sky dusted with glittering stars. It also tempered the sun's ferocious heat the following day, when we both caught up on sleep as our bodies adjusted to interrupted nights.

The Oneata Passage was one possible route through a barrier of islands and reefs that stretched north to south between Tonga and Fiji; the one on the most direct line to our destination of Suva, Fiji's capital on the large island of Viti Levu. At the speed we were making, we would sail through the passage in the dark, a prospect that caused me severe stress. It was five miles wide, unarguably ample for a yacht with a thirteen-and-a-half-foot beam; yet, as I stared at the chart, riddled with tightly packed reef patches and islands, it seemed worryingly narrow.

Before GPS, no sane mariner would have even attempted to take that treacherous route during the day, let alone at night, when they were almost guaranteed to run aground. But of course we did have GPS – even a handheld backup should the onboard one fail – so Gjalt found my concerns ridiculous and highly irksome. He stepped onto his soapbox and cleared his throat for the captain speech once again: Navigation and safe passage were his responsibility, and he would never take a route that would endanger *Stella Maris* or us. Therefore, there was absolutely no need for me to worry. He was upset because he thought I didn't trust him, but that was not the issue. The more I sailed, the more I learnt, the more involved I became. My days of ignorant bliss were over, and I couldn't simply play the bimbo and leave him to it. I had to understand everything we did and feel confident about it.

With the genoa poled out to windward and the mainsail to leeward, we continued to make speeds up to seven and a half knots and reached the Oneata Passage at three in the morning. I had swapped watches with Gjalt so he'd be at the helm when we sailed through it, but I stayed up too. I couldn't possibly have slept and would have just lain awake waiting for us to run aground. (Later, in Australia, a friend told me she was once so certain they would run aground during the night that she went to bed with her shoes on, ready for the inevitable trek across the jagged coral.) With the aid of clear skies and a full moon, we could see Oneata

Island on our starboard side; with that land mass clearly visible, the passage through the deep channel turned out to be a pleasant experience, not stressful at all. This didn't stop me dreaming of heavy breakers on a sixty-foot shallow within the channel though. Gjalt had even avoided this seamount especially for me, pandering to my admittedly improbable concern that unknown recent volcanic activity might have reduced the water depth above it.

Having swapped watches, I had to get up in the pre-sunrise gloom of 5 o'clock, but I enjoyed it against the odds because of the serene conditions. It was wonderful to see the white moon turn to gold as it set on the bow to the west, while the sun rose over our stern to the east. The wind eased, and our speed dropped to just four knots, but Gjalt was too tired to get up and hoist the gennaker. I knew we wouldn't reach Suva during 'office hours' at that rate, and I allowed rumours of 150 dollar overtime charges to dominate my thoughts. To avoid staring at the speedometer, I sat on the bow and gazed at the distant islands of the Lau Group as we pottered along. It was illegal to stop there without first obtaining a permit in Suva, because the authorities apparently wanted to minimise outside influence in that part of Fiji.

Eventually, Gjalt was roused into action, and we poled out the gennaker in front of the bow, turning it into a spinnaker to harness the wind that was now coming directly from behind. Soon the wind picked up, and the flat seas didn't roll *Stella Maris*, allowing her to glide along gracefully between seven and eight knots. This was the sailing I'd been promised way back in the Gulf of Mexico.

Of course the perfection didn't last, and after a few hours, the wind died completely. The engine was pressed into action again, and we seared under the full force of the sun. We ate the last of the dorado for dinner, and I settled into another uneventful night watch. In such calm conditions, looking out for ships was easy, and the only disturbance was the engine, which had to run all the way to Suva; a straight stretch of twenty-six hours.

The next morning, the ocean was as smooth as glass, and the sun's heat reflected off it mercilessly. I couldn't complain about our 1 o'clock arrival time, though, which was well within office hours. While I tidied the boat, Gjalt went ashore to check in. We'd been at sea for three and a half days, and although we motored for a good part of the 450 miles, it had been an enjoyable passage.

We were anchored in Suva's commercial harbour, which was full of rusty fishing boats as well as a few other yachts. It was very hot, but the harbour water was an unappealing murky brown, its surface littered with garbage, so I wasn't tempted to jump in and cool off. I hoped for a deluge of tropical afternoon rain that I could stand under, but it never came.

In the distance, far away from human influence, rose a multitude of wooded peaks, a pleasant contrast to the metal, rust, and rubbish in my immediate vicinity. I had three hours to take in my new surroundings, because that was how long Gjalt was gone chasing the paper trail. He reappeared just as I was beginning to be convinced that he had been knocked down. At sea, eight knots was fast and on land cars shot past us like missiles.

Gjalt was not at all impressed with the bureaucracy he'd faced and blamed the British for having introduced it during colonial rule. He had to fill out multiple forms for the Quarantine, Customs, and Immigration departments, all duplicated the old-fashioned carbon copy way. Even after having spent hours with his shoulder to the task, he failed to complete all the necessary formalities, and we had to finish them the next day.

Clearly, alcohol was required, and we headed to the Royal Suva Yacht Club, a wonderful-sounding establishment that lived up to its name. Sitting on the veranda in the balmy early evening, we drank revitalising, inexpensive beer and gazed across the lawn at the harbour. Gjalt wasted no time indulging his long-held desire for curry, something Fiji was famous for thanks to forty per cent of its population being of Indian descent. I chose the other British staple, fish and chips. It was an excellent way to celebrate our safe arrival.

As our final destination was Australia, we needed to get visas. Arriving there without one would mean a fine of at least 3,000 Australian dollars. Many cruisers opted to go to New Zealand because the Kiwis were altogether more welcoming than their Antipodean neighbours, and issued visas upon arrival. The Australian government seemed almost affronted that yachties considered themselves worthy to seek shelter from cyclones in their beloved country. Undeterred, we took a taxi to the Australian Embassy the next morning, making sure to arrive before they closed for business at midday. It must be tough working such long hours in the Civil Service.

Having had our bags X-rayed and searched at the entrance, we were free to take a ticket for a place in the queue. An hour ticked by slowly as we sat with two dozen other applicants, mostly Indians, waiting patiently for our turn. When it came, all we received were the necessary forms and a few short answers we managed to wring from the reluctantly friendly employee on the other side of a glass window. For the honour of even considering our applications, we would have to shell out ninety dollars and wait ten days. The whole experience left Gjalt less than impressed, and I quickly shuffled him out of the building before he could express his opinion too loudly.

We flagged down another taxi to take us to the Health Centre, where we had to pay some kind of quarantine charge. On the way, we found ourselves on the receiving end of an angry tirade from the Indian taxi driver about how lazy and corrupt the ethnic Fijians were. "Only twenty per cent of them are nice," he declared, as if he'd recently conducted a poll. "The rest are awful. Even though Indians make up more than half the population we don't have the same rights as they do. I'm selling my businesses and moving to New Zealand. Many Indians are leaving."

His claim that the ethnic Fijians were crooks was a bit rich, coming from someone who charged us seven dollars for a fare the meter clearly declared was only half that. Even after this discrepancy was pointed out to him, he tried to short-change us by a dollar, but I was on to him by then. If he classed himself as honest, what on earth were those dishonest ethnic Fijians up to?

After a quick transaction in the Health Centre, we were told we had to take our payment receipt to a government office on the other side of town. Thankfully, taxis were cheap, so being driven around the streets of Suva was an affordable luxury. All our drivers were Indians, but the next one was a far more jolly soul than the last, and was very happy living in Suva. "Most of my neighbours are ethnic Fijians," he said. "I can speak Fijian, English and Hindi. It's different from the Hindi they speak in India, a unique version that has evolved here in Fiji."

"Where in India did your family come from?" I asked.

"I don't know. I was born in Fiji, my parents were born here, and my grandparents. I have never been to India. I am a Fijian."

All our Indian drivers insisted that they were Fijian, born and bred, silently imparting that they had just as much right to live there as their ethnic compatriots. The first Indians arrived in Fiji in 1879, brought to the islands by the British to work as indentured labourers on the sugar plantations. When we visited, feelings were still raw following the country's most recent coup in 2000 (there had been two in 1987). Gunmen had stormed Parliament and taken Fiji's first Indo-Fijian prime minister, Mahendra Chaudhry, his cabinet ministers, and many MPs hostage. A year before, the multi-racial government had replaced one dominated by ethnic Fijians, a situation unacceptable to hard-line nationalist George Speight, the gunmen's leader. The gang demanded Chaudhry's resignation and the suspension of Fiji's 1997 Constitution, which had increased the political rights of Indo-Fijians. The military took control of the country and imposed martial law, but it took two months for the last of the hostages to be released, including Chaudhry himself. New elections in August 2001 were won by the United Fiji Party, led by an ethnic Fijian. Speight claimed he had acted to restore the rights of the indigenous population, but others claimed the coup was nothing more than a personal grab for money and power. In 2002, he was found guilty of treason and sentenced to life in prison.

Having produced our Quarantine receipt for inspection (an unnecessary action if ever there was one), we still needed a cruising permit. The next taxi driver also complained bitterly about thieving Fijians before overcharging us for the fare. He also dropped us off at the wrong building, forcing us to walk along Victoria Parade under a scorching sun in search of the right one. When we finally found it, we stumbled inside, sweaty and overcooked, only to be told that cruising permits were issued somewhere else altogether. There seemed to be no end to the bureaucratic nightmare.

Another taxi drove us out of the city and through the

winding streets of a refreshingly leafy suburb to a resplendent wooden mansion with faded colonial charm. It was lunchtime, and we feared we would be sent away, but the helpful staff was happy to accommodate us. With cruising permit in hand, we were finally free to enjoy ourselves.

It was definitely time for a celebration, and that meant curry for lunch. We asked our last taxi driver of the day to take us to the best restaurant in Suva, and soon we were lounging in a soft-cushioned booth in Singh's Curry House. The food was delicious and cheap, our favourite combination, and Singh's became our regular haunt whenever we were in town.

Suva was like a dozen other hot and busy cities we had visited, with too many shops filled with tatty merchandise, most of it made from garishly coloured plastic. Gjalt needed new polarised sunglasses, so we wandered into a shop to see what was on offer.

The Indian shopkeeper seemed suspiciously desperate to make a sale, almost salivating at the prospect of ensnaring a pair of suckers who would unwittingly boost his retirement fund. He hopped onto a stepladder and eagerly selected a white shoebox from his top shelf. It had 'Polarised' written in marker pen along the side.

"Are these *really* polarised?" I asked, peering into the box. It was stuffed full with cheap-looking glasses, each in a clear plastic bag.

"Yes, they are genuine polarised sunglasses," he replied unconvincingly, a nervous quiver in his voice.

"How much are these?" Gjalt asked, holding up a pair.

"Eighty dollars," the man said, managing to keep a straight face.

"You've got to be joking," we guffawed.

"Fifty dollars."

Gjalt put the glasses back in the shoebox.

"Thirty."

We walked to the door.

"Fifteen dollars," we heard as we left.

We were now on red alert for everything on sale in Suva and immediately decided not buy a new digital camera there. We preferred to make do with our genuine disposable camera rather than risk paying for a fake digital one.

We were not averse, however, to investing in the DVDs

we saw for sale. There was a generous smattering of specialist shops to browse through, and each had a fairly broad selection of titles. The quality of the films was far superior to those we'd bought in the Galápagos. They had been professionally pirated, right down to the copyright law printed on the disc.

"It's illegal to sell copies of films where I come from," I told the super-friendly salesman in one of the shops.

"Why is that?" he asked, smiling at me with his arrestingly prominent teeth, his bright eyes wide open in genuine befuddlement at such an unfathomable hindrance in the world of commerce.

On the hot walk back to the Royal Suva Yacht Club, we came across a fishing tackle shop that sold beautifully made, and surprisingly cheap, squid lures. Gjalt became a regular customer and was drawn inside every time we happened to walk past. His tackle box began to bulge with the double-skirted, multicoloured works of art that simply had to guarantee success.

Back at the Yacht Club, I couldn't wait to wash away the heat and dust of Suva. The shower called to me, my first opportunity to stand under free-flowing fresh water in four months. The last time I'd been able to indulge in such luxury was under the cold-water, open-air affair at Atuona in the Marquesas, beside the laundry sinks. Now I had complete privacy and hot water to boot. It was not an occasion to be rushed.

The Fijian paper trail might have come to an end, but the Australian one was only just beginning. I spent the following morning filling out the visa application forms and drafting a letter to the case officer explaining why Australians should stoop so low as to let us stay in their precious country. It seemed a bit rich for a nation descended from convicts to be so picky about yachties who just wanted a safe place to sit out the cyclone season. Gjalt, meanwhile, visited a cruising couple who were already knee deep in the procedure, hoping to extract information that would increase our chances of getting what we needed: namely, a multiple-entry visa lasting eighteen months. He returned all fired up, rejected my letter after a cursory glance, and instantly set about writing a new one. I tried not to be upset about being ridden roughshod over and did attempt to see the merits of his point of view, but it was no good. I was irked that my opinion carried less weight than his, so grumpiness took hold of me and wouldn't let go.

Suddenly I simply had to get off the boat, but at that very moment it started to pour with rain, so I was trapped. My mood just got blacker and blacker and I sank into a hole so deep I couldn't pull myself out of it.

When the rain finally stopped and we escaped the confines of the boat, we trudged around Suva in stony silence, its distractions not improving the atmosphere between us. Back at the Yacht Club, we sat on a bench by the security gate and made up so we could face our chirpy friends at the bar inside. We were in no mood to join them for a group dinner, so we made our excuses and returned to *Stella Maris*, where we discussed why everything had turned sour that day.

Just as on previous occasions during our trip, I felt I had no control over important aspects of my life, that I was dominated by Gjalt's will. I'd lost the independence I'd had during my working days and the self-assurance that a career in the oil industry had given me. As a petrophysicist, I'd been responsible for obtaining well data using rigs that cost 400,000 dollars a day; now, I sometimes felt like a child, expected to obey orders without question.

We were practically joined at the hip. We did everything together and hardly had any time to ourselves. In Houston, we'd led separate working lives, sharing only the evenings and weekends. Now we were together twenty-four hours a day, and I suppose it was inevitable that we would get on each other's nerves every now and then. Not many couples would be able to endure such constant intimacy, especially on a forty-one-foot boat, and surely all the ones who did argued at least once in a blue moon.

The next day was declared grumpy-free with various penalties to be imposed on violators. This was made especially necessary because we had to go to the Australian Embassy in the morning. After waiting for one and a half hours, we were allowed to hand over our application forms (couldn't they just have a letterbox for people to put them in?), and only ten days later would we get an answer. A trip to Singh's Curry House was called for, and the delicious food managed to put us in a good mood.

After three days in Suva, we were sick and tired of its hot, crowded streets and longed to move somewhere more peaceful. We left in strong winds and sailed close-hauled to the small island of Mbengga, twenty miles southwest of Viti Levu. We entered the sheltered waters behind the fringing reef through the curiously named Sulphur Passage and immediately tucked into Malumu Bay, a mile-long cut in the island running from north to south. We didn't think we could find any better protection from the elements than would be afforded by the sloping hills of this bay, and we moved all the way in, anchoring close to a small island at the head of it.

The shore was lined with impenetrable mangroves, and without sand or clear blue water to swim in, no one had built anything to attract tourists. Our only neighbours were the large fruit bats that soared around the trees on the small island. The absence of human life and its attendant noise and activity was in complete contrast to Suva; it was just what we needed.

The wind stayed strong for the next few days, and occasionally a gust would sweep over the surrounding hills and shoot through the bay like a bullet. In the pitch dark of midnight, one of these gusts pushed *Stella Maris* with such force that her anchor was dislodged from the soft, muddy bottom. Gjalt's ears were tuned to detect unfamiliar noises even in sleep, so he was quickly alerted by the sound of the anchor dragging. He woke me up and we rushed on deck.

In the darkness, Gjalt stepped on the wrong anchor winch button and paid out chain instead of bringing it in. As a result, we moved from a water depth of twenty feet to just nine (we'd anchored in forty), and with a draught of just six feet, we were soon going to run aground. Gjalt paid out the entire length of chain before he noticed his mistake, so while he rethreaded it through the shackle, I motored gently forward to keep *Stella Maris* away from the shallows. Eventually, he brought up the anchor, and we moved back into deeper water in the centre of the bay. We set the anchor alarm but only slept fitfully until first light, when we put out a second anchor. It was then that we discovered the fishing line we'd left over the side had coiled itself around the prop, but thankfully it had broken before causing any damage. We'd learnt another lesson: no fishing lines in the water when at anchor.

After three days, the gusting wind showed no sign of abating. We'd had enough of the wind tunnel experience and suspected life was calmer away from the bullet-producing hills of Malumu Bay. We moved some ten miles west to Yanuca, an attractive island within Mbengga's fringing reef that held little appeal for us since it was home to a small tourist resort. From there, though, we were easily able to slip out of the encircling reef at first light and head for the Navula Pass on the southwest coast of Viti Levu Island.

We were extremely happy to escape the grey gloom that had hung over us for the past few days, and it felt good to be underway again. It was the end of September, and our time in the Pacific was ticking away at an alarming rate. Strong southeastly winds sent *Stella Maris* racing downwind at seven and a half knots like a thoroughbred set free.

A large container ship appeared without warning on our starboard side, emerging unnervingly from the early morning mist that shrouded the coast. The encounter made us stare hard into the fog until it lifted, once we'd moved further westward. The strong winds over the previous few days had generated some impressively large waves, but *Stella Maris* had no trouble skipping over them, and we had a lovely, comfortable sail.

The waters along the south coast of Viti Levu turned out to be fertile fishing territory. We had three strikes: the first got away; the second took one of Gjalt's brand new, highly prized fishing lures (causing a certain amount of distress); and the third was a massive dorado that stayed on the hook.

The fish was so strong we had to slow the boat down to reel it in. I furled the genoa and then turned *Stella Maris* into the wind, a manoeuvre that demonstrated how rough the conditions would have been had we not been sailing a downwind course. *Stella Maris* crashed into the raging waves as Gjalt and I wrestled to bring the fish onboard. By this time, our routine was well practiced, and I held the rod while Gjalt gaffed the dorado through the gills. Then I gripped the tail as Gjalt thrust a knife into the brain. It was an impressive bull, the sex obvious from its large humped head, and it had a thick, muscular body over four feet long. Gjalt made the necessary incisions to bleed it, and in no time at all, the stern was covered in a pool of bright red blood. It was a grisly scene, as if a hideous murder had been committed there, which I suppose it had. Needless to say, Gjalt was drenched in blood himself, and bucket after bucket of seawater had to be hauled aboard to scrub both him and the yacht of the gore.

The further west we went, the more the weather improved, and by the time we reached Navula Passage, we were basking in bright sunshine. We sailed smoothly through the wide gap in the barrier reef and straight into Momi Bay, a sheltered spot just two and a half miles away. Gjalt prepared sashimi, and we wolfed it down in the cockpit, savouring every morsel as the sun dipped towards the horizon.

Momi Bay was a haven of calm after the wind tunnel on Mbengga Island. We awoke the next morning well rested and keen to visit Musket Cove, a famous cruisers' anchorage in the Mamanuca Island chain. Nestling between the largest islands in the group, Malolo and Malolo Lailai, the cove was bought by an American in 1880 for the bargain price of one musket. Since then, Malolo Lailai had fallen victim to tourism, sprouting a marina, two major resorts, timeshare condominiums, and a nine-hole golf course. We had the anchor down for just five minutes before deciding we absolutely hated it.

There must have been forty or fifty yachts crammed together in the anchorage, and it wasn't immediately obvious why. The location between the sandy islands was pleasant (well, it would have been without so many boats) but unspectacular, and there was clearly a lot of tourist activity, something cruisers have the freedom to avoid. We had spent a long time scouting around for the best spot to drop our anchor when a German hollered that his was directly beneath us, a sure sign of the simmering tension caused by overcrowding. We made the token gesture of moving a smidgen further away (there wasn't space to move far) and lowered our anchor.

We both assessed the situation in silence: the lack of swing room, the close proximity of hostile neighbours, the hordes. We both felt a strong desire to leave welling up inside us. Then, out of the blue, the deciding factor hove into view around the corner of one of the islands.

A speedboat came tearing into the anchorage towing a gigantic, inflated banana. What kind of person invents such a thing? How does he pitch it to investors? "It's a sure bet – an inflatable banana! People will love it!"

And the sad thing is, they did. Squealing gleefully as they bounced along were four pasty, overweight tourists in orange life jackets, all of whom would have benefited from consuming a banana every now and then instead of being dragged along on one. If going to sea atop a giant piece of fruit had been our idea of paradise, we would have stayed, but as it wasn't, we made a quick exit.

While we were leaving, we saw a yacht ahead of us, motoring between one of the islands and some rocks, a route we were sure was unsafe. I was just about to check the chart when we saw the yacht nosedive into the water, its stern bucking up into the air shortly afterwards. It had rammed into a reef at full throttle. The hull looked as if it was made of steel and seemed to have survived the collision intact, because the boat soon continued on its way. The incident unsettled me, and I kept a manic vigil for reef and rock hazards as we sailed to the marina at Denarau on Viti Levu. Enchanting tropical island gems were scattered throughout these Fiji waters, but so were treacherous reefs, and it was clear that my nerves were going to be tested.

Denarau Marina had all-round protection from the wind, and we joined several other boats in the shallow lagoon. Onshore we inspected the facilities to see if it was a good place to haul out. There was a suitable travel lift, but the slings looked too frayed for our liking, and the area in which *Stella Maris* would stand while we worked on her was small. There wasn't much of a workshop or anybody to help with the bushes should that be necessary, so we were glad there was an alternative marina at Vuda Point a few miles to the north.

For now, we were happy to have found a calm spot for the night, and we had a drink at the restaurant beside the marina. Our waitress wore a name badge that read 'Cute Claire', but there was little cute about her, as far as we could tell. She pecked at the younger (cuter) waitresses like a bitter old hen, criticising them in front of customers and taking obvious joy in their embarrassment. She listed a range of services her family provided, but her offers were made with a sinister tone that warned against entering into any transactions with her. Denarau Marina was the departure point for fast catamarans to the outlying islands, and her attitude fit the familiar negative effect mass tourism has on the local people caught up in it.

It started to rain during the night, and the downpour continued throughout the next day, but we had to venture out to investigate the facilities at Vuda Point Marina. We ignored the mafia taxi drivers who were waiting to pounce on tourists and hitched a ride into Nadi with the crew of a luxury motor yacht. Once in town, we found a grizzled taxi driver who said he would take us on a round trip to Vuda Point for 20 Fijian dollars. Unlike all the taxi drivers we'd come across in Suva, this one was an ethnic Fijian.

"It'll be twenty dollars there and twenty dollars back," he announced, as soon as he pulled away from the kerb.

"You just agreed to twenty dollars for the round trip," Gjalt argued. "Stop the car and let us out."

"Okay then, thirty dollars"' he tried, but we didn't appreciate his sneaky tactics, or his assumption that we were tourist fools who could be easily parted from our money, and turned him down flat.

"All right, twenty dollars," he agreed reluctantly, but after driving on in uncomfortable silence for a while, he began to ramble constantly about how far away Vuda Point was. Trouble was clearly brewing. While the roads did weave further inland than we'd expected, the driver was so aggressive and rude that we didn't feel inclined to pay him more than he'd agreed to.

At Vuda Point Marina, there were two travel lifts, both of which were superior to the one at Denarau. It was clear that it was the best place for *Stella Maris*, and we returned to Nadi, glad that we'd found a good solution. The burly taxi driver's already dark mood, however, deteriorated on the way back. As we approached Nadi, his intermittent complaints about the low fare became an incessant stream of outrage. The instant he stopped the car, I leapt out and stood up against a shop window, putting myself as far from the imminent trouble as I could without actually running away.

The argument between Gjalt and the cantankerous Fijian quickly became ugly, and I knew I'd have to intervene to stop it getting out of hand.

"Do you want a fight?" the Fijian growled. "If you don't pay I will fight you."

"You agreed to take us for twenty dollars. If the money we gave you isn't good enough, give it back," Gjalt said.

"I'm going to call the police."

At this point, I stepped forward and offered an extra five dollars on the grounds that he'd waited for us while we looked around Vuda Point Marina. He was an unpleasant man who freely agreed a price and set about changing it from the very beginning, but it had been a long trip, and it was worth the extra money. If he had taken a friendlier, less hostile tack, we would gladly have paid him more, but trying to bully us into submission only made us determined not to give in.

The encounter left a bad taste in the mouth. It seemed that such animosity between locals and visitors was an unfortunate side effect of tourism, but perhaps Fijian taxi drivers – both ethnic and Indian – just liked to try their hands at increasing the fare one way or another.

We bought boat supplies in a small shop where an obliging Indian directed us to a good restaurant in town. It was several notches down from Singh's, lacking a clean and pleasant ambience and serving chicken curry riddled with bones and unfamiliar body parts, but at least it was cheap.

Sick and tired of taxi drivers and their upwardly mobile fares, we decided to hitch-hike back to the marina, even though it meant getting drenched in a torrential downpour. Amazingly, a car actually stopped to give us a lift, despite our sodden state. The driver turned out to be a Pacific Airways steward, a man who spent his working life being friendly and accommodating. Thankfully, it spilled over into his private life too.

The staff at the marina restaurant could have taken a few leaves out of his book. A large group of us ate there that night, and we were treated to Cute Claire's simmering aggression and barely concealed dislike of foreigners. There was no escaping the dark shadow of tourism in that part of Fiji.

Early the next morning, we sailed the five miles north to Vuda Point Marina. Gjalt was required to manoeuvre *Stella Maris* stern first into the haul-out slip, and I had to scurry around like a crazed lunatic to catch the lines thrown from the men onshore and secure them to the cleats. Once *Stella Maris* was resting securely in the slings, we climbed into a waiting boat and were taken ashore. We both had lumps in our throats as we watched *Stella Maris* being hoisted out of the water and swaying gently in the slings, but the experienced operator soon placed her safely on land. It was a huge relief that everything had gone so smoothly.

Gjalt immediately started to work on the rudder while I set about scraping the keel, which, to our dismay, was encrusted with barnacles. The creatures had positively feasted on the antifouling that was supposed to ruin their appetites. It was satisfying to chip at the barnacles and watch them fall away, like the childhood joy of picking scabs but without the blood.

Everything was going swimmingly until Gjalt removed the rudder and discovered that the top bush sent from England didn't fit onto the rudder post. He had been afraid of that back in Tonga, but when Gjalt double-checked with the supplier he was assured that we'd been sent the correct bush. He was absolutely livid. Fortunately, Jeff, a practical New Zealander who was the yard's go-to man for anything that needed to be fixed or fabricated, knew someone in the nearby town of Lautoka who could machine rudder bushes. And as luck would have it, our ever-helpful Brazilian friend, Caju, visited us that afternoon in a rental car, so he and Gjalt set off to track the man down.

After several strangely relaxing and gratifying hours spent de-barnacling, I was covered from head to toe in molluscs and antifouling alike. A shower was still the height of luxury to me, and I stood under the streaming water until I was transformed back into a presentable human being. Then I joined Gjalt and Caju, recently returned from a thankfully successful trip, in the Yacht Club's outdoor bar.

The view of the sea and the sandy islands shimmering tantalisingly in the distance was a good reward for a hard day's labour. I couldn't resist a cold beer, but it was the wrong medicine for a headache that was steadily developing after several hours working in the heat. It didn't stop me from enjoying yet another chicken curry, though, and after swallowing two aspirins back on *Stella Maris*, I fell into a deep sleep. Unfortunately, the beer came back to haunt me at three in the morning when I woke up desperate for the toilet. I had to get dressed, climb down the ladder propped against the boat, and trudge to the facilities. This most unappealing aspect of living on the hard was made worse that night by a sudden burst of torrential rain that turned the earth into slippery mud.

I thought I would have a nice and easy second day, but the keel was in such a state that we decided to strip it down completely and apply new antifouling. I spent the entire day scraping away at it with a variety of implements, an exhausting task made worse by the searing heat and the antifouling's inclination to reattach itself to me. Meanwhile, Gjalt collected the newly machined rudder bushes. We held our breath as he tried them out for size and exhaled with relief when they fit perfectly. Over time, though, we knew the fit would become tighter because the bushes were made from nylon, which swells a little when in contact with seawater. They would have to be replaced using a better material once we were in Australia, but as long as they got us there, we'd be happy.

The next day, I coated the keel in new antifouling while Gjalt concentrated on the rudder operation. With two burly men holding the rudder in position, he attempted to insert the holding pin. Try as he might, he just could not push it all the way through, and then he couldn't pull it back out again either. Jeff came to the rescue with the optimal tool from his extensive collection, but when the pin finally reappeared, it was bent. Luckily, we were able to buy a replacement for it in Lautoka, and Gjalt worked until after dark to put everything back together again. When we moved the rudder, though, it felt stiff; far too stiff. We weren't sure if this was simply due to the heavy steel rudder moving in air rather than water, but the last thing we wanted was to get back in the water only to have to be immediately hauled out again.

During our fifth day on the hard, Gjalt removed the rudder again and sanded down the spacer rings and holding pin just enough for the rudder to move a little easier. When it was back in place, it turned much more smoothly, and we were glad we'd taken the extra time to improve the fit.

That afternoon, *Stella Maris* was lowered back into the water, where she belonged. When she was released from the slings, I pushed against a concrete post to prevent her from scraping against it and promptly dislodged my shoulder from its socket. I was desperate to get the joint back in place because I had to jump ashore and secure *Stella Maris* in her berth. I stretched out my arm and frantically wiggled it around until I felt the ball pop into its socket, making me instantly useful once again.

After numerous attempts to get information out of the Australian Embassy (involving several phone cards and disconnections), we were finally told that we'd been granted visas. We were allowed to collect our passports the following day, a rare case of perfect timing.

We left *Stella Maris* safely tied up in the marina while we took a cheap taxi to Suva and back, a round trip of 400 kilometres with no scams or arguments this time. Hanif, the amiable Indian driver, drove to Nadi to find a third passenger, and a smartly dressed Fijian woman took the front seat while Gjalt and I spread out in the back. This sharing of taxis seemed to be the normal way for locals to get to Suva.

It was nice to see something of inland Fiji and get a glimpse of how people lived away from the big towns and the coast. There were many houses made from corrugated iron, some clearly home to extremely poor people, and everywhere we looked, washing was hanging out to dry as if Wednesday were National Laundry Day. As we drove past gently rolling hills, I put my brain in neutral and let the scenery flow past my eyes, a relaxing experience occasionally spiced up by Hanif's desire to become intimately familiar with the car in front. He would accelerate towards it, stop a foot or so from the rear bumper, hang in its slipstream until the next blind bend, and then make it eat his dust.

In spite of his hair-raising driving style, Hanif deposited us safely at the Australian Embassy, right on schedule at nine thirty. We settled down for the usual hour-long wait, only to be called to one of the windows after just two minutes. The woman who handed us our passports looked normal enough, but when we dared to query the visas we'd been given, she sprouted six new hideously ugly heads and snapped at us with razor-sharp teeth, revealing her true identity as Scylla, the sailor-eating monster of Greek mythology. Despite extracting every possible piece of useful information from other cruisers, despite writing a long letter explaining why Australians should deign to let us spend the cyclone season in their country, despite producing bank statements to prove we wouldn't sponge off the state, despite sitting in the Embassy for hours and finally driving 400 kilometres to pick up our passports, we'd still only been given visas that insisted we leave Australia every six months. What possible sense was there in that? There was only one reason we could think of: the government could make more money granting visa extensions than it could if it issued longer-term visas in the first place.

If we arrived in November, our first six months would be up in May, just after the cyclone season had ended. At that time, we intended to be sailing north along the east coast, making our way up and over the top of the country to reach the Indian Ocean, not diverting to one of Australia's neighbours to restart the clock on our visas. It isn't exactly the easiest place for sailors to nip away from, after all; New Zealand lies some 1,000 miles away, New Caledonia would be 700 miles back where we came from, and Papua New Guinea is 450 miles north of Cairns, and something of a crime hotspot to boot. It was this unwillingness to be accommodating that had cruisers sailing in droves to New Zealand.

We tried to explain the situation to the seven-headed monster, but she was determined to be as unhelpful, dismissive, and downright hostile as possible. The fact that her animosity emerged in a heavy Italian accent, without even a hint of convivial Australian twang, somehow just made matters worse. Her attitude did nothing to cool Gjalt's boiling anger, and I had to drag him away when he began to imitate The Dude's best friend Walter by proclaiming very loudly that we wouldn't dream of going to their bulls**t country now anyway.

Sitting on a bench outside the waiting room, we considered our options. We could have a last-minute change of plan and sail to New Zealand instead. There, we would be welcomed with open arms and granted visas upon arrival. Or, as we intended to fly to Europe to visit family and friends, we could time our return so we would sail away from Australia during the subsequent six-month period. If that didn't work out, we could hop across the Coral Sea to Papua New Guinea.

The situation would not have been so bad (bad, but not *so* bad) if every applicant received the same treatment, but everyone we spoke to had been given a different visa – all issued by the same Embassy. They hadn't been granted according to fixed rules, but something altogether more vague, like the phase of the moon or the case officer's hormone levels or just whether he was in a good mood or not. There was nothing to be done but think of The Dude's friend Walter again, who would have said, "F**k it Dude, let's get a curry," so off we went to Singh's to eat away our frustrations.

Hanif picked us up at two in the afternoon, right on time again, and he didn't bother getting a third passenger for the trip back. He was a Muslim and told us about the suicide bombings in Bali a few days earlier. "I was shocked," he said. "It's very sad that Islam is tarnished by the actions of a few fanatics."

I enjoyed sitting on the back seat watching the world go by and talking to Hanif about his life in Fiji and the country's politics.

"I think there'll be another coup after next year's election if an Indian becomes Prime Minister. That's why there was a coup in 2000, even though the ruling party had both Indian and ethnic Fijian members. There has been talk of granting an amnesty to George Speight and others who took part in the coup, but many people are not happy about that."

(Hanif's prediction of a coup in 2006 came true, but not because an Indian became prime minister. The ruling United Fiji Party narrowly won the elections but was deposed by the military for allegedly pursuing policies that would benefit the ethnic Fijian majority at the expense of the Indian community. The government had proposed a bill to grant amnesty to those involved in the 2000 coup and another to grant ethnic Fijians greater land and sea rights.)

"My daughter is getting married soon," Hanif said, changing the subject to something more pleasant and closer to his heart. "My wife and I were approached by the groom's parents. We arranged a meeting and my daughter liked him."

"How old are they?" I asked.

"She is twenty-one and the groom is twenty-three. The wedding will cost me 5,000 dollars. I have to buy clothes for the bride and our family, furniture, jewellery and food.

My wedding was also arranged by my parents twenty-five years ago and I'm still happily married," he said cheerfully.

After almost a week in the marina, working hard on *Stella Maris'* maintenance, we were ready to escape. We filled up with diesel and water at the fuel dock and set sail for the furthest reaches of the Mamanuca Island Group, some twenty-five miles to the northwest. It was a glorious day with good wind for sailing, but I could not allay my fear of the booby trap reefs and spent the whole trip on red alert.

The Navadra anchorage was stunning, an area of clear blue water protected to the south and east by three high islands with wide, sandy beaches. Being exposed to the west and north meant the anchorage could be rolly, but when we arrived, it was dead calm. We jumped over the side to go snorkelling and discovered a massive sloping wall of soft corals close to shore, the most beautiful and abundant we had seen in the Pacific. We felt as though we'd returned to paradise after a long journey across the desert.

We walked around the largest of the islands until a steep rock face, too crumbly to conquer, prevented us from going any further. From there, we sighted the first of three yachts to arrive that afternoon, one of which had a dive compressor that roared like a 747 during take-off. It ran for hours, destroying the tranquillity, a particular crime at sunset, the cruising world's sacred hour of the holy sundowner.

That evening, the wind picked up, and Gjalt's sixth sense took him topsides, where he saw one of the yachts drifting towards us. He jumped into our dinghy and went over to inform the captain that his boat was on the move. By the time the man was ready to re-anchor, his boat was just a few feet from ours, and I stood on the bow, fenders at the ready, to protect *Stella Maris*.

"Which direction is the shore?" the captain yelled as he prepared to steam off into the pitch dark. This was not encouraging. Gjalt accompanied the yacht in our dinghy and helped the crew put out a second anchor. We stayed on watch in the cockpit until one in the morning when, to our relief, conditions eased.

The strong winds made the anchorage quite rolly, and after daybreak, boats departed one after the other, until we were all alone. We considered leaving as well, but the sudden solitude was too precious to give up; we only had to share this heavenly world with a few goats and chickens that roamed the islands – our kind of neighbours. We moved *Stella Maris* to a spot that afforded slightly more protection from the swell, which gradually reduced during the day as the wind died down.

By this stage of our adventure, we were finally learning to stop looking ahead to the next destination, where we expected the water to be bluer and the coral more captivating. Tourism was rife in this part of Fiji, and our idyllic private haven of Navadra had escaped its clutches. We weren't about to leave it sooner than we had to, and we stayed until the weather gods persuaded us to go.

After two calm days, huge swells began to roll in from the west, rocking *Stella Maris* from side to side throughout the night. When we got up at dawn, it was to the sight of large waves crashing onto the expansive submerged reef in the centre of the anchorage. It was alarming to see such ominous breakers just a short distance from where we were.

We decided to move to a mooring further from the reef, but we couldn't raise the anchor. With the seabed sixty feet below us, Gjalt donned scuba gear and unwrapped the chain from around a large block of coral while I winched it aboard. Tied to the mooring, we waited for the sun to rise high enough to highlight the shallow reefs, and then we set off for an anchorage that was eighteen miles to the north.

It turned out to be a slog of a close-hauled trip with persistent, strong winds kicking up uncomfortably choppy seas. After four hours, we entered a protected channel between two islands at the southern end of the larger Naviti Island and anchored a good distance from the other yachts there. We soon realised that we were sitting in the current that was flowing through the centre of the channel and went in search of a better spot. As we moved past a flashy super yacht, the crew ordered us not to anchor close by, something we found particularly irritating, as we had no intention of staying anywhere near them. This altercation was just one reason we preferred less crowded anchorages, and while this one was pretty, it couldn't match Navadra.

So the next morning, we sailed the thirty-five miles back to Lautoka to check out of Fiji. It was nearly mid-October, and we still wanted to visit Vanuatu before heading for Australia. Gjalt gave me the day off while he took care of the navigation, and I relaxed for the first time, mostly because the reefs were visible far in the distance, thanks to the sun beaming down from high in the clear sky behind us. We enjoyed a wonderful fast sail for the first few hours, but when we reached the aptly named White Rock, the wind dwindled, forcing us to motor-sail the final stretch to Lautoka.

Deciding to throw thriftiness to the wind, we picked up a mooring beside the attractive Bekana Garden Resort, only to discover that it cost less than two dollars a night! We were surprised at how pleasant the anchorage was, because we'd heard bleak reports about boats being covered in the black soot that belched out from nearby sugar factories. The soot did materialise during the night, but it was the pungent smoke hanging stubbornly in the still air that bothered us more. The stench, combined with a stealth attack by giant, bloodthirsty mosquitoes, disturbed our sleep. We battened down the hatches and doused ourselves in DEET in order to survive the night.

The next day, we went into Lautoka to check out and buy fresh provisions for the four-day passage to Vanuatu. I felt unwell, having fallen victim to a rather unpleasant bladder infection, and consuming a greasy lunch of sausage and chips did nothing to improve my condition. I'd been unable to stomach the carcass segments adrift in the chicken curry on offer, which would certainly have made me feel even worse.

Walking around the uninspiring town in the stifling heat was a strain, so I sat outside the gloomy covered market and let Gjalt do the shopping. As he took out his wallet to pay, he noticed a shoe-shine man rushing towards him. He turned in time to push away his attacker, and in the skirmish, a knife dropped to the floor. The man quickly picked it up and ran off. We'd been warned in Suva to be wary of pickpockets and muggers, but we hadn't had any trouble until then.

Back on *Stella Maris*, we prepared to go to sea. We were looking forward to Vanuatu, a land of fiery volcanoes and fascinating tribes, a country we hoped was less overrun by tourism than Fiji. But the cyclone season was fast approaching, robbing us of time for our explorations.

STELLA MARIS RELAUNCHED AFTER BEING HAULED OUT, VUDA
POINT MARINA, FIJI

# 16.

# One Wedding and a Funeral

*A small community living in the Pacific island chain of Vanuatu has become one of the first to be formally moved out of harm's way as a result of climate change. The villagers have been relocated higher into the interior of Tegua, one of the chain's northern most provinces, after their coastal homes were repeatedly swamped by storm surges and aggressive waves linked with climate change.*

– United Nations Environment Programme,
  December 2005

We set off early in the morning and had a good sail south to Mapolo Passage, through which we gained freedom from the reef-infested waters of western Fiji. The passage was wide and clearly marked by sandy islands on either side.

It was another gorgeous day, but out on the open ocean, the waves were large and confused, so the trip got off to a very bumpy start. The rough motion made me tired and I went down below to succumb to the fatigue. When I got up a few hours later, I watched the islands of Fiji fade on the horizon.

I took the first watch and enjoyed being underway again; the moon was bright, the skies were clear, and the music on my Walkman made the time pass quickly. I went to bed in calm weather, but by the early hours of the next morning, the sea had become so rough that I was woken up by *Stella Maris* being vigorously rocked from side to side. Even worse, I suffered a relapse of my bladder infection, which I foolishly exacerbated by drinking coffee to stay awake during my watch. (As I had to rush to the toilet at least a dozen times in two hours, it certainly did that.) It was a miserable watch. When I was in the cockpit, it rained, and when I went to the toilet, I fretted about whether a nearby fishing boat would suddenly alter course while I was indisposed. After three very long hours, I was hugely relieved to hand over to Gjalt and fell into bed exhausted.

I was somewhat revived by a long sleep and felt steadily better as the new day wore on, which was just as well because the weather grew steadily more demanding. The wind began to howl, and *Stella Maris* took off, sailing mostly above eight knots, even reaching nine at times. The seas were very big but not confused, as they had been the day before, so it was still a comfortable ride – so comfortable, in fact, that an opportunistic seabird hitched a ride on our solar panels, sliding merrily across them in its liberally produced guano before flying away.

On our third day at sea, the wind eased, the ocean flattened out, and I was well on the road to recovery. *Stella Maris* cruised along at a good pace. Just as we were discussing what to have for dinner that evening, we caught a dorado the exact length of the fish filleting table on the stern. The act of catching and killing such a magnificent creature wore more on Gjalt's conscience each time. The man who had ripped off the skin of a fish with his teeth was being steadily shoved aside by a vegetarian. Whilst this new man was cleaning the catch, a large manta ray launched out of the water close by and somersaulted in the air three times. To our amazement, it repeated the spectacular trick twice more before disappearing beneath the waves for good. We came across so little marine life at sea that it was an incredible stroke of luck to be in the right place at the right time to see such a majestic creature fly so magically out of its element.

During the night, the wind direction kept changing, so we had to pole the genoa in and out several times, interrupting our sleep. We caught up the following day, which was just as well because conditions deteriorated towards evening.

The wind was strong and steady, often gusting to near-gale force. *Stella Maris* was sailing so fast that we were going to reach Port Vila, the capital of Vanuatu on the island of Efate, at night. We had a rule not to enter an anchorage we had never been to before in the dark. A pitch-black world is very different from a daylight one, with or without harbour lights, and plenty of cruising boats lie at anchor without a light. Therefore, we sailed with only a reefed main and headed south of Efate Island. The seas hit *Stella Maris* broadsides on, making for a very rocky ride, and at one point I was 'blue-walled' by a monster wave that climbed onboard and drenched me from head to toe.

When we hove-to, conditions became more bearable, but with our normal routine broken we were both overcome by tiredness. It was cold, too, which didn't make keeping watch any easier. Soon after we started sailing towards the island, the wind eased, and just making progress instead of killing time transformed the wild night into a pleasant one. I snatched some sleep, and when I got up we were entering the channel leading into the protected harbour of Port Vila.

We anchored in the area designated for new arrivals, and it wasn't long before the Quarantine officer came onboard. All he required of us was the completion of his form and thirty dollars for his trouble.

Gjalt was not enthralled by our proximity to town and its unattractive buildings, so we moved a short distance to go behind the half-mile-long island of Reriki and picked up a mooring. Port Vila looked a lot more pleasing from our new vantage point, so it was worth the ten-dollar-a-night fee, a luxury we wouldn't normally have contemplated.

Vanuatu gained its name and independence from joint British and French rule in 1980. The nation was called the New Hebrides by Captain Cook when he arrived there in 1774, because the rugged islands reminded him of those off the west coast of Scotland. When an Irish seaman discovered sandalwood in 1825, contact with Europe grew and fourteen years later, the first British missionaries turned up to establish Christianity. They introduced a common language, called Bislama (pidgin English), which was intended to stop the natives from killing and eating each other – something they apparently did often, and with great enthusiasm, due to 'misunderstandings' that arose because practically every village had its own language. I'm not a fan of missionaries, with their unbridled need to bend others to their will, but I was thankful that cannibalism was no longer practised in Vanuatu, as sailors had been devoured in the past.

When we walked into Port Vila, our fragile land personas

were agitated by the heavy traffic along the main street; we hadn't expected so many cars. There was also evidence of a tourist industry, although it was of the laid-back, take-it-or-leave-it variety that was a lot less annoying than the inflatable banana-riding kind. A quick investigation of scooter hire ruled it out (we weren't about to pay sixty-five dollars for eight hours on a moped). Restaurants were also expensive, certainly compared to Fiji, but eventually we found a nice place overlooking the harbour that served our favourite 'special occasion' meal of hamburgers and French fries at an acceptable price.

The open-air market was packed with tables display-ing mouth-watering fruit and vegetables. As we walked around, Gjalt suffered the misfortune of a run-in – quite literally – with a large, unidentifiable fruit that was lurking mischievously on the floor. The impact thrust a thick stalk under the nail of his large toe, severing its connection to live tissue and poling it vertically up into the air. The fruit was sent skidding along the ground and suffered severe lacerations, while Gjalt hopped on his uninjured foot, swearing profusely and trailing blood as he hobbled away from the scene. It was a case of kick and run (or kick and limp to be precise), and I was left surrounded by a small crowd of watchful natives. I felt nervous, adrift in a sea of serious brown eyes, and I had the distinct impression that they were looking to us to pay for the damaged fruit. I hurried after Gjalt and voiced my thoughts to him, but he was outraged that I had the audacity to be concerned with anything other than the fate of his toe.

I wasn't sure that the feelings of the ni-Vanuatu stall holders should be so lightly dismissed. They looked distinctly wild, their hair sticking out defiantly in all direc-tions and their eyes burning with the same intensity we'd seen in the descendants of the Marquesas Island warri-ors. Most of the women, however, wore demure, curiously named 'Mother Hubbard' dresses, flowery smocks of a highly decent Christian nature, with frills and lace around the collars, cuffs and hems. Although the men wore decid-edly mundane shirts and trousers, it remained obvious that we had arrived in a country that was totally different from anywhere we'd set foot before and that was exciting.

W e left the hustle and bustle of Port Vila to go to Port Havannah on the northwest coast, a half-day's sail away. Nosing into a protected channel between Efate and the six-mile-long island of Moso, we dropped the anchor in an enticing patch of turquoise water bounded on both sides by lush vegetation and sandy beaches. To the northeast rose the dramatic peak of an extinct volcano, reminding us that we were in a chain of islands that had been formed by violent eruptions originating deep within Earth's molten layers.

The village of Sunae was a short distance from us on the bank of Moso Island, and we dinghyed over to seek permission from the chief to anchor and walk on his land. Some villagers were sitting on a wooden bench beneath a shady tree, so we beached the dinghy close by and walked over to introduce ourselves.

"Is it possible for us to see the chief?"

"I am the chief," replied the oldest man, a warm smile revealing yellowish brown teeth and a large gap where his incisors used to be. He had an aura of wisdom and dignity that was not diminished by his simple outfit of shorts and t-shirt.

"Is it all right for us to anchor here?" Gjalt asked.

"Yes, of course. You are most welcome. You can anchor, swim, and walk on the island. Nobody will bother you; I guarantee that you will be safe. The only thing we cannot give you is water. We have not had rain for a very long time and the well is getting dry. Sometimes we have to go across to the mainland to get water."

I presented the chief with a bag of gifts: pens, folding brushes with mirrors in the handles (courtesy of Continental Airlines), and some clothes and toys for the village children, many of whom had gathered around us. The women seemed particularly taken with the brushes, giggling as they caught sight of themselves in the mirrors.

We were invited to join Chief Kalfau on the bench, and he spoke to us so quietly that we had to lean in close to hear him. He answered our questions slowly and thoughtfully, giving weight to every response. This carefully measured way of speaking, together with his kind face and large glasses, reminded us of the Dalai Lama. His expression could turn from earnest to joyous in an instant. "I am seventy-two years old," he told us proudly. "If you want to

299

live a long life, it is in your own hands."

To the other side of me sat the chief's son-in-law, who told me that one of the chief's six sons was getting married the next day.

"You are welcome to come to the wedding," he said.

The chief reiterated the invitation before we left, and we accepted gladly. We couldn't believe how lucky we were to have been offered such a unique opportunity to glimpse a slice of real life in a Vanuatu village.

We said goodbye and dinghyed to the northern tip of Moso Island, where we strolled along the sandy beach. When a young, bare-chested man brandishing a huge machete strode towards us, we were glad we'd sought permission to come ashore.

"Have you seen the chief?" he demanded sternly, but grinned two rows of perfect white teeth at us as soon as we said we had. "I'm collecting coconuts for my brother's wedding," he said, explaining the deadly weapon in his hand. "He's getting married tomorrow."

When we told him we had been invited, this youngest son of Chief Kalfau flashed his dazzling smile again, said farewell, and continued on his way.

That evening, with the moon large and bright and the water so flat that even the light from individual stars was reflected in it, we decided the time was right to test the apparent stress-relieving properties of kava. We'd bought a small bushel of the herbal plant in the Suva market in case we needed a gift for a Fijian chief, but as we hadn't met any, we decided to give it to ourselves. It didn't turn out to be a particularly generous gesture, however, because the drink we produced from it had the texture and flavour of muddy straw. Kava is very popular in Fiji, so no doubt our methodology was to blame (we really had no idea what to do with what essentially resembled dried grass), but we did, at least, feel mellow afterwards, and our tingling lips confirmed that we were under the influence of an illicit substance.

At first light the next morning, it was so calm that not a single ripple disturbed the water's surface. The tranquillity was enchanting; the only sound was the dawn chorus of birds on the island. Then, out of the liquid mirror emerged the arched back of a dugong, followed by its distinctive whale tale, which rose gracefully into the air before slipping back into the water. A relative of the manatee, the dugong is listed as an endangered species. Chief Kalfau later told us that the villagers used to eat the harmless creatures, also known as sea cows, and although they were now protected, the one I'd seen was Port Havannah's sole survivor.

Gjalt went for a swim in search of the dugong, while I embarked on mission impossible: finding clothes free of rust, grease, or fish blood stains for him to wear to the wedding. Then I hunted through every single cupboard for suitable wedding presents. I found pillowcases still in their original packaging, a brand new towel, a long piece of exotic material salvaged from our old four-poster bed, and some toiletries – not bad after nearly a year at sea.

The dinghy ride to the village was a long upwind run that thoroughly drenched my wedding outfit. A small group of young men laughed with near hysteria as we made landfall, a rather disconcerting welcome that I struggled to understand. We finally put it down to my bedraggled state, because soon enough, young children came to touch my wet clothes and then ran away giggling.

We thought the wedding had been cancelled, as the villagers were simply going about their normal business, but an old man with a bandaged hand led us to Chief Kalfau, who was standing by the church. He was dressed smartly in a festive Hawaiian shirt, black trousers, brown lace-up shoes, and – of all things – a baseball cap. When he turned around, we saw that it had 'Suicidal' embroidered on the back.

"The wedding is delayed because the cake has not arrived from Port Vila," he told us, clearly agitated by this organisational failure. "The cake should have been delivered yesterday, but the fellow who went to collect it got drunk."

He accepted our bag of wedding presents, and took us to sit in the communal dining area, which was artfully decorated with ribbons and balloons and cut bougainvillea stems rich with brightly coloured blossoms.

"The pastor is from the Neil Thomas Ministries," he said quietly. "He agreed to perform the ceremony only if there was no custom. There is only one living God, but we still have some custom ways."

The bride came from the island of Malekula, and she and the groom belonged to the Neil Thomas Ministries, an organisation founded in Australia some thirty years earlier that followed a Methodist doctrine. Sunae village had been successfully converted to Christianity by Presbyterian missionaries in the nineteenth century, but we understood the villagers incorporated some customs into their religion. What these customs were remained a mystery to us, as it seemed intrusive to ask for details. On some Vanuatu islands, many people still practiced their old ways and lived in so-called 'custom villages'. Those ni-Vanuatu wore grass skirts or penis-sheaths, not common attire for Christians. We later learnt that Chief Kalfau had decreed that the Sunae women could only wear trousers while working in their gardens and never in the village. Some of the visiting Malekula women wore trousers, and he clearly did not approve.

As the delay continued, the chief took us on a tour of his village, leading us along a wide, sandy path that ran parallel to the shore. Houses were scattered around it on either side, most built from panels of corrugated iron, each with a terrace to one side and a corrugated iron roof supported by wooden poles to shade it from the sun. Some houses had pretty gardens, with tropical trees and flowering bushes, guarded by a private fence. There was also a newly installed hand pump that provided easy access to the precious water, an innovation the chief demonstrated with obvious pride.

Chief Kalfau explained how the villagers lived as one community, cooking and eating together and sharing chores according to a rota. There were names written beside certain tasks on a piece of cardboard hanging up in the dining area. One man was assigned the task of giving food to the women to cook, and the women always made lap-laps (a traditional Vanuatu dish of grated root vegetables), which were baked for an hour on a fire, covered by stones. The men brewed the tea and cooked soup in a huge caldron. One of the women told us that there were three sittings each for breakfast, lunch, and dinner, with the children eating first. Each family had a garden on the mainland to grow vegetables, because the soil was too poor on Moso Island. Everyone was required to contribute food to the community, but they could make money by selling any surplus at the Port Vila market.

"It is no good for a man to work for anyone but himself," the chief said, "because then he becomes a slave. Living our way, we can work and rest whenever we want." From our own newfound position of freedom, we could easily sympathise with his point of view. Village life in Sunae certainly seemed to be very organised and harmonious.

The chief took our wedding presents to his house and collected his Bible. By the time we got back to the corrugated iron church that doubled as the community hall, the wedding party was waiting by the door, ready to go inside. It had been decided not to wait any longer for the missing cake.

The wedding party wouldn't have looked out of place in an English church. The bride wore a white gown, her face covered by a long veil, and the groom was dressed in a black morning suit, with a bow tie to perfectly complement his white shirt. Each had their attendants: a smartly turned-out best man and seven bridesmaids in matching fuchsia dresses that reminded me of the red dress I'd worn at my sister's wedding. The youngest girls had flowers woven through their hair, and all of them held attractively arranged bouquets of white and red flowers with green sprays mixed in.

The women of the village wore their traditional brightly coloured Mother Hubbard dresses. The men, meanwhile, looked as though they just hadn't bothered at all, as they lounged around in shorts and t-shirts. Perhaps it was appropriate, then, that most of the men stayed outside and listened to the ceremony on huge loudspeakers that had been set up for the occasion. We joined the women inside the church and had the honour of sitting with Chief Kalfau on one of the wooden benches.

The service began with a portly man trying to rouse the congregation using the melodramatic style favoured by evangelical preachers in the USA. He spoke fervently into a microphone, and his enthusiasm boomed out of the stadium-sized loudspeakers that were placed on either side of the hall. He spoke in Bislama, so we could only understand snatches of what he said, but there was no mistaking his animated plea for everyone to join him in raising their hands – which nobody did.

After a few minutes, the warm-up man stepped aside,

and the pastor took centre stage, also speaking Bislama. He began by addressing the bride and groom, apparently explaining their obligations as husband and wife. I was alarmed at the frequent use of the words 'submit' and 'obey' when he spoke to Linda, the bride, but to my relief, I understood that Jimmy, the groom, was subsequently told he was not allowed to boss his wife about. Later, I caught a reference to Genesis, at which point Chief Kalfau began flicking through his Bislama Bible, as if wanting to verify what the pastor had said.

The microphone seemed to fail when the wedding vows were exchanged, because we could have heard a pin drop, but when the singer, dressed in white shorts and an arresting yellow shirt, burst enthusiastically into song, it was clear there was nothing wrong with it. The congregation joined in with the more sedate hymns that followed, and not long after that, the ceremony was over. Jimmy lifted Linda's veil and dumped it on her head in such an unattractive heap that an old lady rushed forward to rearrange it. Then the pair signed the register and left the church to receive the guests, who filed out, grim-faced, to the happy refrain of the cheerful singer.

Gjalt and I took our place in line and shuffled out into the sunshine. The bride and groom were shaking people's hands, and they couldn't have looked more disconsolate if they'd just been sentenced to death. The bride's mother hugged her daughter tightly, and they both sobbed as if they would never see each other again. This promptly set one of the bridesmaids off too. Amidst all this misery, my broad smile seemed so conspicuously inappropriate that I quickly adopted a neutral expression before I caused any offence. The bride and groom shook our hands with the lightest of touches, not raising their eyes from a glum examination of the ground.

Chief Kalfau invited us to sit in the shade of a large tree while he took his Bible back to his house. The good news was that the wedding cake had arrived at last, and we were both brought a piece, along with a welcome glass of orange juice. Then we followed the villagers to the communal dining area, where an impressive spread had been laid on for the occasion. There were large trays of rice, meat, chicken, manioc, yams, and salad, and everyone was given a generous helping of whatever they wanted. The meal was delicious, and we ate it with Chief Kalfau, sitting on raffia mats some women had laid down for us beside the large tree.

Linda and Jimmy and their attendants ate together in a group apart from everyone else, but they all stared dejectedly at their feet without saying a word to each other. Meanwhile, we listened with deep interest to the chief as he told us about some of their customs. We were particularly rapt when he spoke of *nakaemas*, or black magic. It was still practiced in the northern islands such as Malekula, he said, which was where Linda came from.

"Be careful if you go there," he warned. "They have the power to kill you if they want. They could use a dog, or a cat - it might just brush past you and you wouldn't even notice it. but later you will die. A man in this village did nakaemas, but it is tabu. I sent him to prison in Port Vila, and he stayed there for one year. As chief, my word is law. The ability to run a village is in the blood, and it must stay in the family. I will decide which of my sons will become chief after me and no one will question it, because it is my right.

"You have to be careful of the Big Nambas," he said. "Many missionaries have been killed on the outer islands, because they tried to make the Big Nambas stop their custom ways. Only one missionary was killed on Efate. God must have wanted it that way. The missionary interfered in politics, which was not right. There is only one living God, but everyone is free to believe what they wish to believe. We are each responsible for managing our own lives."

"What do you think of the Jon Frum cult?" I asked, interested in his views of the people on the island of Tanna, who worshipped an American deity by that name.

"It is their way, and they are free to choose. It is not right for outsiders to come and tell people how to live in their own country," he said.

He told us about a great chief, King Roymata, who brought peace between the warring, cannibalistic tribes of neighbouring villages by inviting them to share food, thereby making them brothers. "When he died, his wife and servants were buried alive with him."

"That was not good," I said.

"It was their belief," he answered, softly. "On Judgement Day, the living God will decide what the afterlife holds for all of us; heaven, or hell. Our actions will have consequences."

Later in the afternoon, Catrine, an eloquent woman with bright, lively eyes came over to talk to us. She was visiting her daughter, who lived in the village with her boyfriend, and was helping with the wedding. "Oh, I hate nakaemas," she said. "I am afraid of it. If someone practicing nakaemas chants your name in a song, you will be compelled to go to them. Then they will kill you, but bring you to life again so you will go back to your family and die in front of them a few days later."

After several hours in the village, we decided it was time for us to go. We wanted to see the ceremony of the bride being delivered to her new home by her family, but it was held up by a broken guitar string. The chief's help was needed to find a solution, so we wanted to free him from any pressure he felt to entertain us. We had probably taken up too much of his time as it was, but we'd been fascinated by every minute of it.

Chief Kalfau said he wanted to give us a present and walked away in the direction of his house. When he returned, he presented us with a rolled-up raffia mat, tied with twine and decorated with fresh bougainvillea flowers. "Thank you for accepting my word," he said, as he shook Gjalt's hand.

It was a lovely gesture at the end of a special day, and we left surrounded by smiling faces and waving hands.

That night, music and laughter drifted to us from the village, but early the next morning, we awoke to sounds that couldn't have been more different. Gone were the festive voices of celebration, replaced by prolonged and tormented wailing from both men and women. It made us question the true nature of the marriage that Linda and Jimmy had seemed so unhappy about.

We decided to explore away from the village and dinghyed through a small boat pass at the northern end of the Port Havannah channel. We did some wonderful snorkelling in crystal-clear water, although Gjalt nearly drowned when he slipped into the water head first and snagged his trunks on a protuberance on the dinghy. One second he was having fun, and the next he was submerged upside down, watching his life flash before his eyes. Luckily, I was there to rescue him. I unhooked his trunks, and he dropped free; it would have been an embarrassing way to go.

That afternoon and evening, the blood-curdling wailing started up in the village once again. We were completely perplexed and even worried that we were somehow responsible. *Did we upset them or anger the chief in some way?* We realised it was unlikely, since we'd even been given a parting gift from the chief when we left, but it is always possible to make a blunder by misunderstanding another culture. The wailing was totally alien to our European sensibilities and deeply disturbing to listen to. The Presbyterians may have succeeded in converting the people of Sunae village to Christianity, but they hadn't changed something fundamental within their souls. The wailing we heard rose up from the depths of despair, and it became clear to us that something terrible had happened: someone had died. All kinds of scenarios ran through our minds. *Did the bride kill her husband on their wedding night? Did the chief die?* We dared not intrude to find out.

But when the wailing started again the next morning and we saw people walking along the water's edge towards the village and boats going back and forth between Efate and Moso Island, we simply had to find out what had happened. The day before it had seemed indecent to enquire, but now it seemed indecent not to.

We decided to go for a walk on Efate in the hope of finding someone who could tell us what was going on. We paddled into the mangroves, tied the dinghy to a tree, and walked to the house of one of the chief's sons. It was a basic corrugated iron structure, but there was a modern pickup truck parked beside it. No one was home. By this time, the wailing had begun again, and it was so raw and so full of pain that it was almost frightening.

When we reached the start of the paved road, we found many parked cars. There was a sign by the water that read, '*Sapose yu nidim boat, ring im bel*'. This was where the boats had crossed to Moso Island. We carried on walking, and a truck full of men passed us. When they greeted us with a friendly wave, we were reassured that we weren't the cause of the trouble.

We turned back and met two young men on the way; they had just come from the village. We told them we had been at the wedding the day before, and finally, we discovered the reason for the wailing.

"Somebody died," one of them said. We immediately

thought it must have been an older person, but they told us it was the chief's youngest son, Pani. We were shocked, because this was the machete-wielding young man with the bright smile, whom we'd met the first day we went ashore. He had been so happy, so alive, and now, less than two days later, he was dead.

After the evening wedding party in the village had finished, some young people had gone across to Efate to continue celebrating. In the early hours of the next morning, Pani had been hit on the back of the head with a rock by one of his friends when they got into a fight over a girl. He was only in his early twenties. Finally the bouts of wailing made sense: first when the news had reached the village, then when the police came to arrest the culprit, and finally that morning when Pani's body had been returned for the funeral.

"You can go to the funeral," the young men said, but we decided it would be intrusive. Attending a wedding was one thing; attending a funeral was quite another.

Still, we knew that we had to go and pay our respects, no matter how awkward we felt about it. Chief Kalfau and the villagers had made us so welcome, we could hardly just weigh anchor and leave.

It was impossible to predict how two cruisers would be received at such a time of grief, but as soon as we landed the dinghy, we were greeted as warmly as before. We said we'd heard the news and wanted to see the chief, but only if we weren't intruding. A well-spoken man called Will said we had done the right thing by coming and that our visit meant more to them than a material gesture. He took us to Abel, another of the chief's sons, who walked us to his father's house.

Abel had the same nervous giggle as his younger brother Pani had had.

"We had not expected this," he said.

We waited in line to see the chief, who sat on the stoop of his house, clearly devastated. He looked stunned, as if he couldn't believe what had happened. He was wearing the same loud Hawaiian shirt he'd worn to the wedding just two days before as well as the 'Suicidal' baseball cap, which had lost its humour and become almost ominous. It was horrible to see the chief so upset, having lost a son so unexpectedly and violently. Several mourners shook our hands, including an adorable young girl, who thrust her hand out earnestly, looking me straight in the eye. To the side of the house, a group of women sat sobbing in the shade of an awning.

When it was our turn to see the chief, we offered our condolences, and he thanked us for coming. He told us about the blow to the back of Pani's head. "We had not been expecting this," he said, echoing Abel's words. "I hope I will meet Pani again; with our Maker."

"I hope that we will meet you again," Gjalt said, and the chief returned this sentiment. After saying all we could, we headed back to the dinghy.

As we were leaving, we met the chief's brother. He had tears in his eyes, and as he held my hand, I told him I hoped they would find the strength to get through this difficult time. We could not have wished to meet such warm and generous people, and we felt deeply sorry that such a tragedy had happened to them.

We had wanted to give the villagers of Sunae some children's clothes and toys before we left, but now that all seemed silly and insignificant. On the day of the wedding, Chief Kalfau had told us that living a long life depended on one's own management. It turned out that didn't always hold true. We decided to head back to Port Vila the next day to check out. The weather forecast predicted the return of the trade winds, the absence of which had given us such peaceful days at anchor, and we needed them to make our final passage across the Pacific. It was the last week of October, time to head for Australia.

We left the anchorage early the following morning, sad to leave. As we passed the village, the chief stepped out from the shade of the tree he'd sat under when we first met and waved goodbye with both arms. The village would be in mourning for five days, and then there would be a feast. We hoped no cruisers would stumble haplessly into the village during that time, but we were certain that if they did, they'd still receive the warmest of receptions.

Back in Port Vila, we checked out and did some final shopping. We gave the remainder of the kava to a waitress at our regular burger haunt; we didn't think the pernickety Australian Customs officers would be too pleased to find the hallucinogenic substance on our boat.

I wasn't ready to leave Vanuatu. It was an exciting country that we'd barely scratched the surface of. We had considered racing north to the other islands, which sounded fascinating (the dangers of black magic apart), but we'd simply run out of time. It was impossible to do the vast Pacific justice in a single cruising season. It was clear that one day, we would have to return.

SUNAE VILLAGE, EFATE ISLAND, VANUATU

THE WEDDING PARTY GREETS GUESTS AFTER THE CEREMONY,
SUNAE VILLAGE, EFATE ISLAND, VANUATU

THE WEDDING PARTY EATS TOGETHER AFTER THE CEREMONY,
SUNAE VILLAGE, EFATE ISLAND, VANUATU

A Calm Morning In The Sunae Village Anchorage,
Efate Island, Vanuatu

# 17.

## Arriving Down Under

*The Great Barrier Reef is perhaps the best managed Marine Park in the world, but it is not immune from climate change. Increasingly frequent El Niño events superimposed on a rising trend in temperatures will impede the recovery of coral cover from previous bleaching events. We are at risk of seeing the most pristine coral reef system degrade over the next few decades, with macroalgae (seaweed) taking over from the coral, and drastic changes to fish populations and biodiversity generally. This is already happening in large areas of the reef as a result of climate change and other impacts.*

– *The Implications of Climate Change for Australia's Great Barrier Reef,* WWF-Australia and the Queensland Tourism Industry Council, February 2004

The 1,000-mile trip to Bundaberg would lead us north of New Caledonia's outer reefs and take about a week. We got good trade winds from the start and had a fantastic first day, covering 170 miles. We'd sailed close to full moon for most of our passages across the Pacific, and although that good fortune had now come to an end, Venus shone brightly enough to light up the ocean on my first watch.

On the second day, the sun remained hidden behind a thick bank of clouds that made the world grey, wet, and miserable. Luckily, the winds remained strong, and *Stella Maris* continued to make excellent progress. At midnight, we passed north of the reefs at the top of New Caledonia, another country we would have to explore on our next visit to the Pacific.

The sun returned the following morning and with it came calmer conditions. When the strong wind disappeared, we

hoisted the gennaker and enjoyed a relaxed day sailing
smoothly over a benign sea. I watched a school of flying fish
launch six feet out of the water like a squadron of Harrier
Jump Jets at take-off and then cruise so far that seagulls
were able to swoop down and pick off one or two of them in
mid-flight. I'd only ever seen such fish fly low to the waves
before, crashing into the water like kamikaze pilots; this
high-altitude formation flying was a new and impressive
sight.

On the third night, the wind picked up, and we went
back to sailing with the main and the genoa. Far from
any hazardous reefs, I was able to relax on my watches,
except for a few moments when the moon emerged above
the horizon and imitated a huge ship steaming full speed
ahead towards us. Once it had revealed its true identity,
its magical crescent added to the tranquillity of a peaceful
night.

After a fourth day of fast sailing, we skirted the northern
tip of Chesterfield Reef, an extensive shallow bank of reefs
and islands that stretched north to south some 450 miles
east of Bundaberg. We were now able to steer a course
southwest, and since winds were southerly, they suddenly
began to scream over the deck, sixty degrees off the bow.
We reefed the sails, but night watches became wild and
bumpy, and I was happy to hand over to Gjalt and snuggle
into bed down below. But as we were in the vicinity of reefs
once again, I ended up having nightmares about sailing at
high speed through crowded anchorages and treacherous
mazes of shallow hazards. After nights such as these, it
was a relief to wake up and find that we were safely over
deep water.

The winds finally eased off a little the following evening,
and we took the reefs out of the sails to maintain an average
speed of seven knots. The seas were quite lumpy, so we
had a somewhat bumpy and testing ride, but we were able
to fish again and caught a good-sized dorado, our last fish
of the trip. By this time, though, Gjalt no longer derived
any joy from catching fish; he had even withdrawn his
birthday request of a brand new reel.

During our last night at sea, we had enough wind to
make eight knots, but this wasn't fast enough to get us
into Bundaberg before sunset the next day. It was an
incredibly starry night, and I watched a host of meteorites

streak across the sky, one of which actually exploded in a brilliant white flash.

Six days after leaving Port Vila, with eighty-three miles still to go, the wind started to die. By early afternoon, we were ambling along between four and five knots, using the gennaker. In the gentle conditions, I tidied and cleaned the boat and threw the remnants of our fresh food overboard, so as not to invite the wrath of Australia's zealous Quarantine officers.

We saw one coastal freighter but no other boats. A Customs Coast Watch plane flew overhead, and we received a polite call on the radio warning us against stopping anywhere before clearing in at Bundaberg. We actually found it reassuring to have confirmation that we were approaching Australia. There was not even a hint of land on the horizon, and our echo sounder wasn't working; its display insisted we were in deep water instead of the a hundred feet or so indicated on the chart. It was a disconcerting feeling to see no sign of the world's largest island when it was supposed to be only a dozen miles away.

As the final vestiges of daylight began to fade, we at last sighted land. It turned out to be The Hummock, Bundaberg's highest point at just ninety-six metres above sea level. For Gjalt, it was weird to think we would soon be safely tied up in a marina similar to the one we'd left in Texas eleven months before. The great responsibility he had assumed for us and for *Stella Maris* would be over. The trip had demanded an enormous amount of focus from him: boat maintenance, boat repairs, navigation, weather, the Panama Canal transit, negotiating atoll passes, and secure anchoring; the list of his responsibilities was long. The thought that all the stress would end filled him with a strange feeling of fatigue rather than the relief he'd expected.

By 9 o'clock, we were at the start of the channel leading to the Bundaberg Port Marina, and having been told that it was an easy night entry, we decided to head in. The channel was very well marked, its abundant flashing red and green lights lining up like an airport runway, but we had the misfortune of arriving just as a fleet of fishing boats was on its way out. These boats had their arms extended to each side and were zigzagging haphazardly, making it a challenge for us to stay within the channel ourselves. In the pitch dark, it amounted to two miles of high stress, and when we finally arrived at the marina, it took us a while to find a safe spot to anchor for the night. Once we had, exhaustion sent us to bed, where we zoned out until the following morning. The Pacific Ocean was sadly behind us, but we had realised our dream: we had sailed across it to Australia.

The next morning, we cleared in, and contrary to expectations, the Australian Quarantine and Customs officers were very pleasant; one of them even became a good friend. I'd been so careful not to arrive with any prohibited food that the Quarantine officer didn't confiscate a single item, the first time this had been the case for him, he said. We saw enormous yellow bags full of illicit produce being hauled off other yachts and wondered what on earth they contained.

We booked into Bundaberg Port Marina for a month and rented a car to visit other marinas before deciding whether to stay there for the entire cyclone season. As we drove south along the east coast, we had the unpleasant feeling that we'd sailed across the Pacific only to end up back in the USA. The monotonous, unimaginative architecture of familiar restaurant chains and sprawling shopping malls was depressingly similar. Everyone was busy blindly running in the hamster wheel of consumerism, fuelling the capitalist engine without thinking too hard about the consequences. Fresh from living happily with very little on a small boat and seeing how beautiful nature is away from the influence of man, this so-called civilized world seemed vulgar and ignorant to us. Humanity is obsessed with keeping the economic machine turning, manufacturing disposable goods to sell to consumers who've been brainwashed into believing happiness lies in the possession of the latest gadget. The monster has to be fed at all costs, and we'll chew through the Earth's resources and push species to extinction to do it. How can our lives be good, when so much destruction is needed to pay for them? When will we realise that less is more?

We returned to the Bundaberg Port Marina and booked in for the cyclone season. It was pleasant and uncrowded, it had all the facilities we needed to work on *Stella Maris*, and the staff were helpful. It just happened to be in the middle of nowhere. Still, the flat countryside made Gjalt feel right at home and before long, I felt the same way.

We had taken the old-fashioned, long way to Australia. It was an incredible journey across the world's largest ocean, and we'd stopped at some of the most magical and peaceful islands on Earth along the way. Like all good things in life, that journey passed far too quickly, but there was not a single moment we regretted. We had wanted to escape from the so-called 'real world', to sail far out, and that was exactly what we did. The freedom we found on the ocean allowed us to become part of a world so enchanting that we had no choice but to keep going. As soon as the cyclone season was over, we carried on sailing and ventured even further out, into the Indian Ocean and around the Cape of Good Hope into the Atlantic.

But that's another story.

CORINNA MAKES FRIENDS WITH THE AUSTRALIANS

# *Acknowledgements*

In addition to the organisations quoted at the beginning of each chapter, I would like to thank the following sources for providing information used in the book:

Wikipedia
The BBC
The Panama Canal Authority
Galápagos National Park
Charles Darwin Foundation
Jacob P. Lundh *(Galápagos: A Brief History)*
Robert Louis Stevenson *(In the South Seas)*
The San Diego Union-Tribune *(The Wreck of the Emerald Jane)*
The Global Coral Reef Monitoring Network
The Planetary Coral Reef Foundation *(Health of the Bora Bora Island Reef, 2004)*
*Ahoy – Mac's Web Log (History of the* Seeadler, *Mackenzie J Gregory)*.

# Useful Cruising Books

*World Cruising Routes*
– Jimmy Cornell, International Marine/Ragged Mountain Press

*Circumnavigation: Sail the Trade Winds, Volume I - Fort Lauderdale to Fiji*
– Sue Moesly, Wescott Cove Publishing Company

*Cruising Guide to Belize and Mexico's Caribbean Coast, including Guatemala's Rio Dulce*
– Captain Freya Rauscher, Wescott Cove Publishing Company

*Charlie's Charts of Polynesia*
– Charles E. Wood, Charlie's Charts

*Landfalls of Paradise, Cruising Guide to the Pacific Islands*
– Earl R. Hinz, University of Hawaii Press

*The Moorings Tonga, Vava'u Islands Cruising Guide*
– The Moorings

*The Cruiser's Handbook of Fishing*
– Scott Bannerot and Wendy Bannerot, International Marine/McGraw-Hill

*SeaLife: A Complete Guide to the Marine Environment*
– Marc Dando, Michael Burchett, Edited by Geoffrey Waller, Smithsonian Institute Press

# The Author

Corinna Weyreter was born in 1968 in Surrey, England. She graduated in astrophysics from the University of Birmingham and became a petrophysicist with Shell for the opportunity to work overseas. After fifteen years with the company, she resigned to sail across the Pacific with Gjalt van der Zee, and *Far Out* is the story of their adventure. Having reached Australia, they decided to continue sailing, and their voyage took them around the world to the Azores, where they now live. They plan on taking *Stella Maris* to sea again soon.

CPSIA information can be obtained at www.ICGtesting.com
Printed in the USA
LVOW01s0017051213

363886LV00029B/2042/P